ITALY
IN THE MAKING
1815–1846

CHARLES ALBERT
(*About the year* 1815)

ITALY
IN THE MAKING
1815 TO 1846

By
G. F.-H. BERKELEY

CAMBRIDGE
AT THE UNIVERSITY PRESS
1932
REPRINTED
1968

CAMBRIDGE UNIVERSITY PRESS
Cambridge, New York, Melbourne, Madrid, Cape Town, Singapore,
São Paulo, Delhi, Dubai, Tokyo, Mexico City

Cambridge University Press
The Edinburgh Building, Cambridge CB2 8RU, UK

Published in the United States of America by Cambridge University Press, New York

www.cambridge.org
Information on this title: www.cambridge.org/9780521159159

First published 1932
Reprinted 1968
First paperback edition 2010

A catalogue record for this publication is available from the British Library

Library of Congress Catalogue Card Number: 33-7256

ISBN 978-0-521-07427-8 Hardback
ISBN 978-0-521-15915-9 Paperback

To
MY WIFE

*Non ho detta nulla, che non sia nella mia piu intima,
piu sincera, piu meditata opinione.*

Balbo, Letter to Gino Capponi
of September 29th, 1844.

CONTENTS

MAPS

PREFACE

This volume deals with the period up to 1846, but in reality it is part of a life-study of the whole Risorgimento. Close upon thirty years have passed since my first article on the subject and I hope that this book may be followed by a second dealing with the years 1846 to 1848.

In the course of thirty years I have met men of all parties —old Garibaldians, Piedmontese, Papal Zouaves and other survivors of the great days, and of course hundreds of a more modern date; and I have discussed every possible side of the question with them. At the same time the libraries and archives have proved a mine of information, perhaps unequalled elsewhere; for until 1860 there were nine or ten small nations in Italy each of which had its state archives.

In reality, however, the most interesting part of the study has been watching the development of the new nation formed in 1860; no other in Europe has made so much progress during the last seventy years.

At this present date, anyone who starts to write about the Risorgimento may think himself fortunate in one respect, namely, that since the settlement with the Church he can express his views more freely than heretofore without fear of reopening vexed questions. For a long time the "Roman Question" remained a living issue of unusual bitterness. In Italy, of late years, the leading historians—notably Masi— have tended to take a broadminded view of the situation; but there are few English or American books, I think, in which full justice has been done to the part played by Pius IX during his first two years, 1846–8. It seems best to begin by stating this view because to some extent it has influenced the general plan of my work, although those two years do not come actually within the scope of this volume.[1]

There are so many people to whom I am indebted for kind and courteous assistance that it would be difficult to name them all.

I must begin by making my acknowledgments to the memory of the late Cardinal Gasquet for his great kindness in discussing the whole subject with me, in lending me his books, and in obtaining permission for me to search in the Vatican Archives.

Secondly, to Miss Joan Weld, who has done so much that her assistance has often amounted to collaboration. Next there is the Countess Maria Pasolini who, out of her great knowledge, was abundantly generous to a foreign student. Also to her son Count Guido Pasolini.

In Florence my warmest thanks are due to the Commendatore Dorini for all the trouble taken on my behalf in the splendidly managed archives of the old state of Tuscany; and also to the Marchese Degli Azzi-Vitelleschi, the author of the well-known books *Le stragi di Perugia* and *La Liberazione di Perugia*, for his kind advice and suggestions.

In Rome I am indebted firstly to the British Ambassador for permission to delve in the State Archives; also to Mr A. Randall of the British Legation to the Holy See; also to Commendatore Casanova, Commendatore Rè and Cavaliere Polidori. And I owe a great debt to Commendatore Menghini, Director of the Risorgimento Library and editor of the National edition of Mazzini's Letters, for his constant help and advice; also to General Ezio Garibaldi for much extremely interesting information about the times of his grandfather. At the Vatican I owe my sincerest thanks to

[1] Masi is well known to English readers owing to his having been the Italian historian invited to write the articles on the Risorgimento for the *Cambridge Modern History*.

Monsignor Mercati, Prefect of the Vatican Library, and also to his brother, Monsignor Mercati, Prefect of the Vatican Archives; also to the Rev. Hubert Bastgen.

At Milan, in the Risorgimento Library, Commendatore Monti gave me the kindest assistance.

In Paris I owe my thanks to the British Ambassador, and am deeply indebted for the help afforded by the admirable organisation of the Archives des Affaires Étrangères.

Finally, in London, I must acknowledge with gratitude the practical and prompt assistance which I received from all the employees of the Public Record Office in Chancery Lane.

G. F.-H. B.

1932

INTRODUCTION

THE MAIN LINES OF DEVELOPMENT BEFORE 1846

I

The three years from 1846 to 1849 constitute the first great period of trial and test in the Making of Italy, and undoubtedly mark the chief turning point in its history. To Italians, of course, that statement will seem to be a truism. Outside Italy, however, its full significance is not always realised, and, until one realises it, there is some difficulty in forming a clear idea of the whole subject. That short period is the central moment—one might call it the junction—in point of time: from all sides the important lines of development lead up to it. Then, within that narrow compass of only three years, they reach their crises almost simultaneously, and every single party in Italy is summoned to the test. Their works, their projects and their hearts are tried in the fire. After 1849 those few which have not been consumed emerge from the furnace, and, under the consummate guidance of Cavour, are enabled to become definite working realities in 1860.

The trial is by no means confined to those developments which are within Italy. The following are some instances of these crises during the years 1846–9: in Austria, Metternich's system reaches the beginning of its end; in France, the limited monarchy of Louis Philippe is overthrown and, in Switzerland, the Sonderbund; in Italy, the attempt to set up a Liberal modernised Papacy is wrecked once and for all; in Rome, the Mazzinian Republic is proved to be impossible; in Rome and Florence, the scheme for uniting all the Italian states into a federation is found to be unsatisfactory; in Piedmont, Charles Albert's ideal, *Italia farà da se*—that Italy single-handed can drive out the Austrians—is proved to be only a patriotic dream.

But out of these years of suffering and wrecked ideals, there emerge two or three constructive opinions which have stood the test of hard experience: that Piedmont is the only state worth considering in time of war; that, to drive out the Austrians, a foreign alliance is necessary; and—for rather negative reasons—that Mazzini's principle of union-by-fusion is right, although his republicanism is wrong. During the latter part of the Risorgimento these three conceptions are combined in the Piedmontese diplomacy of Cavour; and he is joined by Garibaldi, a Mazzinian who has resigned his republican creed for the sake of national unity.

The true turning point in the story is, undoubtedly, the year 1846. Up to that time, many different schemes seem equally possible or impossible.

At that moment, there were two leading figures in Italy, Charles Albert and Pius IX. It was Pius IX who, in 1846, gave the word to advance on the path of Liberal development; and this could hardly be otherwise, for no other ruler could make a wide or deep appeal outside his own realm; Charles Albert's influence was mainly confined to Piedmont, and even there he was tied by a promise. It was the Pope alone who could reach the mass of the people in every state alike;[1] and it was he alone who could rouse the parish priest and call the

---

[1] This opinion is becoming more and more generally accepted. Cf. for instance the opinion of Ritter von Srbik (1925): "Up to 1846 the Papacy held that Religion and Revolution were irreconcilable and the nationalist currents, even Mazzini's enthusiastic idealism, had not gripped the mass of the people;...hitherto the national movement had lacked both power to move the masses and an inspiring [literally, fire-lighting] personality as a leader which even Mazzini...was not. But in Mastai-Ferretti, who assumed the tiara as Pius IX, they found the man who of his own impulse transformed the old ideas into the collective passionate will of the majority of the people, and allowed himself to be lifted to the summit of the revolution so long as the existence of the State of the Church did not seem to be endangered by it". Srbik, II, 124.

peasants to action. And it was to the cry of "Viva Pio Nono" that the Liberal advance was initiated all over Italy.

The narrative in this volume (1815–46) is necessarily rather of a preliminary character. In it are traced the main lines of development leading up to the crises of 1846; without such a preliminary narrative it would be impossible to realise the situation which faced Pius IX on his accession in the summer of that year. It will be found that from 1815 to 1846, Charles Albert of Piedmont is the most important figure on our stage: that is to say, up to the end of this volume.

It was in 1846, however, that the great period of trial began; and for the first two years the leading part was played by Pius IX;[2] after which, in 1848, Charles Albert again became the leader of Italy, from the day when war was declared.

All my work has been an attempt to make clear *only* the *main* lines of development of the Italian Risorgimento: the chains of causes and effects: how one idea led to another until the final result was achieved.[3] It is these chains of ideas which

[2] "After the Piedmontese dream there has come the Pontifical dream which is now in progress." Quotation from a letter (October 20th, 1846) of Mazzini, who believed in neither kings nor Popes.

[3] Commendatore Casanova, who is head of the State Archives in Rome, once said to me that foreigners hardly ever write a history of the Risorgimento, but only of one man in it, such as Cavour, Garibaldi, or Mazzini. What he meant, I think, was that some of the finest books of the last fifty years have been lives of individual men. Certainly any English writer who produced a work similar to the Italian general histories would find that his readers had great difficulty in following the main threads of cause and effect throughout the period: there are too many small states concerned. The present volume is an attempt to make quite clear those main threads of cause and effect up to the end of 1846: consequently some of the states—Naples, for instance—can only receive a slight mention. Naples, however, played only a small part in the movement before 1846: "Italy ends at the Garigliano" was a common saying in those days. The state whose history one regrets curtailing is Tuscany, because it was the home of so many of the most interesting men.

are of value now: the actual events[4] of the early period are already well known, and need only be stated briefly to modern students. But before 1849 there were, throughout Italy, some of the ablest thinkers in Europe searching desperately for the right way forward.

II

The present volume only goes as far as June, 1846. My hope has been that a short clear summary of the sequence of ideas and events of the Risorgimento between 1815 and 1846 might prove useful to students and interesting to every one. The following is a brief analysis of the narrative which it contains.

The subject might be approached from a hundred different angles, but perhaps it groups itself most naturally and most conveniently under five headings, namely, the Conservative Reaction, the Revolution, the State of Piedmont, the Papal State, and the Moderate Movement. These are the five chief influences or powers which play a leading part in the development of the Risorgimento. This book begins by describing four of them in its first four[5] chapters; then, in chapters V to XVI are traced their respective developments; and finally, in chapter XVII, their actual situation during the first half of the year 1846 is reviewed.

Thus, broadly speaking, the book is a record of the Conservative Reaction on the one side, and, on the other, of the four main Italian forces which were striving to achieve nationality. Of course the achievement of nationality is primarily a mental process.

---

[4] Some even of the best-known events can only receive a brief mention, if any at all; as, for instance, Confalonieri's imprisonment or Menotti's rising. Their omission is inevitable. The work is selective.

[5] The Moderate Movement does not make its appearance until chapter IX.

From 1815 to 1846 the two great European influences governing the whole political situation are those of the Conservative eighteenth-century Reaction on the one hand, and the Revolution on the other.

I. THE CONSERVATIVE REACTION is typified by Metternich and the Holy Alliance. From 1815 to 1848 he remains in power at Vienna, and his policy is necessarily immovable because any advance towards popular freedom would prejudice the safety of the Austrian Empire.

II. As opposed to him, THE REVOLUTION is constantly at work; in Italy it is organised chiefly by the Carbonari Society until the year 1831: and after that by Mazzini and the Giovine Italia (Young Italy Society). It is (a) fusionist, and (b) republican.

The three chief outbreaks in Italy of political strife between the Revolution and the Conservative Reaction are:

1820–1. The rebellions in Naples and in Piedmont, suppressed by Austria.

1830–4. The risings in Piedmont, in Modena, in the Papal State and elsewhere.

1846–9. The great period of crisis ending in the first War of Liberation.

Within Italy there are two states (out of ten) which, more than the others, bear the seeds of the future; namely Piedmont and the Papal State. The story of the Risorgimento during this early period, 1815–46, is often little else but the history of these two.

III. PIEDMONT,[6] to the north-west of the peninsula.

Its future after 1815 depends mainly on the career of the heir presumptive, Charles Albert. In his life there are three crises; namely, 1821, when he involves himself in the mutiny and emerges from it a discredited prince; 1831–4, when, at the very beginning of his reign, he earns the hatred

---

[6] The chapters dealing with the State of Piedmont are Nos. IV–VI, XII–XIV, and XVII. Between them they supply a summary of Piedmontese history during the period.

of the Liberals by his severity in repressing the conspiracies of those years; and finally the years 1848 and 1849, when he becomes the hero of the first war of Liberation (which does not come into this volume). His character is perhaps the hardest to estimate of any in the Risorgimento. Throughout his life he was misunderstood. His two ill-starred moments, in 1821 and in 1831–4, made him a hated and a marked man. Yet in reality he remained the most convinced believer in Piedmont's mission, and the most persistent enemy of Austria.

The belief of his life was that Italy, led by Piedmont, could drive out the Austrians *single-handed*; and by the year 1846 it had been crystallised in his celebrated phrase "Italia farà da se".[7]

IV. THE PAPAL STATE.[8] Throughout the reign of Gregory XVI (1830–46) its policy remains almost entirely reactionary, and the chief events are the rebellions; firstly those of 1830–4; then in 1843; and finally in 1845 the Moto di Rimini.

These rebellions achieve very small results; but they give rise to two separate programmes of reform which are of importance because, by the year 1846, they become the chief landmarks in the Moderate movement and consequently have some influence on the Liberal policy of Pius IX. These are

1831. *The Memorandum* of the five Great Powers; a scheme of reform for the Papal State.

1845. *The Manifesto of Rimini*; a programme of reform presented by the ex-rebels.

V. THE MODERATE MOVEMENT.[9] During the course

---

[7] "Italy will fend for herself", in the sense that Italy will work out her own salvation without foreign assistance.

[8] The chapters dealing with the Papal State are Nos. IV, VII–IX and XV–XVIII. Between them they give a summary of the Papal State's connection with the Risorgimento.

[9] The chapters dealing with the Moderate Movement are Nos. IX–XIV and XVI. The Memorandum of 1831 appears in chapter VIII, but this can hardly be called part of the Movement, which did not yet exist.

of these troubled years many people become tired of both Revolution and Reaction, of alternate bloodshed and reprisals. There arises a Moderate or reforming movement, half-way between the two extremes. It is the most interesting of the nationalist developments because it is the most thoughtful. It includes nearly all the thinkers of the period, and they set their brains to work out the problems of the Risorgimento; and, consequently, they alone of the parties produce a definite and progressive advance.

The origin of this Moderate movement might probably be traced to the coteries of intellectuals in Tuscany during the years before 1830; also to the Memorandum of 1831, and no doubt to other causes as well; but its three greatest writers were Gioberti, Balbo and Massimo d'Azeglio, all Piedmontese, and its first important success was achieved in 1843 when the Abbé Gioberti published his great book *Del Primato morale e civile degli Italiani*. He was a man who could appeal both to Charles Albert and to the Pope, for he was both a Piedmontese and a priest. His scheme for the making of Italy was a federation of small states, of which the Pope should be the President and Charles Albert the defender; his ideal was to have a Liberal and patriotic Pope for their leader. This book started a new era in Italy. It was followed by the work of Balbo, who substituted Charles Albert for the Pope, and later by d'Azeglio also an Albertist. D'Azeglio's creed was to work by peaceful agitation instead of bloodshed. These were the main tenets developed by the Moderates between 1815 and 1846, with which year this book comes to an end.

In 1846 the scene changes; Pius IX succeeds Gregory XVI and the whole situation is altered. He is Gioberti's Pope come into being. He inaugurates the régime of progressive ideas in Italy, and does not abandon his great effort to be a Liberal Pope, until, some two years later, he is driven from his home by the Revolution.

Between 1846 and 1849 we have the period when (as already

stated) all of these five main forces and influences are tried in the fire of revolution and war. Some portions of them are consumed. The Conservative reaction loses Metternich. Mazzini's republic is found to be impossible, but his principle of union-by-fusion survives. Charles Albert's idea that Italy can defeat Austria single-handed ("Italia farà da se") is proved to be impossible, but his establishment of the hegemony of Piedmont survives. In the Papal State the conception of Gioberti's Pope and the Liberal Papacy are abandoned, and the federal scheme of the Moderates is found to be unsatisfactory.

Out of all the patriotic schemes and hopes existent before 1848, there remain in being after 1849 the Albertist doctrine of Piedmontese hegemony in Italy, and the Mazzinian creed of an Italy united by fusion and not by federation. To these, Cavour adds his plan of a French alliance against Austria; and under his guidance the Making of Italy is accomplished in 1860.

LIST OF AUTHORITIES

A. PUBLISHED SOURCES

ALBERTI, MARIO DEGLI. *La politica estera di Piemonte sotto Carlo Alberto, secondo il carteggio diplomatico del Conte Bertone di Sambuy.* 1835–46.

AMIGUES, JULES. *L'état romain depuis 1815 jusqu'à nos jours.* 1862. Notes and documents by Farini.

ANZILOTTI = ANZILOTTI. *Gioberti.* 1922. The latest work on Gioberti; a useful book from all points of view.

Archivio triennale = *Archivio triennale delle cose d' Italia dall' avvenimento di Pio IX all' abbandono di Venezia.* 3 vols. 1851. The republican statement of their case in 1851. A collection of documents mostly of 1848 and 1849.

D'AZEGLIO = D'AZEGLIO, MASSIMO. *Degli ultimi casi di Romagna.* 1846.

D'AZEGLIO, *Lettere* = D'AZEGLIO, MASSIMO. *Lettere a sua moglie.* 1876.

D'AZEGLIO, *Proposta* = D'AZEGLIO, MASSIMO. *Proposta di un programma per l' opinione nazionale italiana.* 1847.

D'AZEGLIO, *Ricordi* = D'AZEGLIO, MASSIMO. *I miei ricordi.* New ed. 1910.

D'AZEGLIO. Other works consulted. *Correspondance politique.* 2nd ed. 1867. *Lettere a Giuseppe Torelli.* 2nd ed. 1870. *Raccolta degli scritti politici.* 1850. (This includes *Degli ultimi casi* and the *Proposta* mentioned above.)
Massimo d'Azeglio was one of the most interesting figures of the Risorgimento. No one else had so wide and so varied a knowledge of all classes of Italians as he had. It is well to remember that the *Ricordi* was written in 1864 when, inevitably, his anti-Papal feeling would have been at its strongest.

BALAN, Prof. PIETRO. *Pio IX; la chiesa e la rivoluzione.* 2 vols. 1898. *Storia d' Italia.* 1878. A strongly Papal writer.

BALBO = BALBO, CESARE. *Delle speranze d' Italia.* 2nd ed. 1844. See chapter XIII of the text and also under Manno.

BARANTE = DE BARANTE, Baron. *Souvenirs.* Vol. IV. 1894.

BASTGEN = BASTGEN, Rev. HUBERT. *Die römische Frage. Dokumente und Stimmen.* 1917.

BASTGEN. Other works. Article in *Rassegna storica del Risorgimento.* 1914. Father Bastgen's work is thorough, and documented throughout; drawn from the Vatican Archives.

BAUDRILLART, Monsignor. *Dictionnaire d'histoire et géographie ecclésiastique.* 1912.

BEAUCHAMP = DE BEAUCHAMP. *Histoire de la révolution de Piémont.* No date; bound with Santarosa. Useful to read in conjunction with Santarosa's account of the Piedmontese rising of 1821.

BERSEZIO = BERSEZIO, VITTORIO. *Il regno di Vittorio Emanuele.* 2 vols. 2nd ed. 1895.

BERTI = BERTI. *Vincenzo Gioberti.* 1881.

BIANCHI, *Curiosità* = BIANCHI, NICOMEDE. *Curiosità e ricerche di storia subalpina.* 8 vols. 1874–81.

BIANCHI, NICOMEDE. *Memorie del Generale Carlo Zucchi.* 1861. The extremely interesting memoirs of the old Napoleonic officer who lived to see Italy united in 1860. See also under Zucchi.

BIANCHI, *Storia* = BIANCHI, NICOMEDE. *Storia documentata della diplomazia europea in Italia dall' anno 1814 all' anno 1861.* 8 vols. 1865–72. Bianchi's work is of course monumental: it is Piedmontese in sympathy; valuable for its documents. Their perfect accuracy has lately been questioned, but one doubts that, as a whole, their importance will ever be much diminished.

Bollettino del ufficio storico. Stato maggiore del reale esercito. Various dates.

BROFFERIO = BROFFERIO, ANGELO. *Storia del Piemonte.* Three parts. 1849–51. Brofferio was a republican and a revolutionist; he is describing events in which he took part, but his politics have spoilt his history.

BUNSEN = BUNSEN, Baron. *A Memoir of,* by his widow, Frances Bunsen. 2 vols. 1868. A very able man; his memoirs and his letters are necessary for 1831. It was he who drafted the Memorandum.

Cambridge Modern History. Vol. XI: *The Growth of Nationalities.* 1909. See also under Masi.

CANTÙ, CESARE. *Cronistoria.* 3 vols. 1872 *et seq.* This work is so long, diffuse and desultory that these defects nullify the vast erudition of the author.

CAPPONI, GINO. *Lettere.* 1886.

CARLO ALBERTO, King of Piedmont. *Memoriale.* April 1821. *Détails sur ma Régence. Ad majorem Dei gloriam* (1839). *Letters,* 1821–3. For all these see note 6 on p. 59 of text, also under Manno and Fiorini: Bianchi mentions another Memoriale of Charles Albert, but it is apparently not in print. He was also the author of various other works.

Carte segrete ed atti ufficiali della polizia austriaca in Italia. 3 vols. 1851–8. Interesting, but not very useful. Said to have been compiled by Manin, the Venetian patriot.

Catholic Encyclopedia, The. "Gregory XVI." "Pius IX."

CERRO, EMILIO DEL. *Cospirazioni romane.* 1899.

CIBRARIO = CIBRARIO. *Notizie sulla vita di Carlo Alberto.* Cibrario was a senator and a friend of Charles Albert. His book was for many years the standard Life of the king and will always be valuable.

COLOMBO, A. *Dalle riforme allo statuto di Carlo Alberto.* Good documents but mostly for 1848.

COPPI. *Annali d' Italia dall' anno* 1814.

C. DE BEAUREGARD = COSTA DE BEAUREGARD. *La jeunesse du roi Charles Albert.* 1872. A psychological study, partly based on the diary of his uncle Silvano Costa, who was Charles Albert's equerry.

CRÉTINEAU-JOLY. *L'église romaine en face de la révolution.*

DEBIDOUR, *Hist. Dip.* = DEBIDOUR. *Histoire diplomatique d'Europe.* Vol. II. 1871. A classical work on European diplomacy.

DELLA ROCCA = DELLA ROCCA. *Autobiografia d' un veterano.* 1898.

DURANDO, GIACOMO. *Saggio politico e militare della nazionalità italiana.* 1846. See chapter X of the text.

FABRIS = FABRIS, CECILIO. *Gli avvenimenti militari del* 1848 *e* 1849. 3 vols. 1898.

FALDELLA, GIOVANNI. *I fratelli Ruffini.* 1895. *Massimo d'Azeglio e Diomede Pantaleoni.*

FARINI = FARINI, Dottor LUIGI CARLO. *Lo Stato Romano dall' anno* 1815–50. 4 vols. 1850. Dr Farini was one of the ablest men of the Risorgimento. He was a Mazzinian till 1844; a conspirator in Romagna in 1831, 1843 and 1845, in which latter year he turned Moderate. His History is the most brilliant and informative of the contemporary works; it is indispensable. He is a fighting Moderate who attacks with equal vigour his old Mazzinian associates and his Conservative enemies.

FIORINI = FIORINI. *Scritti varj di Carlo Alberto.* This includes the three narratives published by Manno. Also the *Simple récit des événemens arrivés en Piémont.* Also ninety-four letters written by Charles Albert between 1821 and 1823.

GALEOTTI. *Della sovranità e del governo temporale dei Papi.* 1847.

GAMBERALE = GAMBERALE, BICE. In the *Rassegna storica del Risorgimento* for 1927, an article called "Gli inizi del pontificato di Gregorio XVI. La conferenza diplomatica e le riforme". This article is a most valuable contribution based on documents in the Vatican, Berlin and elsewhere. See also under Unpublished Sources.

GAMS = GAMS. *Die Geschichte der Kirche Christi im XIX Jahrhundert.* One of the standard Church histories.

GENERALLI. *La corte di Roma.* 1866. *Il governo Pontificio.*

GIOBERTI, VINCENZO. See under *Primato.*

Giovine Italia, Protocollo della. See under *Protocollo.*

GORI = GORI, AGOSTINO. *Storia della rivoluzione italiana durante il periodo delle riforme* (1846–Marzo, 1848). 1897. This is probably the best book on the period 1846–8; the work of a lawyer. The only drawback is that there is sometimes difficulty in finding the subject required.

GUALTERIO = GUALTERIO, F. A. *Gli ultimi rivolgimenti italiani. Memorie storiche.* 6 vols. 1850–1. A good contemporary historian of the period up to 1847 with useful documents. He is a Moderate and an Albertist. According to M. Vidal, he represents the views of Villamarina, Charles Albert's Liberal minister.

DE GUICHEN = DE GUICHEN, Vicomte. *La révolution de juillet 1830 et l'Europe.* 1916. Useful for the French view of the Papal question in 1831.

HANCOCK, W. K. *Ricasoli and the Risorgimento in Tuscany.* 1926. A sympathetic and informative study of the Tuscan Risorgimento.

HERGENRÖTHER = HERGENRÖTHER, Cardinal. *Histoire de l'église.* French translation by the Abbé Belet. 1892.

HILLEBRAND = HILLEBRAND. *Geschichte Frankreichs von der Thronbesteigung Louis Philipps bis zum Fall Napoleon III.* Band III. 1879. A valuable history, though in some points superseded by the discovery of new material.

JOHNSON, Rev. HUMPHREY. *The Papacy and the Kingdom of Italy.* 1926. A short and excellent handbook on the Papal question.

KING, BOLTON. *Mazzini.* Everyman edition. 1919. The standard English Life.

KOCH, JULIUS. *Deutsche Geschichte.* IV. Sammlung Göschen. 1924.

LA FARINA, GIUSEPPE. *Storia d' Italia dal 1815–50.* Vol. II. 2nd ed. 1861.

LAGRANGE, F. *Life of Monsignor Dupanloup,* translated by Lady Herbert. 1885. Useful for the history of the French Church at this period.

LEMMI = LEMMI, FRANCESCO. *La politica estera di Carlo Alberto.* 1928. *Il Risorgimento.* (Guida Bibliografica.) 1926.

LE ROY BEAULIEU. *Les catholiques libéraux.*

LUZIO = LUZIO, A. *Gli inizi del regno di Carlo Alberto.* 1923.

LUZIO, A. Other work. *Carlo Alberto e Mazzini.* 1923. Interesting historical essays based on documents in the Turin Archives.

MAGUIRE. *Rome; its ruler and its institutions.* 1857. The author visited Rome in 1857 and his work is valuable for its well-informed and vivid descriptions of the leading personalities of the day. Written from a Papal point of view.

DE MAISTRE. See under *Simple récit* and Un Savoyard.

MANNO = MANNO, ANTONIO. *Informazioni sul ventuno in Piemonte.* This includes three writings of Charles Albert in his own defence. *Memoriale* (April 1821), *Détails sur ma Régence* and

Ad majorem Dei gloriam (1839), also narratives of Balbo, Gifflenga and others.

MANNO. *L' opinione religiosa e conservatrice in Italia dal* 1830–50 *ricercata nella corrispondenza di Mons. Giovanni Corboli Bussi.* 1910. Letters of Monsignor Corboli Bussi. Valuable and interesting, but more so for 1848.

MASI = MASI, ERNESTO. *Il Risorgimento italiano.* 2 vols. 1917. A comprehensive and well-balanced work. One of the best general histories.

MASI, *Nell' Ottocento.* 1922. Perhaps the most inspiring essays on this period.

MASI, *Il segreto* = *Il segreto del re Carlo Alberto.* 1890. An interesting essay on the early part of Charles Albert's life, especially the conspiracy of 1821.

MASI, ERNESTO. *La rivoluzione di* 1831 *e le società segrete in Romagna.* 1890. *Il Risorgimento nei libri.* 1911. A critical bibliography of works on the Risorgimento. Also in the *Cambridge Modern History,* vol. XI. An article called "Italy and Revolution".

MASSARI = MASSARI. *Le opere inedite di Vincenzo Gioberti.* Vols. IX, X. Biography and letters. 1861.

MATTER, PAUL. *Cavour et l'unité italienne.* 1922.

MAZZINI, *Scritti* (E.N.) = MAZZINI, GIUSEPPE. Collected works (National edition): full title is *Scritti editi ed inediti. Edizione Nazionale.* 1906 *et seq.* An admirably printed series of volumes with painstaking and informative notes by Commendatore Mario Menghini. When completed it will include all Mazzini's writings.

MAZZINI, *Scritti* (A.E.) = MAZZINI, GIUSEPPE. Collected works (Author's edition): full title is *Scritti editi ed inediti. Edizione diretta dal Autore.* This edition of Mazzini's works is valuable for the "Proemi" or Prefaces. Those to the first eight volumes are written by himself; those to vols. IX–XII by Aurelio Saffi after Mazzini's death.

MENGHINI, MARIO. *La giovane Italia.* 1902. In *Rassegna storica del Risorgimento,* 1916, an article called "Rinaldo Andreini e i moti di Romagna del 1845". Gives an interesting and at times amusing account of the risings in Romagna, 1843–5.

METTERNICH = METTERNICH. *Mémoires.* French translation. 2nd ed. 1880.

MINGHETTI, MARCO. *I miei ricordi.* 3 vols. 4th ed. 1899. Memoirs of this Bolognese barrister, one of the ablest of the Moderates.

MONTANELLI = MONTANELLI, GIUSEPPE. *Memorie sull' Italia.* 2 vols. 2nd ed. 1853. The author was one of the most prominent revolutionists in Tuscany, 1846–9.

MONTI = MONTI, ANTONIO. *Pio IX nel Risorgimento italiano.* 1928. The latest book on Pius IX. It contains some interesting new documents.

Mowat, R. B. *History of European diplomacy*, 1815–1914. 1923. A very useful outline of the diplomatic history of the nineteenth century.

Nuova Antologia, 1927. Article by Marcus de Rubris.

Nuovo Atlante, 1820. An atlas with fifty-two maps and a volume of descriptions.

Orsi, Pietro. *Histoire de l'Italie moderne*. French translation by Bergmann. 1911. One of the accepted histories of the time, but owing to its general brevity it rather loses value when dealing with individual episodes.

Orsini, Felice. *Memoirs and Adventures*. English translation by Carbonel. 1857. Memoirs of the well-known Felice Orsini. An interesting record of the ideas of a revolutionist.

Pasolini, Giuseppe. *Memorie raccolte dal suo figlio*, 1815–76. 2 vols. 4th ed. 1915. The same, translated and abridged by the Countess of Dalhousie, 1885. Count Desiderio Pasolini has compiled a charming record from the papers of his father Count Giuseppe, who was a close friend of Pius IX both before and after he became Pope. Pasolini was a Liberal and a Minister in Pius' constitutional government, and afterwards in that of the Kingdom of Italy. *Carteggio con Marco Minghetti*. Vol. I, 1846–54. 1924. A valuable collection by Count Guido Pasolini of the letters exchanged between his grandfather and Marco Minghetti. Not many of these were written before 1848 and therefore do not concern the present volume.

Pelczar = Pelczar, Monsignor Josef, Bishop of Rito. *Pio IX e il suo Pontificato sullo sfondo delle vicende della chiesa nel secolo XIX*. Italian translation from the 2nd Polish ed. 3 vols. 1909. A good, thorough and painstaking work, written of course from the ecclesiastical point of view. It also contains a useful review of the pontificate of Gregory XVI.

Predari = Predari. *I primi vagiti della libertà in Piemonte*. 1860. Predari was a central figure among the Liberal writers in Turin and was thus in a position to describe the whole of their movement from the inside. His book is indispensable.

Primato = Gioberti, Vincenzo. *Del Primato morale e civile degli Italiani*. 1843. See chapter XI of the text.

Protocollo = *Protocollo della Giovine Italia*. 6 vols. 1915–22. Invaluable for the history of the Mazzinian movement. It contains an abstract of all the letters sent out and received by the Headquarters Committee of the Giovine Italia. Edited with useful notes and explanations by Commendatore Mario Menghini.

Quintavalli, Francesco. *Storia dell' unità italiana*. Hoepli, 1926. The Hoepli Manual of the period.

Rass. stor. = *Rassegna storica del Risorgimento*. The organ of the Società Nazionale per la Storia del Risorgimento. Various dates.

RAULICH = RAULICH, ITALO. *Storia del Risorgimento politico d' Italia*. Vol. III (1844–8). No date.

REVEL = REVEL, GENOVA DI. *Dal 1847 al 1855*. 1891. *Negoziati per lega doganale a Modena e a Napoli*. 1847. Useful and exhaustive studies based on original documents.

Revue des Deux Mondes. Janvier 1923. Article "L'Italie Libérée".

RICHARDS, E. *Mazzini's Letters to an English family*. 3 vols. 1920.

RICOTTI = RICOTTI. *Della vita e degli scritti del conte Cesare Balbo*. 1856. An account of Balbo's life and writings written soon after his death.

RINAUDO, COSTANZO. *Il Risorgimento italiano*. *Conferenze*. Vol. I. 1911.

RINIERI = RINIERI. *Lo statuto e il giuramento del re Carlo Alberto*. 1899.

Risorgimento, Il. The predecessor of the *Rassegna storica del Risorgimento*. Various dates.

Rivista Italiana. Nuova serie. Vol. II.

RODOLICO = RODOLICO, NICCOLÒ. *Carlo Alberto, Principe di Carignano*. 1930. The latest work on Charles Albert's life before he became king: very interesting and well-documented.

ROMANO, GAETANO. *Dizionario d' erudizione ecclesiastica*. No date. The author, who was an "Aiutante di Camera" to both Gregory XVI and Pius IX, gives under the heading "Pius IX" a month-to-month record of some interest but not of any great value.

ROSI = ROSI, M. *Storia contemporanea d' Italia*. 1922. A useful general history of the Risorgimento.

RUBRIS, M. DE. Article in *Nuova Antologia*. 1927.

SAFFI, AURELIO. *Ricordi e scritti*. 14 vols. 1893. *Storia di Roma, 1846–9*, included in the above and written in 1852. The most cultured writer among those of the Mazzinian movement. Unfortunately he makes Mazzinianism his whole creed, and consequently his work has little value except as a specimen of the ideas of his group.

SAINTE-AULAIRE, Comte DE. *Souvenirs, 1832–41*. 1927.

SANTAROSA = SANTAROSA, Count. *De la révolution piémontaise*. 1847. Narrative of the Piedmontese movement of 1821 by the revolutionary leader Santarosa. On certain points it comes in conflict with Charles Albert's account. Apparently the whole truth has not yet been finally established.

SAVOYARD = SAVOYARD, UN. *Les trente jours de la révolution piémontaise*. March, 1921. This is generally attributed to De Maistre, and considered to have been inspired by Charles Albert himself. It is more or less an answer to Santarosa. See also below *Simple récit*, etc.

SEGRÉ, ARTURO. *Il tramonto di un regno e l' alba di un regno nuovo.* 1912. For the early years of Charles Albert. Interesting for the extracts he gives from reports of Barante, then French ambassador at Turin and a shrewd observer.

SILVA = SILVA, PIETRO. *La Monarchia di Luglio e l' Italia.* 1917. One of the latest books on the subject; interesting and useful for the documents and authorities he quotes. A little biased by enthusiasm for the Risorgimento.

Simple récit = *Simple récit des événemens arrivés en Piémont.* 1900. This has also been attributed to De Maistre. (See above, Un Savoyard.) This edition includes ninety-four letters of Charles Albert's written during the years 1821–3.

SOLARO = SOLARO DELLA MARGHERITA. *Memorandum.* 1852. An invaluable account of della Margherita's term of office, 1836–44. He is a firm Conservative but an assertor of his country's independence against Austria.

SPADA = SPADA, GIUSEPPE. *Storia della rivoluzione di Roma.* 3 vols. 1868 *et seq.* The chief Papal historian of the years 1846–9. His book was written during 1858 and 1859 but not published until ten years later. From small beginnings he rose to be a partner in the Torlonia Bank. He was living in Rome; collected his material methodically from day to day; and has left an immense mass of documents in the Vatican Archives. Within his limits Spada is virtually irrefutable; unfortunately his limits are rather circumscribed. He seems to have had no desires for Italian nationality or for popular liberties. He found things perfectly satisfactory as they were.

SRBIK = SRBIK, HEINRICH RITTER VON. *Metternich der Staatsmann und der Mensch.* 2 vols. 1925. The latest and most authoritative life of Metternich. An exhaustive work, more useful for reference than as a textbook.

STERN = STERN. *Geschichte Europas seit den Verträgen von 1815 bis zum Frankfurter Frieden von 1871.* Vols. IV, V, VI, VII. 1916. An admirable and well-documented general history.

STILLMAN. *The union of Italy.*

THAYER, WILLIAM ROSCOE. *The dawn of Italian independence.* 2 vols. 1894. *The life and times of Cavour.* 1911.

THUREAU DANGIN = THUREAU DANGIN. *Histoire de la révolution de juillet.* 8 vols. Interesting and well-written though somewhat diffuse. The writer is a Moderate in politics and his book contains much matter not published before.

TIVARONI = TIVARONI, CARLO. *Storia critica del Risorgimento.* Vols. IV, V, VI. "Italia durante il dominio austriaco" (sub-title of vols. I, II, III). An ex-Garibaldian. In 1859 he volunteered; in 1866 he fought in Cadore; in 1867 he was at Mentana; a democrat historian, astonishingly impartial. His is probably

the most impartial and the best general history of the Risorgi-
mento, especially for foreigners. It consists of nine volumes.
Vol. I: Italy before Napoleon. Vols. II and III: Italy under the
French (up to 1815). Vols. IV, V and VI: Italy under the
Austrians (up to 1849). Vols. VII, VIII and IX: Italy, 1849–70.
He is a great historian.

TORELLI, GIUSEPPE. *Ricordi politici.* 1873.

TORELLI, LUIGI. *Pensieri di un anonimo Lombardo.* See chapter X
of the text.

VACCALLUZZO = VACCALLUZZO, NUNZIO. *Massimo d'Azeglio.* 1925.
An excellent life of Massimo d'Azeglio. It is of interest both
to the student and to the general reader.

VANUCCI, ATTO. *I martiri della libertà italiana.* 1860. An account
of the sufferings of the revolutionists.

VERCESI, ERNESTO. *Pio IX.* 1929.

VESI, ANTONIO. *Rivoluzione di Romagna del 1831.* 1851.

VIDAL = VIDAL, C. *Charles Albert et le Risorgimento.* 1927. Written
in French. The last and best Life of Charles Albert; indispensable. It does not deal with events before his accession
in 1831.

VIDAL, *Louis Philippe* = VIDAL, C. *Louis Philippe, Metternich et la
crise italienne de* 1831–2. 1931.

WHITE MARIO, JESSIE. *The birth of modern Italy.* 1909.

WHYTE, Rev. Dr A. J. *Early life and letters of Cavour.* 1925.

WISEMAN, CARDINAL. *Four last Popes.* Cardinal Wiseman knew
Gregory XVI personally. An interesting book but does not
touch the pontificate of Pius IX.

ZOBI. *Storia civile della Toscana.* 5 vols. 1850–2.

ZUCCHI = *Memorie del generale Carlo Zucchi,* edited by BIANCHI.
The extremely interesting memoirs of a wonderful life.

B. UNPUBLISHED SOURCES

LONDON. Public Record Office, Chancery Lane. These reports of
the British diplomatic and consular representatives are invaluable. They certainly exhibit a higher general level of
efficiency than any others known to the writer. They are
referred to in the text as F.O.

ROME. State Archives. (Archivio di Stato.) Reference in the
text = Rome S.A.
Vatican Archives. They contain invaluable material for the
pontificate of Gregory XVI. For that of Pius IX they have not
yet been thrown open to the public; an exception has, however,
been made most kindly with regard to the "Fondo Spada",

which contains a vast collection of material both printed and unprinted for 1846 to 1849. Reference in the text = Vatican Arch.

PARIS. Affaires Étrangères. Reference in the text = Paris A.E.

I have also to acknowledge my great debt of gratitude to Signorina Bice Gamberale for permission accorded me to use her collection of hitherto unpublished documents relating to the Papal question during the years 1830 to 1834. On these was based the exhaustive study which she published in the *Rassegna storica* for 1927. Of those hundreds of documents very few had ever appeared in print; they were from the Berlin Archives, the Vatican Archives and elsewhere.

Chapter I

THE WORLD-INFLUENCES AFFECTING ITALY, 1815 TO 1846

I. THE CONSERVATIVE REACTION

The whole history of our continent between the years 1815 and 1846 is, of course, the story of a struggle between the principles introduced by the French Revolution and those that survived from the old régime. Broadly speaking, it may be said that on one side there stood the eighteenth-century absolutist reaction primarily represented by Austria, Prussia and Russia, the powers which are commonly referred to as the "Holy Alliance",[1] while, on the other side, was "the Revolution", with its branches extending into every nation.

Between these two extreme phalanxes there were the governments of France and England. In Italy, and distinct from either political combination, was the Papacy, whose religious influence nearly always lay on the side of Conservatism.

Broadly speaking, one may say that the whole situation in Europe dated entirely from the settlement at the close of the Napoleonic wars. In 1815, the Congress of Vienna and the Second Treaty of Paris had made a final delimitation of the national frontiers.[2] France was reduced to a minimum. Prussia received a great increase of territory. The newly-formed Germanic Confederation, which included most of

[1] Metternich himself tells the whole story of its foundation, vol. v, p. 193 of his *Mémoires*.

[2] Congress of Vienna, Art. 58. In Europe the supreme authority was divided between Austria with a population (1818) of 29,769,263; Prussia (1816), population 10,349,031 (including Poles); France (1826), population 31,858,937; Russia with at least 40 millions in Europe; the British Isles with 20,893,584 (of whom 6,801,827 were in Ireland). Also the Germanic Confederation, a bulwark against French aggression.

Prussia, after 1816 was to consist of thirty-five small states and four free towns, and was to be directed by a Diet of Plenipotentiaries. Austria, too, received an increase of territory,[3] and, apart from that fact, was to supply the President of the Germanic Confederation; Russia had been allowed to re-annex a considerable portion of Poland. These treaties constituted a definite permanent basis for the future and were guaranteed by the five Great Powers above-named.

This settlement wins a certain degree of approval from writers on diplomacy, on the grounds that it brought peace to Europe for nearly half a century. But, surely, there is a great deal to be said on the other side of the question. It is true that the Congress of Vienna brought peace among the Great Powers; but it did so mainly because it provided each of them with a sufficiency of spoil, and because, in any case, they were temporarily sick of war. Similarly the treaty is defended on the ground that it set up a balance of power so stable that "it remained substantially intact until 1860".[4] But it did so at far too great a cost of injustice and suffering. It did so at the price of partitioning whole populations and handing over tens of millions of free men and women to one or other of the dominating governments, just as if they were so many herds of cattle.

In reality the settlement of 1815 was responsible for most of the suffering in Europe, until finally it was overthrown by the Great War. Its faults were twofold: it drew frontiers where the inhabitants on either side of the line did not want frontiers, and it imposed absolute rulers on peoples which were too far developed to submit to absolutism. Hence it arrayed nationality against Conservatism and created scores

[3] In Italy she received the northern provinces of Lombardy and Venetia (about 4,700,000 souls).

[4] "Yet, though chipped and changed here and there in the next forty years, the Vienna settlement remained substantially intact until 1860 and gave Europe nearly half a century of comparative quiet." Mowat, *History of European Diplomacy*, 1815–1914, p. 5.

of revolutionary movements where they need never have existed: and consequently it is responsible for an immeasurable amount of human suffering.[5] The settlement in fact went far towards putting Conservatism and law-and-order in the wrong everywhere. Under its provisions there were probably as many subject peoples as free in Europe.[6] It began by a re-partition of the Poles: most of those living in the Grand Duchy of Warsaw were handed over to the government of Russia: some of them (Posen and West Prussia, including Danzig and Thorn) were allotted to Prussia; and Austria took most of those inhabiting Galicia and some others as well.[7] Nearer home, one reads that the Belgians were duly delivered to the King of Holland, and Norway was ceded to Sweden. In Italy the five million

---

[5] Cavour's opinion in the *Revue Nouvelle* of May 1st, 1846: "L'organisation que l'Italie a reçue à l'époque du Congrès de Vienne fut aussi arbitraire que défectueuse. Ne s'appuyant sur aucun principe, pas plus sur celui de la légitimité violée à l'égard de Gênes et de Venise que sur celui des intérêts nationaux ou de la volonté populaire, ne tenant compte ni des circonstances géographiques ni des intérêts généraux, ni des intérêts particuliers que vingt ans de révolutions avaient créés, cette auguste assemblée agissant uniquement en vertu du droit du plus fort éleva un édifice politique dépourvu de toute base morale. Un tel acte devait produire des fruits amers".

Massimo d'Azeglio's opinion was even stronger: "We believe that all the troubles (*disturbi*) which have occurred since 1815, in the ordering of Europe; that all the ill will and the revolutions of those thirty-two years, the unrest, the moral disquiet which has agitated society...that all these have been caused by the enforced and unnatural order given to Europe by the Congress of Vienna. The dispositions by which it aimed at laying a stable foundation for European peace and tranquillity, have become, on the contrary, the germs of all the wars and of all the revolutions and disorders which have taken place from the day of the Congress to to-day...".
D'Azeglio, *Proposta di un programma per l' opinione nazionale italiana*, chap. VI.

[6] *V.* Congress of Vienna, Articles 1, 23, 65, 93, 98, etc.

[7] "I am heartily sorry for the Poles." Palmerston, speaking of the failure of the Polish rebellion in 1831. *V.* Bulwer, *Life of Palmerston*, II, 147.

inhabitants of Lombardy and Venetia were forced back under the German bureaucracy of Austria, and the rest of that peninsula was parcelled out under absolutist rulers. And there were plenty of subject peoples whose names do not appear in the treaty; for instance, Greece and other Christian populations in the East were left to the Turks—and so forth. In short, one may say: the nineteenth century has always plumed itself on its abolition of the slave-trade; but, owing mainly to the Congress of Vienna, it will always be remembered as having been pre-eminently the century of enslaved nationalities.

Against such a settlement revolutions were inevitable, and conditions remained so until after the Great War of 1914–18. What was perhaps its most disgusting feature was its cynicism: the fact that after twenty years of war hardly a gleam of higher idealism is to be found. Prussia, for instance—the Prussia of the poet Körner and of the Tugendbund—had just emerged from a glorious patriotic fight for freedom, but no sooner is the armistice proclaimed, than her diplomats throw all such notions to the winds and simply annex everything and everyone possible.[8] This point of view was actually sent to the

---

[8] The following is a specimen of Körner's patriotic poems which called the whole German race to arms:

> "Wie heisst des Sängers Vaterland?—
> Jetzt über seiner Söhne Leichen,
> Jetzt weint es unter fremden Streichen.
> Sonst hiess es nur das Land der Eichen,
> Das freie Land, das deutsche Land.
> So hiess mein Vaterland!"

This may be rendered, quite roughly:

> "What name is thine, my Fatherland?—
> Wilt thou remain forever weeping
> While unavenged thy sons are sleeping?
> The land of oaks was once thy name.
> The free Land: the German Land.
> 'Twas once thy name, my Fatherland!"

Körner's *Werke*, Verlag von Th. Knaur, I, 11.

Looking back on them to-day Körner's songs seem rather a scathing indictment of the policy of Prussia—and of the other Great

Congress of Vienna in 1815, by Angeloni, an Italian whose writings afterwards had considerable influence on Charles Albert:

> To conquer Napoleon you have invoked two principles: freedom and nationality...do not dispose of Italy according to the mere wish or convenience of this or that family, but according to the needs and wishes of the people.... (Cibrario, *Notizie sulla vita di Carlo Alberto*, p. 21.)

Prussia, however, was certainly no worse than the rest of the allies.

II. THE REVOLUTION

It has been said that the history of the period is simply that of a struggle between the Conservative reaction and the "Revolution". As to which principle is right there is practically no discussion nowadays: the Revolution laid down that in each nation the people should rule, and with this doctrine I imagine almost everyone nowadays would agree. But in the first half of the nineteenth century it was by no means a matter of general acceptance—which is not altogether surprising when one remembers that in those days very few of the sovereign people could either read or write, and that those who could do so often fell a prey to the unscrupulous journalism of the time. Thus, even in England, and indeed even as late as the year 1890, one of the commonest maxims quoted among the Conservative classes was: "Everything for the People; nothing by the People"; a phrase which nowadays would win very little sympathy. Moreover the Revolution, though doubtless right in principle, was usually hideous in practice; it had been

Powers as well—during the following hundred years. Speaking of the Congress of Vienna Sir Archibald Alison, F.R.S.E., says that "territories inhabited by thirty-one million six hundred and ninety-one thousand persons were at the disposal of the allied powers and there was for each enough and to spare" (Alison, *Hist. of Europe*, Ch. xcii).

bred amid the political orgies of 1789, and had taught its votaries to glory in reckless theories, violence and bloodshed. Hence the horror with which it was generally regarded by peaceable men. Perhaps the best way to realise how our great-grandfathers viewed the Revolution is to consider our own feelings to-day (in 1930) concerning Bolshevism. Throughout the nations of Western Europe there are undoubtedly many people who regard the fundamental principles of Bolshevism with sympathy; but nevertheless there has been everywhere a general agreement among them, in fact a keen anxiety, to prevent those principles from spreading inside their own country, because they fear an upheaval that would make red havoc of all existing government, of religion, and of social organisation, and would re-enact the stories which, rightly or wrongly, they have heard from Russia. This present-day frame of mind is very similar to that which animated the Holy Alliance[9] and the Conservative classes between the years 1815 and 1848: the feeling that all over Europe they had to be on the watch against a pack of wild animals which any day might break out of its nets and tear them in pieces: and that if one single beast could break loose at any given point (such as Paris, Rome, Warsaw or elsewhere), his cry of triumph would bring the whole pack at their throats.[10]

And undoubtedly they were right. Twice the Revolution broke its bonds, namely in 1830 and in 1848—when the people

[9] Metternich constantly harped upon this string. In 1831 he wrote to Paris: "Notre ennemi c'est l'anarchie; nos amis sont ceux qui la repoussent" (Our enemy is anarchy; our friends are those who repel it), Metternich, v, 156. And in 1834 he says: "We declare that these attempts at propaganda are crimes", *ibid.* p. 600.

[10] This simile was used at the time. Even Louis Philippe, who had been a soldier of the Revolution, and had fought at Jemappes, regarded it as a wild beast. In 1840 when he was protesting against the Treaty of London he said to the Austrian and Prussian representatives: "You are ungrateful: you want war and you shall have it. And, if necessary, I'll unmuzzle the tiger (referring to the Revolution). He knows me and I know how to play with him". Debidour, *Histoire diplomatique d'Europe*, i, 381: and other works.

rose in Paris and overthrew the existing régime—and before a year had passed, blood was flowing in half the cities of Europe. There is nothing more catching than the spirit of revolt. Before the end of 1831, Belgium, Poland,[11] Modena, Parma, most of the Papal provinces, and various states in Germany, had followed the example of Paris, and France and Austria were almost at war with one another. Similarly in 1848, nearly the whole of Europe rose in rebellion, from Ireland to Hungary and Naples.

Thus the Revolution was most undoubtedly an international movement, and the people who claimed that it was always right were as much mistaken as those who held that it was always wrong; because, though springing everywhere from the same original principles, it developed on rather different lines in each separate country. In fact, one might classify it roughly under the following headings:

Firstly, those cases in which it took the form of a national rebellion of one people against another: as, for instance, the rebellions of the Greeks against the Turks; or the successful revolt of the Belgians against Holland in 1831; or the glorious rising of the Poles against Russia in the same year. Each of these was, in fact, a patriotic fight for freedom.

Secondly, when it took the form of a struggle for a freer kind of government: when Paris, for instance, in 1830, dethroned Charles X; or when the Roman Catholics in the British Isles won their emancipation (1829). In these

[11] When in 1831 Metternich persuaded the Poles to treat for Peace, the Princess Melanie wrote in her journal: "We shall prevent the Russians from risking the loss of a battle which might be decisive for all Europe".

"(From Belgium) the movement of revolt was spreading like a train of powder into Germany, at Aix-la-Chapelle and at Cologne, was crossing the Rhine, driving the Duke of Brunswick from his state, and forcing the Grand Duke of Hesse-Cassel, the King of Saxony and several other sovereigns to promise constitutions to their subjects; and was re-arousing at the universities the spirit of the Tugendbund and the Burschenschaft". Debidour, *Hist. dip.* I, 281.

episodes there was often nothing more alarming than militant Liberalism; but O'Connell's agitation created a considerable sensation on the continent, especially in France and Italy, because it was the first successful movement of the kind.

Thirdly, there was the social, the worst form of revolution. This, of course, we have seen in our own day in Russia, just as our great-grandfathers saw it in France in 1789; a rebellion not merely against a foreign nation or against a despotic home-government, but against the whole fabric of law-and-order, the richer classes, the existing institutions, the Church and (as in the French Revolution) even against Christianity itself. It was outbreaks of this nature which disgusted moderate men and compelled the Church to preach against freedom.

Chapter II

REVOLUTION: MAZZINI

MAZZINI'S MOVEMENT

I. HIS CREED

Of Mazzini's movement, which, of course, is among the two or three greatest in the Risorgimento, one is compelled to say that it partook of all the three types above-named. It was, in the first place, a noble, and an extraordinarily persistent uprising against the foreigner; it was also a struggle for national unity and for free institutions; but thirdly, in practice it was partly a revolt against the existing social order. Mazzini himself was a convinced republican of the extreme type; a man who preached liberty, equality and fraternity, and the right to obtain them by the use of the gun.[1]

Of Mazzini's personality we need give no description:[2]

---

[1] "Every member is to provide himself with a dagger, a gun and 50 cartridges", Plan of the Young Italy Society, Art. 6. Mazzini hated the dagger but he did not entirely exclude it. It must be remembered that he and his followers would have been ready enough to fight in the open, but such a contest was hopeless. Mazzini denies that traitors were condemned to death, as was commonly believed. Mazzini, *Scritti* (A.E.), III, 42.

"Even to-day I do not believe that the salvation of Italy can come from the Monarchy; at least not of the Italy which I mean and which we all meant a few years ago." *Ibid.* I, 51.

[2] Born at Genoa, June 22nd, 1805; died at Pisa, March 10th, 1872. His father was a doctor and a professor at the University; his mother, Maria Drago, a cultivated and enthusiastic woman to whom he owed much of his inspiration. Mazzini himself was by training a lawyer and literary man. The rebellion of 1821 made him an Italian nationalist. In 1827 he began political writing and before long joined the Carbonari; 1830, was imprisoned in Savona and then banished from Piedmont; 1831, went to Geneva and thence to Marseille; spent 1831–33 at Marseille founding the Giovine Italia Society which took the place of the Carbonari then moribund; 1831, addressed his celebrated letter to Charles Albert;

everyone interested in the Risorgimento has read of the
tragedy of his life :[3] the forty years spent in disinterested work
and suffering for the sake of his ideas. His beliefs were profoundly honest, amounting in fact to a religion which he had
reached after passing through long periods of suffering.

As to the primary causes of his strange career, hardly anyone
has pointed out that he—the seer whose whole mental being
was consumed in patriotic imaginings—had been born into
this world a man without a nation. In earlier times his natural
patriotism would have been laid at the feet of the ancient
republic of Genoa; but, by the Treaty of 1815, Genoa "la
superba" had been handed over forcibly to Piedmont. By law
he was a subject of the House of Savoy, though, like many
Genoese, he felt no loyalty to it. His whole soul went out to
the great united Italy—in fact to a nation whose very existence
was deemed impossible except by himself and a few political
dreamers.

Let us now examine the scheme which Mazzini offered as
a preferable alternative to the settlement of 1815.

His political and religious conceptions were not limited to
Italy; they comprised a whole world-system; in fact he
preached them as a religious creed,[4] and therein lay their
power; but here we can only summarise them very shortly.

1832, was banished from France but stayed on secrectly for a
year; 1833, started an army plot in Piedmont; 1834, organised
an abortive invasion of Savoy; failure; in 1837, banished from
Switzerland, he went to live in London; 1840, renewed the activities of the Giovine Italia Society; 1844, the episode of the Bandiera brothers—Mazzini's letters opened by Government; 1848,
he returned to Italy for the war; 1849, chief Triumvir of the
Roman Republic. The rest of his life, too lengthy to be summarised
here, was spent in organising revolution.

[3] Mazzini, *Scritti* (A.E.), IX (Saffi's Introduction).
[4] "Ours was not a political association (*setta*) but a patriotic
religion. Political associations may die under violent treatment:
religions never do." Mazzini, *Scritti* (A.E.), V, 112. This is true,
but of course any combination of religion and politics tends to
promote bigotry in each of them, and is no more justifiable in a
republican association than in any other.

Mazzini held that perfect freedom was necessary for the full development of man—that is to say, for Progress.[5]
It was necessary therefore to begin by securing freedom; and already the first stage in this process had been completed by the French Revolution, which had established the Liberty of the Individual Man. The second stage, he held, was actually in progress during the nineteenth century: it consisted in the now-free individuals associating themselves together in order to form free nations; for nations are necessary to the full development and ordering of mankind. Once that could be accomplished, the third phase would follow: all mankind would be organised as a vast association of free nations (sister-republics) to carry out together their mission on earth by methods of peace and mutual love.[6]

According to that Law given by God to Humanity all men are *free*, *equal* and *brothers*: and similarly, all nations are free, equal and brothers.[7]

But in Mazzini's religion there could be no rights without corresponding duties; that was perhaps the finest trait in his belief.[8] The individual was a being with a duty; and similarly the nation was a being with a definite duty: "Life is a mission".

Europe[9] was the recruiting ground. The political ordering of Europe must necessarily precede every other work. And that ordering can only be carried out by peoples: by peoples which live in the free brotherhood of one faith; by peoples which all believe in one common aim, and each of which will have a definite part and a special mission in the enterprise. "The question of the nationalities was, and is for me, and should be for all of us, a very different matter from a mere tribute due to our rights or to our local pride; it should be the

---

[5] The Dilucidazioni (explanations) to the Statuto of the Giovine Italia, given out in 1833.
[6] Mazzini, *Scritti* (A.E.), xii (Saffi's Introduction), xv.
[7] *Ibid.* p. xxiii.
[8] *Ibid.* p. xvi.
[9] Mazzini, *Scritti* (A.E.), v, 214.

sharing out of European work....In any case," he added later, "for me, Nationality was the question which would give its name to the century."[10]

The question remained: Who was to spread abroad these doctrines throughout Europe? To this Mazzini replied: There are three great families of peoples: the old Helleno-Latin now represented by Italy; the Germanic represented by Germany; and the Slav represented by Poland (for Russia is still asleep). These three nations—Italy, Germany and Poland —are to be the initiators of the new ideas in Europe.[11]

Association therefore—association of individuals into nations and of nations into a world-power—was the watchword of Mazzini's political creed. But to summarise his incomparable pages seems rather like reducing a war-song of liberty to terms of x. As to his religion, therefore, we will merely say that its chief principle was the dogma of the *Continuous Progress of Humanity*, a progress due to the constant action of Eternal Truth and its Law on the intellectual and moral faculties of man. The Law of God was the Supreme Guide: and those men who were ablest and best would become *interpreters* of the Law, and would institute the education of the race.[12]

[10] Cf. also Mazzini, *Scritti* (A.E.), xii (Saffi's Introduction), xxiii: "Every people has a special mission which co-operates toward the general work achieved by Humanity. That mission—which is determined by its ethnographic, territorial and historical conditions— constitutes its Nationality: and Nationality is sacred".

[11] From this idea arose his plan of founding the Giovine Europa (Young Europe) Society, which became a sort of central association of the national societies. It will be seen that the plan whereby Italy, Germany and Poland were to head new national movements would hardly commend itself to Austria; nor indeed to Prussia or Russia. Mazzini, *Scritti* (A.E.), v, 38.

[12] These doctrines of course did not satisfy the Church—Mazzini himself knew this. He said: "The school which I tried to promote and which was the germ of the *Giovine Europa*, rejected—from its very first lines, namely from *one single God: one single master, namely the Law of God; one single interpreter of the Law, namely Humanity*— rejected (I repeat) all doctrine of external Revelation of an immediate and final character, and substituted for it the slow, continuous, indefinite revelation of the designs of Providence through the *collective* Life of Humanity". Mazzini, *Scritti* (A.E.), v, 38.

This doctrine of Progress necessarily involved inviolability of Thought and of Conscience: and also inviolability of Liberty and of Association. Even heresy was inviolable—for it might announce new aspects of the Truth.

These tenets of course were supremely unpalatable to the Holy Alliance and to the European religious authorities of those days.

The above is a brief sketch of Mazzini's general ideas; but of course in the foreground he beheld with a pathetic enthusiasm his beloved Italy a united republic, the Terza Italia, the third re-incarnation of Rome, once again lighting the path of civilisation for all the other peoples in the world. He himself has said so:[13]

In those days, from that still immature conception there flashed out—as it were from a star of the soul—an immense hope: Italy reborn to Humanity; and—owing to her missionary zeal for spreading her élan of belief in Progress and Fraternity—greater by far at the present time than in the days of old.

Just as the French Revolution had freed the individual, so now there was to be an Italian Revolution which should free the nations. This conception had a far stronger hold on Mazzini than is generally realised. So deep was his feeling that Italy must fulfil a great mission of inaugurating the new era of free nations, just as France had inaugurated that of the free individual, that he found comparatively little pleasure even in her final unification and emancipation; because it was not the work of the Revolution and did not inaugurate a new era.[14]

He believed—and was his belief entirely without justifica-

[13] Mazzini, *Scritti* (A.E.), 1, 40.

[14] Even as early as 1830 and 1831 when he was founding the Giovine Italia (Young Italy Society) Mazzini describes his motives in the following terms: "I will merely remark that, even then, the motive which generated every design was not merely a political motive, not merely the idea of improving the lot of *one* people which I saw dismembered, oppressed and degraded; it was a presentiment that Italy, when she arose, should be the *initiator* of a new life; and of a new and powerful Union among the nations of Europe". Mazzini, *Scritti* (A.E.), 1, 39.

tion?—that in Europe there existed a great void: the void due to the absence of genuine and holy authority. Might not this suggest the mission reserved for the Terza Italia, the third Italy?[15]

For the association of the peoples with a view to the Progress of Humanity, it is necessary, he said, that the peoples must each have a real existence:

And the people have no existence where, owing to a forced union of races or families, there is no unity of belief and moral purpose; these factors alone constitute nations. The division of Europe, as sanctioned by the Treaties of 1815—with its inequalities, its compulsion to lean on a Great Power, and the internal divisions within each nation...interposed an insurmountable obstacle to every normal and sure development of liberty. To re-make the map of Europe and re-order the peoples according to the special mission assigned to each one of them by its geographical, ethnological and historical conditions, was therefore, the first essential step for everyone.[16]

True: but these views set Mazzini in direct opposition to the Treaty of 1815 and to the five Great Powers. No real attempt was made by Europe to complete this part of his programme until after the Great War.

[15] "In ancient days Rome, following close upon the flight of her eagles, had ploughed and sown the whole known world with the idea of Right as being the fountain-head of Liberty. Then, later, when she seemed to be no more than a sepulchre, there had arisen a fresh unifying influence—the Popes—who upon the idea of Right had superimposed the idea of Duty, and—duty being common to all men—had founded the principle of Equality. Why should there not arise a third Rome, the Rome of the Italic People...a third and more vast Unifying Influence...which should harmonise earth and sky, Right and Duty, and should proclaim—not to individuals but to the peoples—a message of Association so as to teach those men who are now equal and free, their duty in this world?" Mazzini, *Scritti* (A.E.), I, 39.

[16] "The pact of Humanity cannot be signed by individuals but only by peoples which are equal and free, with a name, conscience and life of their own, and a national flag." *Ibid.* V, 20.

"To enable Europe to make any genuine advance, to arrive at a new synthesis and consecrate to its working-out all the forces that are now consumed in internal struggles, it was necessary to draw its map afresh." *Ibid.* p. 21.

II. HIS REVOLUTIONARY MACHINE

After examining Mazzini's doctrines, our next enquiry must be as to the political organisation, in fact the revolutionary machine, which he created. Broadly it was twofold: firstly, his scheme of Italian Revolution by means of the Giovine Italia, or Young Italy, a national society founded in 1831; secondly, his European federation of revolutionary movements under the Giovine Europa, or Young Europe, committee, founded at Berne on April 19th, 1834.

(1) It was, of course, in the Giovine Italia, in dreams of a young and ideal Italy, that Mazzini found his true inspiration. His work in this connection (April 1831) began with a letter, now celebrated, to King Charles Albert of Piedmont, appealing to him to lead the Revolution. The letter produced no result.[17] But Mazzini, though an exile (from Piedmont), living in squalid lodgings at Marseille, was already hard at work day and night founding the Giovine Italia, whose secret branches were to be established in all the chief towns of Italy, and were to be stimulated and kept in touch with the central committee by means of his newspaper, the *Giovine Italia*.[18] And this period (1831 to 1833) is perhaps the finest of his life: these were two wonderful years of striving, of intense poverty, miserable and yet splendidly happy because they were spent in successful patriotic effort. Every one knows the story of this handful of exiles without money, Mazzini, Lamberti, the Ruffinis, Usiglio, Lustrini, La Cecilia and several others; of their successful printing of the newspaper; of their getting it smuggled through the custom-houses and distributed in thousands of Italian homes.[19] Almost at once the new

---

[17] Mazzini never expected it to produce any results. He wrote it because some of the revolutionists were pinning their faith on Charles Albert, and marking time themselves. Mazzini wanted to prove to all Italy that Charles Albert would do nothing.

[18] Mazzini, *Scritti* (A.E.), I, 394; III, 312.

[19] In August 1832 the paper was suspended and Mazzini was exiled from France as well as from Piedmont; but he continued in

Society, arising out of the ashes of the old Carbonari,[20] founded branches all over Italy and was received as a kindred force by the French and Polish committees in Paris and in Switzerland. It aimed at action: "nous voulons remuer cette terre jusqu'aux entrailles". It was an appeal to youth as opposed to age—he would accept no one over forty years old— and therefore to enthusiasm; and above all things it was a call from the Ideal; its votaries were to be the regenerators of Europe, and it exacted from them a noble standard of morality and self-sacrifice.

Its organisation was as little complicated as possible. It consisted of

(i) The Central Office (Congrega), which always met outside Italy. It gave instructions, communicated signs of recognition, dealt with the press, diffused their newspaper, etc. etc.

---

hiding at Marseille, and persisted in his work for over a year. "Our people scattered themselves among the small villages near the centre of our work: we arranged for the transporting of the writings as soon as they came off the printing press: and as for me I began then, that method of life which kept me, for twenty-two years out of thirty, a voluntary prisoner within the four walls of a tiny room. They never found me....I remained a whole year in Marseille, writing, correcting proofs, corresponding and holding interviews at midnight with men of the Party, newly-arrived from Italy, and also with some of the heads of the republican party in France." He says, however, that the worst weapon employed against him was slander. Mazzini, *Scritti* (A.E.), III, 32 *et seq.*

[20] One may date the zenith of the Carbonari as having been between 1821 and 1831. After that the Giovine Italia takes their place. Mazzini claims that by the middle of 1833 he had a stronghold in the Genoese territories, in Tuscany, and in the Papal State, and had friends in Naples (Poerio); and that in Piedmont he had had some success, though the work progressed more slowly there. Among the towns in which the Giovine Italia was spreading its propaganda he mentions Livorno, "which inspired Pisa, Siena, Lucca and Florence". He also mentions Perugia; also Bologna and the towns of Romagna, Rome; and of course Genoa. The movement had aroused such enthusiasm that it was necessary to strike while the iron was hot; hence Mazzini's early attempts at insurrection. Mazzini, *Scritti* (A.E.), I, 398; III, 314.

(ii) The Provincial Offices in Italy. Each of these directed the work of its province; composed the signs for the province; transmitted messages and reported monthly to the Central Office.

(iii) The Ordinatori (Organisers). In each city there was an Organiser. His work was under the Provincial Offices, and was similar to theirs under the Central Office.

(iv) The Propagatori, or initiators. Their special work was to initiate new members; they fulfilled also the duties of an ordinary member.

(v) The Semplici Affratellati, or ordinary members. Their duties were to communicate information to their Propagatore; to spread the principles of the Society; and to hold themselves ready for action.

Every affratellato was to have his *nom-de-guerre* (pseudonym), a dagger, a gun and fifty cartridges.

They all subscribed monthly to the Provincial Office, and this money was spent on the province, except a quota reserved for the Central Office.

The signs and passwords were different in each province, and were altered every three months. This system seems to have defeated the police; for we hear that the revolutionary network all over Italy was hardly ever betrayed for years to come.

Thus the machinery was simple and practical; but in its actual working Mazzini did not always show himself very business-like. He was certainly too prone to trust to the numbers on paper of those who received his journal and joined the Society; no doubt their sympathy was genuine, but of course many of them had no intention of answering a sudden call to arms. And in framing its policy of action he overlooked the immediate difficulties—a fault of which, to his dying day, no failure could ever cure him.

(2) The second development of Mazzini's conception—the wider scheme—consisted of his European federation of revolutionary movements under the Giovine Europa or Young Europe committee. Who but Mazzini could have conceived and carried out such an idea in days before railways or

telegraphs? By means of this international organisation, the Holy Alliance was to be met by an equally holy federation of revolutionary societies! This Young European committee was to be formed of delegates from the already-existing national committees, such as those of the Giovine Germania (Young Germany), Giovine Polonia (Young Poland), Giovine Italia (Young Italy) and, before the end of 1834, by the Giovine Svizzera (Young Switzerland), newly organised with its network of committees. The purpose of this scheme was to found a defensive and offensive alliance for pushing on Mazzini's aims, and, at any given moment, to secure a simultaneous outbreak of revolution all over Europe.[21] It was a gigantic conception, ghastly as the results might have been; one cannot but admit that. This Pact of Brotherhood was composed by Mazzini and signed by seventeen men— Mazzini and five other Italians, the rest being Germans and Poles representing their respective peoples; and many of these men lived to see the fall of Metternich.

Seventeen unknown men and Mazzini! Nevertheless, by combining the cause of Italian freedom with that of inter- national militant democracy, they were able to command a kind of ebbing and flowing sea of revolutionary forces all over Europe. Its flood tide came in 1848, when some of the subject nations were temporarily set free, and since then its work has been completed by the Great War, 1914–18.

III. CRITICISM OF MAZZINI'S MOVEMENT

Truth compels one to say that, however beautiful, his programme was extremely unpractical: much of it was far ahead of his time: and as revolutions cause great suffering,

[21] "The ideal of the Giovine Europa was the organisation on federal lines of European Democracy under a single directing body, so that the insurrection of one nation would find the others ready to support it with action...." Mazzini, *Scritti* (A.E.), v, 37. They started at once upon their network of national committees; their secret oaths and their affiliations; and they adopted an emblem— which, rather poetically, was a spray of ivy.

a revolutionist should beware of following after visionary ideals.

Firstly, as to his aims: the primary aim of Mazzini's scheme was to unite all Italy into one indivisible republic: that is to say, it was twofold: namely (*a*) republican, and (*b*) founded on union-by-fusion. Of these two items, (*a*) the idea of a Mazzinian republic reached its zenith in 1849, and after that year never again appeared in the foremost place as a constructive scheme: but (*b*) his idea of uniting Italy, by simply fusing all her states into one, eventually carried the day as opposed to union-by-federation or any other scheme of united states in Italy. Nowadays this form of unity seems natural, and the young generations can hardly realise that they are born in a united Italy which for twenty or thirty years had little existence except in Mazzini's brain: during the first half of the nineteenth century each Italian state rejoiced in a separate national tradition, language, government, history and, sometimes, literature: the Florentines, for instance, gloried in their splendid national art, and in speaking the true language of Dante: the Venetians remembered the wonderful story of their city on the lagoons during a thousand years; and the Piedmontese were loyal monarchists, proud of their brave House of Savoy. So that Mazzini's union-by-fusion was not to be thought of for the time being; and in fact it never became practicable as long as it remained linked to the idea of a republic.[22]

Nevertheless, his truest claim to greatness lies in the fact that he was the apostle, in the proposed Italian state, of this principle of union-by-fusion. Undoubtedly it was he who

---

[22] "Though the efficacy of this association had been far from slight when diffusing *generally* the principles of liberty and nationality, yet as a society for preaching republicanism or for planning conspiracies it had lost ground every day" between 1834 and 1840. This is the opinion of Cornero, who was a member from 1832 onwards, and he seems to have been a man of ability; in 1845 he worked for Massimo d'Azeglio in Romagna. *Archivio triennale*, III, xviii.

first saw the modern Italy of to-day, the "Terza Italia", as she was destined to be. For a long time fusion was not possible, but eventually it became so.

Secondly, as to his methods: as a practical scheme of rebellion his programme was quite unworkable. To fuse the whole of Italy into one single republic would involve too many processes: firstly, simultaneous insurrections in each state; secondly, the elimination of all the existing governments; and finally, the fusion of the whole country into one democracy. It was an easy plan on paper—his idea seems to have been that there were enough associates on the roll of each town to carry out a popular rising there; he believed in the power of the masses. But the magnitude of the scheme[23] made it quite impossible. As there were nine monarchical governments in Italy, it involved war simultaneously against nine armies and nine sets of vested interests; also against the Austrian Empire; also against the Treaty of 1815 and the five Great Powers of Europe which had guaranteed it; and at the same time the fusing into one single indivisible republic of many millions of people who were neither unitarians nor republicans, and could hardly understand each other's dialect. Added to which, in the towns many of his followers, though sympathetic, were apathetic, and in the country most of the peasants only wanted to be left alone.

This condemnation of Mazzini's plan is not merely an opinion after the event. The scheme was condemned at the time by working revolutionists such as Dr Farini[24] and

[23] For plan of the Giovine Italia, *v.* Mazzini, *Scritti* (E.N.), II, 59.

[24] Here, for instance, is the opinion of Luigi-Carlo Farini, by profession a doctor, who was one of the leaders of revolution in 1832, and who afterwards wrote an excellent history of the period. He complained bitterly that the plan meant war against every one at the same time: "It [the Young Italy Society] did not propose merely to change a state from being absolutist and narrow into being constitutional and broadminded, nor only to try alterations within an Italian province. Its aim was to conquer the whole of Italy and rule her according to the dogma of Young Italy: namely as a

Professor Montanelli, who were as genuine rebels as could be found in Italy.

Mazzini's reasons for preferring a republic to any other form of government may be summarised as follows:

Because monarchy would bring with it aristocracy "which is a source of inequality and corruption to the entire nation".

Because monarchy would certainly lead to *Federalism*, owing to the difficulty of selecting any one monarch to rule all Italy. And Mazzini disapproved of Federalism because it would mean an assemblage of courts with all their appanage—such as diplomacy. It was undemocratic, "it would betray the people and ruin the Revolution". Yet Federalism was at that time the only possible form of unity.

Because in order to move a whole people, one must have an aim that speaks directly and intelligibly to *their own* rights and advantage.

Because, as the Young Italy Society is in opposition to all the monarchs of Italy,

we are compelled, if we would avoid remaining alone in the arena, to call to our side the peoples, raising above us a banner of the people and invoking them in the name of the principle which to-day dominates every revolutionary manifestation in Europe.[25]

democratic republic, one and indivisible. War therefore against all the Italian governments and all the Italian princes; war of ideas against princedom and monarchy; war against the Austrians, and against Europe, the guardian and guarantor of the treaties. The Young Italy Society gathered in obols from the meagre purses of the exiles: these constituted the funds of its treasury. It recruited on foreign soil, with an oath of life and death, Italian and Polish exiles, young men of personal courage and ready to face the dangers: these were its armies. It conspired with the republicans of France—and they were its allies", etc. These are Farini's rather caustic remarks (written after he had become a Moderate) about the Young Italy Society.

V. also the opinion of Montanelli, a leading revolutionist, the founder of the Fratelli Italiani Society. Montanelli, *Memorie sull' Italia*, p. 40.

[25] D'Azeglio wrote after the fruitless attempt at Rimini in 1845: "Even if consulted, the Italians *en masse* would have refused to rise in arms, because in the masses, especially in Italy, there is a

The most unfortunate feature of his scheme was that it excluded all others. It led Mazzini, for instance, on three separate occasions to attack Piedmont, which was the only Italian power capable of resisting Austria; also to work secretly against Pius IX's policy of reform; and later to oppose Cavour's party throughout the whole country.

It is venturesome to try and sum up so well known a character, but the following is an endeavour. He was a born visionary; but as a propagandist, or rather as a preacher of ideas, he was absolutely peerless—his writing was like a flame. As an organiser he was great only within certain limits, but he had a wonderful power of pushing on his movement. Yet he was not a wise judge of immediate and active enterprises nor a skilful director of rebels. It was his self-sacrifice, his power of arousing enthusiasm, his genius with the pen, his mental audacity when conceiving schemes and when sending men to the slaughter,[26] and, above all, his marvellous persistency which made him a power in Europe off and on during forty years. In each generation he sent young men to the slaughter, lest the national movement should die down and become merely a memory.

practical common sense which is not always to be found in individuals". And he continues: "The greater number having neither civil education nor even the beginnings of political understanding (and this is the condition of the masses in our country) moves only for its needs, its desires or its material sufferings". D'Azeglio, *Gli ultimi casi di Romagna*, p. 13. But, he continues, the people are right not to rise: "Because to rise in small numbers is useless, and to rise in large numbers is impossible". Even if they won freedom from their own government they would then have to fight disordered and unarmed against the Austrians. Gioberti was even more scornful about the possibility of successful revolution in Italy.

[26] This of course is the quality which makes a revolutionist dangerous. It is not very common; usually he is an altruist ready to offer his own life but not to order others to do so. An Italian once said to me that Mazzini "kept the sacred fire alight by throwing in batches of young men generation after generation". This is perhaps an exaggeration.

During the period of Mazzini's leadership there must have been hundreds of soldiers and policemen killed or wounded by Mazzinians who, one remembers, never wore uniform. Yet he is rarely condemned; because fundamentally he was justified by the circumstances around him. He was living in the Europe of that day, a continent which everywhere was disgraced by slavery;[27] that is to say, where nearly every weak nation was enslaved by some stronger power. And such dominations by force cannot possibly be maintained without a whole system of fraud: in their interests the truth must be suppressed; therefore free speech, free writing, free assemblage and justice in political trials are reduced to a minimum; secret service, the opening of letters and the spreading of slanders are systematised; and the law of course is used as a weapon of retaliation.[28] Such conditions create men far more violent than Mazzini.

The moral effects of such a domination are the worst imaginable: for instance, Mazzini—the very soul of kindliness —has been condemned because he did not entirely exclude the use of the stiletto. In reality none of the weaker nations

[27] "In this century, in which slavery of the individual is an object of universal abomination, in which the more powerful and more civilised nations are making such efforts to blot out the stain from the world; in this century, in which we believe it to be unjust that a man should keep in fetters the will and actions of any other man and direct them to his own advantage, and profit by his toil while leaving him nothing for himself but his life and the most restricted necessaries of existence, who can assert that that which is unjust between man and man is just between nation and nation?" D'Azeglio, *Gli ultimi casi*, p. 11.

[28] Under Metternich's Italian régime free speech, free writing and free assemblage were necessarily curtailed: the secret service was very efficient; the opening of letters was systematised; the law and its law-courts were of course on the side of the government in political cases. Without these methods his government could not have been maintained for long; nor could any other of the same type. It was a good government of its kind: successful, pleasant and benevolent to anyone who had no sense of natural patriotism. Even Massimo d'Azeglio preferred it to the régime at Turin and spent ten happy years in Milan under its wing.

could exclude it. If the strong abuse their strength, the weak, in self-defence, will abuse their weakness. It was the presence of the Austrian soldiers in Lombardy and Venetia that justified Mazzini. Obviously when one nation dominates another it creates a situation in which rebellion, murders and other acts of resistance, such as those of the Mazzinians, will result inevitably—as certainly as night follows day—and always have so resulted since the world began.

The mental condition developed among the men of the Revolution can be exemplified in a final quotation which shows the intense idealism, self-sacrifice and vindictiveness that Mazzini inculcated in his young followers:

Nations are not regenerated materially unless and until their moral regeneration is complete. . . .
Freedom is the first-born offspring of the virtues. . . . Be virtuous; remain unstained. Be such that no friend can blush for you, and no enemy strike at you except by calumny.
Virtue is self-sacrifice.
Thought is action.
These maxims alone can give life and triumph to our brotherhood. Spread them with unvarying persistence. Be active. Let not one minute of your life pass without service to the holy cause; and let there be no thought in your soul that is not a thought of progress and of your native land. But at the same time be cautious and prudent. A flame must burn in your breast; it is the flame of liberty, the sun of our soul. Let it be powerful, inextinguishable, one whose light shines and illumines but does not consume: so must the flame in your breast disperse the darkness by the fulness of its victory. And let it not be merely as a rapid and ineffective gleam: accumulate grief on grief; concentrate your ardour for revenge; make the Italian race your treasure. Never forget; but let your face be cold and smiling when a fire is burning in your heart. The dagger of Harmodius was wreathed with myrtles from the feast of Venus. Imitate Harmodius and suffer. One single imprudence, one single impulse, even though generous in itself, may ruin our enterprise, may set Italy back by half a century and may earn you the execration of all good men. Mazzini, *Scritti* (E.N.), ii, 68, 69.

Chapter III

REACTION: PRINCE VON METTERNICH AND ITALY[1]

I. PRINCE VON METTERNICH

It would be impossible, probably, to find a more complete contrast between any two human beings than that which existed between Mazzini, the man who meant to free Italy, and Prince von Metternich, the man who meant to keep her in subjection. Broadly speaking they were both in the wrong; because the one preached schemes that were not yet possible and the other represented ideas that were no longer true. Thus it was a struggle between antitheses, not merely between individuals, but—as both men realised—between principles, systems, epochs and ideals. Indeed the tragedy of this period lies in the fact that it is the story of a war of ideals: the national ideal; the democratic ideal; the ideal of loyalty to the throne; the ideal of the Catholic Church and the ideal of empire. And the beautiful land of Italy was their chief battle-ground.

For a period of no less than thirty-nine years, from 1809 to 1848, Prince Clemenz Lothar von Metternich remained the principal director of Austrian policy; and during most of that time he may be called, undoubtedly, the leader of European diplomacy.

Strangely enough, he too was a man almost without nationality.[2] He was not an Austrian and never entirely became one. His early home had been in the Rhineland, and

---

[1] For Metternich's life the authorities mainly relied on have been his own *Memoirs and Letters*, and *Metternich der Staatsmann und der Mensch*, by Heinrich Ritter von Srbik. Of course other lives and works have also been consulted, such as Friedjung's *Oesterreich von 1848 bis 1860*.

[2] *V.* Srbik, I, p. 53.

his only sentiment of patriotism—of the genuine inborn love-
of-country which ennobles men—consisted of a memory of
the wooded hills and castles between Bingen-on-the-Rhine
and Bonn. Most probably a romantic remembrance of those
princely days of his youth may have followed him through the
whole of his life. But after 1815 his home-land, the prince-
bishopric of Treves, had been allotted to Prussia; before the
Revolution it had been an electorate of the Holy Roman
Empire.

He was born in 1773, the son of an Austrian diplomat and
Count of the Empire. Up to the age of fifteen his education
had been entrusted to a priest and to a Protestant tutor, but
after that date (1788) he was sent to France to the university
at Strasbourg.[3] His true and life-enduring lessons, however,
were those provided for him by the French Revolution.[4]
During the next four years he saw the whole of that human
eruption from start to finish: he saw it begin in the university
lectures and discussions; and he saw it end by turning into
sans-culottism. In 1790 he was obliged to leave Strasbourg
and he went to Mainz University. In 1791 he was driven
from Mainz and went back to his father, who had an appointment in Brussels. But Belgium was soon seething with strife,
so his father sent him for a few months to England. Meanwhile their own home had been overrun, plundered and
annexed,[5] and in 1794 both father and son arrived in Vienna,
financially at a low ebb and seriously out-of-grace with the

[3] At the completion of Metternich's education he wrote French
with greater ease than German. *V.* Srbik, 1, 61.
[4] "The mental position and the teachings which I drew from it
have never abandoned me during the long course of my public life."
Ibid. 73.
[5] "In July [1794] Treves fell into the hands of soldiers in red
caps [of liberty]. Soon Cologne and Bonn, and on the 23rd of
October Coblenz, the home-town of the Metternich family, suffered
the same fate, and the house of the now officeless Minister lost all
its [belongings] on the left bank of the Rhine: three and a half square
miles of land, 6200 subjects and 50,000 florins of annual revenue."
Ibid. 79.

now irritable authorities. These lessons remained graven on
Metternich's mind for life. Throughout all his long thirty-
nine years of hegemony in Europe he had one primary object
in view: to prevent a fresh outbreak of the Revolution; and
not only to prevent but to forestall it in lectures, newspapers,
speeches or even thought. His motto was: Never again.

Henceforth he classed all revolutions—whether social,
liberal or national—as social: as an attempt by the mob to
plunder the rich.[6] In reality, of course, they are entirely
different from one another, but the Settlement of 1815 had
banded them together by blocking the way simultaneously
against all three.

Thus Metternich emerged from his early years of suffering
rather a typical eighteenth-century reactionist; laborious,
thorough, symmetrical in mind (so to speak) and given to
political generalisations; the champion everywhere of "strong"
government and determined at any cost to maintain law-and-
order by force, and—quite another thing—to maintain the
existing law-and-order by force. In the course of his work
he had evolved certain principles, which since then have
been called his "system"; but in practice his guiding motive
was that the imperial-aristocratic form of government must
always remain an unalterable pier of safety; below it the
waves of popular movement might sway to and fro according
to the storms or the tides, but they must never be able to rise
to its level. Metternich's true enemy in life was not to be
found among the foreign nations, however hostile, for they
were unlikely to go to war with him: it was the Revolution.
In 1815 these views chimed in with the general desire for
peace: so he soon became the supreme director of the Austrian
peoples, for whom in reality he had no special affection.

During his earlier days one can sympathise with him. But
in political principles he remained unchanged for forty years—

---

[6] Metternich afterwards said that the chief principle of the
Revolution was: "Ôte-toi que je m'y mette" (Clear out so that I can
take your place).

a rampart, of course, against mob-invasions, but at the same time a barrier throughout Europe against Liberal development and against the rights of nationality. The reason for this extraordinary immobility was that he was a Conservative by necessity. For him no other creed was possible.

As director of the Austrian policy he inevitably represented imperialism pushed to the point of absurdity; an Empire without any genuine national basis; in fact, as time went on, a governmental organisation rather than a people. Austria was an assemblage of different races, whose lands had fallen to the Hapsburgs by marriage, by treaty, or by conquest, and who therefore acknowledged the Emperor as their feudal chief; but it could hardly be called a nation. As a matter of fact, although it perpetuated the throne of the Holy Roman Empire, strictly speaking it did not even possess an official name until the year 1806, when Francis I christened it "The Austrian Empire".[7]

This huge remnant of Germanic feudal machinery still wielded immense power, but, like the gods of Valhalla, already it was doomed. It was irreconcilable with Progress. The mere introduction of modern democratic, nationalist or racial ideas into its realms might easily disrupt the whole organisation; and this fact was plainly perceived by Metternich.

---

[7] "La manière particulière dont s'étaient réunies les différentes parties de l'Empire, et cette longue succession de Souverains qui pendant des siècles avaient occupé le trône du Saint Empire romain, et gouverné un pays formé d'éléments si complexes, avait fait naître un singulier inconvénient; cet *ensemble*, ce corps politique n'avait pas de nom; il y avait là dans la langue usuelle un vide, un défaut qui se révélait par la dénomination de 'Maison de Habsbourg' ou de 'Maison d'Autriche' qu'on donnait à la famille régnante. Le cas est unique dans l'histoire des États; nulle part on ne s'est jamais servi, dans la vie ordinaire et encore moins dans les relations diplomatiques *du nom de la famille régnante* au lieu du nom du pays même. Ce n'est qu'en 1806 en même temps que disparaissait la dignité d'Empereur d'Allemagne, que l'Empereur François à donné à son Empire le nom *d'Empire d'Autriche*." Metternich, *Mémoires*, French Translation, 2nd ed. 1880, I, 212.

Supposing, for instance, that the seeds of democratic and nationalist movements—which nearly always go together—were sown in Austria, they would produce a whole crop of separate nations: the Empire would develop, not into one national democracy, but into half a dozen different democracies each with its own language and its own assembly. This would be all the more dangerous, in that it would coincide with the racial movements outside the frontiers. There were three possible racial movements—the pan-German, the pan-Italian and the pan-Slav. If any of these should prove successful it would tear from the Viennese government one of its component nations. The making of a pan-Italian nation would mean the loss of Lombardy and Venetia; a pan-Slav movement would threaten Bohemia, and even a merely Polish national rising would convulse Galicia; and, worst of all, pan-Germanism was shortly to become the chief weapon of Prussia in supplanting Austria as the leader of the race. No other nation was in so dangerous a position as Austria.

Consequently Metternich was necessarily opposed, and permanently opposed, to the Revolution; and not only to the Revolution but to every form of Liberal advance. In fact, one might say that the apparently all-powerful Prince von Metternich was in reality rather like a man living over a powder-magazine—anxious at the sight of every spark, and determined that no one should carry a light. Even the successful secession of Belgium from Holland in 1831 seemed to him a disaster, simply and solely because it formed a precedent, and proved, moreover, that the sacrosanct Settlement of 1815 might possibly be defied with impunity. It was not merely actual revolt that he feared, but any conceivable movement or institution that could suggest interference with the existing peace and order or the blessed *status quo*.

Hence it is that in Metternich's letters—often side by side with fine sentences showing immense experience, combined with excellent common sense, perspicacity, realisation of principles, and thoroughness in detail—we find such gems of modern thought as the following:

What is true of religious dogmas is equally true of principles of government. To discuss them is often dangerous and always useless.[8]

Or again:

We certainly are not alone in putting to ourselves the question whether society can exist along with *the liberty of the press*, a scourge unknown to the world before the last half of the seventeenth century.[9]

Or again, the following critical observations about the representative system:

The Faction tries to implant the modern idea of popular sovereignty disguised under the form of the representative system. That is what constitutes—and His Majesty the Emperor is intimately convinced of it—the principal agent of the disorganisation now spreading from one neighbouring power to another. That is the prime cause of the encroachments on the rights of sovereign authority of the German princes.... All other symptoms, however striking, however alarming they may be, His Majesty the Emperor considers merely as the inevitable results of the preponderance which this fatal theory has gained in Germany, in relation to monarchical principle.[10]

He evidently disapproved of a free press, of free discussion and of popular representation. This did not much matter at first, in 1815, when many war-weary people were inclined to agree with him, but, as years went by, his position became more and more difficult, because the conditions of the Austrian Empire made it impossible for him to advance with the times.

In his early days Metternich was completely successful. In 1815 Austria, though four times overthrown during the Napoleonic era, had emerged surprisingly vigorous from those years of divine wrath, or human insanity. She possessed

[8] Metternich, v, 393.
[9] *Ibid.* III, 443.
[10] *Ibid.* v, 627.

a remarkable power of recuperation, largely due to the great reserve of young and hardy populations[11] and undeveloped resources always at her government's call; and under Metternich's able guidance very soon she became the leading power on the continent.[12] But out of all these early diplomatic contests of his, there are only three that seriously concern our present subject which is Metternich's policy in Italy before 1846.

Firstly, in 1815, in conjunction with the Emperor Alexander, he formed the Holy Alliance of Austria, Russia and Prussia (to which various other powers afterwards adhered), originally a noble, religious conception, but one which soon degenerated into a mere league of governments for preventing the growth of revolutionary or Liberal ideas. This aim was natural enough, seeing that two out of the three powers had themselves been conquered and overrun by the Revolution; and the justification of the Holy Alliance is that it aimed at peace[13] and represented the immense weariness which followed upon eighteen years of Napoleonic slaughter. But, as time goes on, one realises that the constant proclaiming of the necessity for

[11] This point was noted by Napoleon III when he was preparing to attack Austria in 1859 (the campaign of Magenta and Solferino). He recalled the fact that when the allies had invaded France in 1814, it was he Austrian battalions which had the finest material within their ranks.

[12] Geographically it was a huge empire consisting of Upper and Lower Austria (German), Salzburg (German), Styria (German), Carinthia (German), Carniola (Slav), Gorz, Istria, Trieste (mixed), Tyrol Vorarlberg (German), Bohemia (Slav), Moravia (Slav), Silesia (German and Polish), Galicia (Polish and Ruthenian), Bukowina (mixed), Dalmatia (Slav), Lombardo Venetia (Italian).

The above list omits several millions of Serbs, Slovenes and Rumans. In 1818 its total population was 29,769,263; in 1830 it had risen to 34,082,469.

[13] "Ce que nous voulons, c'est la paix, la paix morale comme la paix politique....Ce que nous voulons, du reste, est également et uniformément voulu à Saint-Pétersbourg et à Berlin." Metternich, v, 117. The letter then goes on to dilate on the Russian preparations for the reconquest of Poland; a struggle which ended in the suppression of Polish freedom (1831).

restoring law-and-order was often induced by the fact that the
three Great Powers in question had secured a splendid share
of booty in 1815, and wanted to be left alone to enjoy it.[14]

Secondly, in 1818 there was held, at Aix-la-Chapelle, the
first reunion of the five Great Powers of Europe—Russia,
Prussia, Austria, England and France. Louis XVIII was
being invited to join the other great guarantors of the Second
Peace of Paris (1815) to help in maintaining the *status quo*.
These five powers formed the Concert of Europe.

For the next half-century they were able to dominate
Europe—on those occasions, at all events, when they could
work in unison. But joint action could not always be obtained
between nations in such different stages of development.
France, for instance, the mother of the Revolution, was regarded from the first by Metternich as *déclassée*; and after
1830 she became his indefatigable rival in Italy. England,
too, was often on the Liberal side; but on Russia and Prussia
he could nearly always rely.

These differences of sentiment came to a head after the
Revolution of 1830. The raising of the barricades in Paris had
fired the revolutionary spirit everywhere, and Metternich and
his allies were seriously alarmed. As they could each command vast military forces, they realised keenly what an
immense advantage it would be to have a joint right of armed
intervention in any state whose internal unrest was a menace
to the peace of the world or an encouragement to their own
subject populations; and this situation brings us to the last
important heading on our list.

[14] The "Holy Alliance" became little better than a pledge to protect each other's conquests. Austria, Russia and Prussia had shared
Poland and consequently felt bound to support each other in holding
it down. Austria indeed could not possibly acknowledge the principles of democracy or nationality anywhere because they would have
disrupted her whole empire. The other powers were more or less
in a similar difficulty as regards nationality. France in fact was the
only one who could now boldly preach freedom because her conquests had all been taken from her.

Thirdly,[15] in September 1833 there was held a meeting at Münchengrätz, in Bohemia, between the Czar, the Austrian Emperor and the Crown Prince of Prussia, and they decided to form a league for counteracting the policy of France and England. On October 15th, by the Treaty of Berlin, they laid down as a definite principle the *right of intervention* in the internal affairs of any nation whose sovereign called on them for help, and added that if any outside nation tried to prevent their intervening, they bound themselves to joint resistance. This was definite. They intended to intervene and repress any population that rose against its ruler if he invited them to do so. This was a league of princes for holding down Poland, Italy, or any other subject nation; in Italy especially it would find a justification for constant interference.[16]

II. THE LIBERAL POWERS AND INTERVENTION[17]

But France and England were by no means disposed to agree. On November 4th, 1833, France asserted definitely that she would not tolerate intervention in Belgium, Switzerland or Piedmont, and this powerful protection afterwards converted Piedmont into a comparatively secure stronghold from which its rulers could sally out and attack the Austrians. A year later, when the Spanish and Portuguese questions became acute, England, Spain, Portugal and France formed

[15] On this subject, *v.* Metternich, v, 545; Debidour, *Hist. dip.* I, 329; Bianchi, *Storia documentata della diplomazia europea in Italia dall' anno* 1814 *all' anno* 1861, IV, 62, 245; and others.

[16] This principle had already been stated by them at the Congress of Troppau in 1820; and in 1821, at the Congress of Laibach (Austria, Russia, Prussia), the principle had been put into practice. The Austrians, authorised by the other two powers, had intervened with armed force in Naples and in Piedmont, had restored the *ancien régime* in those two countries, and abolished the constitutions granted by their rulers. Now, however, in 1833 they went a step further, and bound themselves by treaty to joint action. Of course these points are dealt with in most histories, for instance, Debidour, *Hist. dip.* I, 147, 153, 185 (Congress of Vienna), 328.

[17] *V.* Metternich, v, 480; also De Guichen, *La révolution de juillet* 1830 *et l'Europe*, pp. 229, 314, 327.

a quadruple alliance (April 22nd, 1834) which, for a short time at all events, became a Liberal set-off against the Holy Alliance. The doctrine of non-intervention, favoured especially by England, was always of Liberal tendency, because it enabled a smaller nation to settle its own form of government unhindered.

It has been necessary to begin by describing (perhaps rather prematurely) this principle of intervention, because it became the basis of Austrian policy[18] throughout the whole period and remained so until 1860, when the battle of Solferino put an end to it and thus afforded the Italians a chance of forming their nation—at the price of ceding Savoy and Nice to France.

III. THE RESTORATION IN ITALY AFTER 1815

In Italy at first there was a certain amount of truth in Metternich's thousand-times reiterated assertion that he was defending law-and-order and saving the country from anarchy. If a successful rebellion had been engineered by the Carbonari (1815–30) or even by Mazzini between 1830 and 1848, quite possibly it might have resulted in anarchy; at all events for some time to come, the various revolutionary sections, even if victorious, could hardly have avoided quarrelling with one another. The conditions of that long narrow mountain-divided peninsula made joint revolt almost

[18] "The principle of non-intervention is very popular in England. Though false at its base it can be upheld by an island state. Our new France, however, has not failed to appropriate it and proclaim it aloud, which is rather like brigands objecting to the police or incendiaries protesting against firemen. We will never admit a claim which is so subversive to all social order: on the contrary we shall always recognise our right of responding to an appeal from legal authority to come to its defence, just as we recognise the right of going to extinguish the fire at a neighbour's house, in order to prevent its reaching our own." This last phrase was exceedingly true of Austria. Metternich, v, 45, October 21st, 1830.

Also: "What is the principle of non-intervention but the most deleterious and active intervention in favour of anarchy?" *Ibid.* p. 128.

impossible. To establish a new régime was a thousand times more difficult than, for instance, in Paris, where the executive machine already existed, and a revolution simply meant changing its operator. In Italy the Revolution might find it easy enough to overthrow the rulers of the small states, but, when they were gone, there was no central government in existence for the whole peninsula, and any attempt to create one would arouse a whole crop of the bitterest rivalries.

For many years to come the idea of a united Italy was impracticable: it was necessary to work through the individual states.

On his departure to Elba in 1814, Napoleon had left the Italian peninsula divided up (broadly speaking) into three nations: the Regno or Kingdom of Italy which comprised Lombardy, Venetia, the Papal town of Bologna with the Pope's four northern Legations and his province of the Marches: in fact the eastern portion of the peninsula from the Alps, southwards to about half-way down the map (to the River Tronto). This constituted a nice kingdom for his stepson, Eugène Beauharnais. Next to it, all the western side of the country, namely Piedmont, Tuscany, and the west of the Papal State, was directly annexed to the French Empire: thirdly, in the south, Naples and Sicily were united as "the Kingdom of Sicily".

In 1815, however, the Congress of Vienna re-divided the whole peninsula into its old historic units. There were just a few exceptions: Venice and Lombardy, for instance, were given to Metternich to form the Lombardo-Venetian Kingdom under the Austrian Empire; and Genoa was given to Piedmont. By this diplomatic restoration modern Italy, henceforth and for ever, was to consist of no fewer than ten[19] small states: and, as far as possible, their hereditary rulers were restored to them and set up on an absolutist basis as the legitimate authority guaranteed by the treaty. But from the

[19] Eleven, if we include Monaco; but the Matignon-Grimaldi take a line of their own.

very first the task of these kings and dukes was far from easy: many of their subjects were still vibrating from the Napoleonic glimpses of a life in which kings and frontiers were only temporary makeshifts; and others were anxious about their vested interests acquired during the abnormal conditions of those hazardous twenty years.

The following is a complete list of these small Italian states in 1815. It shows that, by the Congress of Vienna, most of Italy had been restored to members of the House of Hapsburg and thus came under Austrian influence. Of the ten states, five were under Hapsburg rulers:

1. The Kingdom of Lombardo-Venetia (Lombardy and Venetia) under the Emperor of Austria, Francis I.

2. The Grand Duchy of Tuscany under Ferdinand III, brother of the Austrian Emperor.

3. The Duchy of Modena under Francesco IV, an Austrian Este.

4. The Duchy of Parma[20] under the rule, for her life, of Marie Louise of Austria, wife of Napoleon, and daughter of the Austrian Emperor.

5. The Duchy of Massa and Carrara under Maria Beatrice d'Este; on her death to be joined to Modena.

Three states under Italian rulers:

6. The Kingdom of Sardinia (or Piedmont), consisting of Sardinia, Savoy, Nice, Piedmont and Liguria, under Victor Emmanuel I.

7. The Papal State under Pius VII, consisting of Lazio, Umbria, the Marches, the Legations, Benevento and Pontecorvo.

8. The republic of San Marino; a tiny state.

Two others:

9. The Duchy of Lucca under Maria Louisa de Bourbon; eventually it was to revert to Tuscany.

10. The Kingdom of the two Sicilies (Naples and Sicily) under Ferdinand I de Bourbon. Numerically, according to the totals of population, this was by far the most important state in Italy.

---

[20] Parma, Piacenza and Guastalla. On the death of Marie Louise, Parma was to go to the Duke of Lucca; Lucca was to go to Tuscany; and Tuscany was to give up Fivizzano and some other small territories to the Duke of Modena. (This by the Treaty of Paris, 1817.)

The Ten Italian States
in 1815

Scale

0 10 20 30 40 50 60 70 80 90 100   150   200
English Miles

SWITZERLAND

Canton
Ticino

F R A N C E

Savoy

L. Maggiore

L. Como

A U S T R I A N   E M P I R E

Lombardy

Venetia

L. Garda

Vicenza

Verona

Venice

Novara

Milan

Turin

Piedmont

Alessandria

Piacenza

R. Po

PARMA

Guastalla

Ferrara

Comacchio

Modena

Bologna

Ravenna

Romagna

Imola

Genoa

Faenza

Forli

Nice

Carrara

Lucca

Cesena

Rimini

Massa

Florence

Pesaro

Nice

MONACO

Leghorn

(Livorno)

R. Arno

Pisa

Siniqaglia

Ancona

Onna

Loreto

Recanati

MODENA

TUSCANY

THE

Macerata

Fermo

Isles of Hyères

Siena

Camerino

Assisi

Ascoli

Perugia

Fabriano

Spoleto

PAPAL

Aterno

Elba

Orvieto

STATES

Rieti

Corsica

Viterbo

Castellana

L

Civita Vecchia

Greta

ROME

THE

R. Tiber

Velletri

Frosinone

R. Garigliano

Ponte Corvo

Benevento

Sardinia

Naples

TWO

I Z I A

S I C I L I E S

Cosenza

Calabria

Trapani

S I C I L Y

ITALY
1815 to 1846

Scale

0 10 20 30 40 50 60 70 80 90 100   150   200

English Miles

The populations of all these states, including those under Austrian rule, were increasing rapidly. Cesare Balbo, in his great work *Le Speranze d' Italia*, gives the following table of round figures for the year 1839 (*Le Speranze*, p. 48, note):

Kingdom of the two Sicilies (Naples and Sicily)	8,000,000
Kingdom of the House of Savoy (Piedmont)	5,000,000
Papal State	2,700,000
Tuscany, including Lucca	1,700,000
Parma	500,000
Modena	400,000
	18,300,000
Lombardo-Venetian Kingdom	4,700,000
	23,000,000[21]

Quite apart from the state governments and their loyal supporters, the whole country was very constantly cross-swept by various political creeds and sentiments. One might roughly number them as follows:

[21] Before the war of 1848, which is the moment at which they will most concern us, these numbers are given as follows:

The Kingdom of Lombardy and Venetia	Almost 5,000,000 inhabitants
Tuscany (including Lucca with population of 165,198)	1,699,938 inhabitants
Modena	575,410 inhabitants
Parma	497,343 (in 1851)
The Kingdom of Sardinia	4,916,084 inhabitants, of whom 547,112 were on the island of Sardinia, and 564,187 were French-speaking Savoyards
The Papal State, population of	2,898,115 inhabitants
The Kingdom of the two Sicilies:	
Naples	6,382,706 inhabitants
Sicily	2,046,610 inhabitants

In pre-railway days, the old state patriotism was very strong: and few people remember how small were these states. The population of all Italy, in 1815, was about 18 millions I think; in 1848 it was about 24 millions. This increase was one cause of her advance.

(1) The desire to get rid of foreign rule and influence, especially Austrian. This soon became the most generally spread political feeling.

(2) The desire which existed in every state for reform and for freer institutions.

(3) The desire among some of the people for Italian unity, either

> (a) By fusion into a single republic.
> (b) By fusion under a prince.
> (c) By federation of the states.

(4) State patriotism.

(5) Purely local patriotism, e.g. Sicily longed to be separated from Naples, and Bologna resented being governed by Rome.

(6) A large proportion of the people only asked to be left alone; mainly peasants.

(7) Outside all the above-named movements there was the influence of the Church; rather latent but universal.

(8) The Austrian policy of domination which aimed at extending her influence over the whole peninsula, and especially over the Papal State; and was held in check mainly by the jealousy of France.

Doubtless there could be found various other movements to add to this list.

IV. METTERNICH'S POLICY IN ITALY

Undoubtedly the restored princes and restored aristocracies have been somewhat ill-used by historians. The princes were of the most genuine royal blood—either Hapsburgs or Bourbons—and certainly neither they nor their nobles claimed greater rights than had belonged to their fathers and grandfathers. They were *émigrés* returning to enjoy their ancestral position and property, and were received with joy by their own sympathisers but with hatred by those of the opposite party.

Most naturally, therefore, their chief aim was to prevent the Revolution from winning a fresh hold on the people, and their fear was justifiable: unfortunately the Revolution seldom failed to run into extremes; it nearly always dethroned its ruler.

Nevertheless, one cannot help thinking that, as the years went by, it would have been possible in some of the states, at all events, to initiate the rudiments of representative government. But the princes were afraid to do so; they were nearly all related to one another and, almost unconsciously, they constituted a circle for safeguarding their rights: in some states the very name of Liberal might cause a man to be ostracised. Thus they continued to throw themselves athwart the path of Progress until finally the barriers broke. Unfortunately most of them did not perceive that it was necessary to do something to meet the Liberal ideas: that in France, in England, in America and elsewhere there were parliaments; that in Italy the people who had lived under Napoleonic rule were not likely to submit to eighteenth-century revivals; and more especially that the men who had marched into Vienna as conquerors were not likely to endure calmly an Austrian domination in Venetia and Lombardy. It was this last item which brought matters to a deadlock.

From 1815 to 1846 Metternich's right of intervention gave him a strangle-hold not only within Italy but also within Austria and within the Germanic Confederation. In Italy he meant to repress both types of advance: firstly the pan-Italian, United Italy movement; and, secondly, the grant of Liberal institutions within each small state. As to the Pan-Italian movement, his policy was undoubtedly justifiable at first; but as to the individual states it was much less defensible. After 1830, at all events, he was blocking the way of Progress. Even if the Italian princes had wanted to advance with the times they would not have been allowed to do so by Austria, because, for Austria, Liberalism was impossible. If Piedmont, for instance, were to set up a modern Liberal national government, Milan and Venice would want to follow suit, and their example would spread into the other states of Austria, and perhaps might disrupt the whole Empire.[22]

[22] Palmerston thought that Austria's wisest course would be to give up the Kingdom of Lombardo-Venetia, as being in reality

Metternich's guiding imperial principle was: Divide et impera. He deemed it necessary, in the interests of the Empire, to keep the peninsula divided, and, at first, in every Italian court he found a ready response to his views. The restored rulers lived in dread of anything like popular suffrage, which at any moment might drive them from their thrones; this fear kept them loyal to Austria. They based their authority on legitimate right supported by the Austrian army. There was hardly one of them who, either directly or indirectly, did not owe his crown to Metternich, and in return, of course, they were expected to comply with his policy. They were in fact the marionettes whose strings were pulled by Metternich at the Court of Vienna.[23]

His machinery for administering the Lombardo-Venetian Kingdom was necessarily a bureaucracy: governmental offices supported by an army of sometimes as many as sixty or seventy thousand men; no representative institutions; a strong police and a magnificent secret service. This machinery was efficient and pleasant to live under: on the whole the people were prosperous, and their numbers increased. He seems to

outside her Empire; but Metternich did not mean ever to give up Venetia. He regarded it as necessary for Austrian supremacy in the Adriatic, and Lombardo-Venetia as a barrier against France. "On the Po we are defending the Rhine." Srbik, II, 117. Later on, of course, he advanced still farther forward in order to defend the River Po.

[23] For instance, in 1831, soon after Louis Philippe had seized the throne of France, Metternich practically ordered the Duke of Modena to acknowledge him, and wrote to Apponyi in Paris: "From the day when we come to his rescue we expect at least that he will take our line entirely in politics". Of course many instances could be quoted, but in this one he states definitely what he expects of the petty Italian monarchs, almost every one of whom he had rescued at one time or another from the Revolution. Metternich, V, 120.

Elsewhere he said, referring especially to the Papacy: "It is in their union with us and our allies that the princes of Italy can find their only hope of avoiding the ruin which, without that support, would be inevitable". *Ibid.* p. 352.

have believed that if he could "keep the people amused" they would be satisfied with this régime.

Nowadays it has been said that if Austria had offered some form of self-government to Lombardo-Venetia, instead of trying to turn these Italians into Austrians by means of government offices, she might have succeeded in converting them, or at all events in separating them from Piedmont. If Milan had been made a capital city, she would have been unwilling to give place to the smaller town, Turin. Metternich had some slight perception of this point, but the Emperor was a believer in fusion and determined to treat them all indiscriminately as Austrians.

Consequently, for decade after decade, overlooking the whole scene we see the figure of the great Prince Metternich;[24] calm, logical, narrow-minded, rather contemptuous; an exceedingly hard-working, conscientious, methodical and efficient imperial minister; hardly ever mistaken; a man of such foresight that he could almost mirror the future—but his future did not include Progress, except in material affairs. In reality, what he represented was not so much a nation as a treaty: the Settlement of 1815. His life-work might in fact be described (by an enemy) as being the defence and exploitation of that settlement for a hereditary governing class at Vienna. He would have retorted that he was serving the greatest Empire in the world; that his imperial master could command a glorious army of over a quarter of a million soldiers ready to die for him; and that the Italian question was a frontier difficulty, the special concern of Austria.

From his own letters, and from many other writings, one has a glimpse of that great court as it existed in his day and continued to exist until within living memory: of its splendid

[24] For a favourable account of Metternich's principles, as enunciated by him in the year 1830, in the middle of his career, see a letter addressed by him to his ambassador at St Petersburg relating to Count Orloff's mission: dated October 6th, 1830. *Ibid.* v, 51–8.

entertainments, its glorious military reviews, its diplomats, its white cuirassiers, its women, and its music from Mozart's symphonies down to Strauss' *Blue Danube*. But unfortunately there are other letters and memoirs which reveal the undersides of imperial domination. Concealment is a constant necessity, as much from his own public as from that of the subject peoples: hence the existence of an immense secret service with spies, both Austrian and Italian, all over Italy, and of an imperial office for opening and examining private letters. Every government is to be absolutist for ever, and whole generations are compelled to live under this régime: whole populations deprived of their joy in their native land; members of the same family embittered against one another; patriots compelled to serve under the flag of their conquerors or not serve at all; hundreds of honourable men—such as Silvio Pellico or Count Confalonieri, for instance—rotting in the Spielberg for years, many of them sentenced as political murderers simply because they stood for their own people against the foreigner. He represents all the splendour of imperial domination, whereas the Italian revolutionaries represent only nationality; and a nationality as yet unformed: and so it lasted until 1859.

During the earlier period, as already stated, there is much to be said in favour of Metternich's "system", especially as opposed to the then impossible theories of Mazzini. But as years went by, his domination became a mere repression not only of pan-Italianism but also of the right of each people to develop its political institutions upon Liberal lines. And this repression continued until (about the year 1845) even his allies finally began to perceive that law-and-order can be bought at too dear a price, and that in any case it can never be established permanently by force from outside: moreover, that material prosperity cannot suffice of itself to satisfy the spirit of a civilised community.[25]

[25] Even Kübeck, the Austrian finance minister, perceived this; in his diary for 1831 he said: "Austria demands from the human spirit

The final outcome, of course, arrived in 1859, when Piedmont came forward, not universally welcome, but well-organised and efficient; able to offer law-and-order, free institutions and future national greatness to all Italy: and Piedmont carried the day.

that it should become a eunuch; if it will do that it may have perfect freedom. Therein lies the whole contradiction between Austria and the century, and between Austria and Lombardy. Lombardy has much material prosperity: she has, so to speak, *Embonpoint*, and in spite of this she is not contented; she wants to be allowed to think". Quoted by Srbik, I, 491.

Chapter IV

THE TWO MOST IMPORTANT[1] ITALIAN
STATES, 1815 TO 1846

Of all the Italian governments there were two which contained a germ of independence—namely those of Rome and of Piedmont: and their history virtually includes the history of this period.

First stands Rome—because it was the only town whose primacy was admitted by all the others. Undoubtedly Rome was the ancient imperial city and the city of the Church all over the world. If Italy should ever become a nation, undoubtedly for its capital it would claim Rome. And this was an impression very widely felt even when the town did not number as many as two hundred thousand souls: that it was the capital of the cities of Italy.

In those days quite a large proportion of the space within its circle of Aurelian walls was still free of modern buildings, and consequently the ancient monuments stood forth singly with a far more imposing effect than to-day. As compared with twentieth-century Rome, the town a hundred years ago would have seemed rather like a vast museum of classical and medieval remains. And those great ruins formed as it were a suitable setting for a sovereign who could trace his temporal power back a thousand and fifty-nine years, to the days of King Pepin, ruler of the Franks during the pontificate of Pope Stephen II.

Thus the Pope and his entourage dated their authority from the father of Charlemagne or even earlier. But the Liberals and revolutionists among the population were far more influenced by the recent interregnum under Napoleon.

---

[1] Numerically Naples was more important than either the Papal State or Piedmont, but not otherwise.

During that period there had been no theocratic rule or administrators, but only a modern French bureaucracy with more or less democratic theories which had left their mark behind them. In fact from this temporary deluge the Papacy had emerged theoretically stronger, but, in practice, much weaker than before.

It had been a curious struggle against the conqueror, and in its way wonderfully successful. Napoleon had wanted to have the Roman Catholic religion and the Pope henceforth at his beck and call. But his aggressive movements had been countered by that long and curious phase of passive resistance maintained by Pius VI, and after him by Pius VII against the hitherto invincible emperor. The resistance had continued for over fourteen years, during which the poor old invalid Pius VII was hurried from Rome to Savona and from Savona to Paris and elsewhere; and, though frequently obliged to give way before his opponent's heckling and threats, yet had never been reduced entirely to submission; and finally in 1814 had returned to Rome triumphant when Napoleon was sent to Elba as an exile. It had been a dramatic *dénouement* and it had left a profound impression in the minds of Churchmen. In fact it seemed to them nothing less than a divine interposition. They saw that the world-revolution itself, and even the great Napoleon had come and gone like a winter storm, while the Eternal Church had emerged unscathed from the ordeal. In their eyes this could only be the finger of God. And in the years to come, when Napoleon III and Victor Emmanuel were trying to force their terms upon Pius IX, there were undoubtedly many Catholics, especially among the French royalists, who believed that in due time the Church must again emerge triumphant, and that sooner or later, the third Napoleon and his allies would be relegated to the same limbo as the first.

In 1815 the territories of the Pope were restored to him by the allies, among whom, of course, was Protestant England: and they were guaranteed to him by the five Great Powers of

Europe. The Powers of Europe agreed to the maintenance of a small, more or less international state instituted to preserve the dignity and independence of the Holy See. This was the work of Cardinal Consalvi; "the great Consalvi". It was a signal success for him; but in just one item he seems perhaps to have been ill-advised. It might have been wiser for him to have given up the four northern legations—Bologna, Ferrara, Ravenna, and Forlì. These territories had formed part of the northern kingdom under Eugène Beauharnais and they hated returning to priestly rule; they remained constantly in rebellion until 1860, and in fact it was largely due to them that the Pope eventually lost the rest of his territories.

In 1815, therefore, within the Papal State, the cry was "back to theocratic government". But although the Pope had out-lasted Napoleon the ideas of the Revolution were still there, by no means dead: and were destined, in turn, to outlast the restored eighteenth-century system of the Holy See.

The Papal State lay right across the centre of Italy, stretching from the frontiers of Venetia to those of Naples. As long as this state remained in existence Italy could only be united by federation: and Mazzini's schemes for union-by-fusion remained impossible.

I. THE PAPAL STATE

The Papal State was composed of the following twenty-one territories:[2]

(1) Lazio, consisting of *Rome*, with the Comarca and the three divisions of Viterbo, Civitavecchia and Orvieto.

(2) "The Legations" in the north of the state, consisting of four Legations: Bologna, Ferrara, Ravenna, Forlì.

(3) The Marches (the eastern province), consisting of six Delegations: *Ancona*, Urbino-Pesaro, Macerata, Fermo, Ascoli, Camerino.

---

[2] This is its geographical division. Most of the above territories were also governmental units, but not all of them. The number of government units—Legations and Delegations—was frequently changed between 1815 and 1860. *V.* p. 49, note 7.

(4) Umbria (the western province), consisting of three Delegations: Perugia, *Spoleto*, Rieti.

(5) The Campagna maritima, consisting of three Delegations:
Velletri, Frosinone, Benevento.

The Papal State stretched from Venetia in the north to
Naples in the south. Venetia was occupied by the Austrians,
and they kept their foremost garrisons across the River Po in
the two Papal towns of Ferrara and Comacchio. On the south
the Papal territories of Benevento and Pontecorvo were
embedded in the Kingdom of Naples.

The greatest length of this state was about two hundred
and seventy miles, and its average width was about eighty.
Its population amounted to about two and a half million souls
of whom about one-sixth or one-seventh lived in towns of a
thousand or more inhabitants. Its average revenue was under
nine million scudi, or about £1,800,000 per annum. Its
imports rather greater than its exports: total about twenty
million scudi or £4,000,000 a year between the two.

It was manifestly a difficult task for a government without
much money to administer so long and narrow a strip of
territory, before the days of railways or electricity. And it
was rendered harder by the fact that its two principal towns
were at opposite ends of the country—Rome (about 150,000
inhabitants)[3] at the southern, and Bologna (about 70,000) at

---

[3] Gams, *Die Geschichte der Kirche Christi in XIX Jahrhundert*,
II, 583, quoting the report of the Governor of Rome at the end of
the year 1842. There were 15,000 strangers and 3732 Jews apparently all included in this total.

The Papal State, population of:

  In 1827 2,425,000 (Pelczar, I, 71)
   ,, 1842 2,732,436 (Gams)
   ,, 1850 3,000,000 *circa* (Farini, I, 134, and others)

Rome, population of:

     In 1800 153,004
     ,, 1812 117,882
     ,, 1820 135,046
     ,, 1846 170,199

the northern extremity; moreover Bologna was swayed by a strong local pride and resented being governed from Rome.

Bologna, la dotta, the learned, celebrated for her university, her books, her leaning towers and her colonnaded streets, is a very ancient town and naturally proud of her past. She remembers the traditions of her medieval days and preserves a full share of that old-time sentiment, the patriotism of the walled city, which has played so large a part in the development of the Latin nations. She had first come under Papal protection in the year 1276, so that the connection was of long enough standing; but the modern pushful Bologna was by no means proud of it. Her citizens wanted popular government, and they had, besides, some permanent grievances. Their old pre-Revolution municipal privileges had been abolished by the French and had never been fully restored to them; the Papal laws required revision; the ecclesiastics according to Bolognese ideas were not always good administrators; and in any case the richer classes hated the Papal rule.[4] Under Eugène Beauharnais they had been linked to the industrial-minded north of Italy and not to the tradition-loving south. Moreover, within their own orbit their town might almost be called a capital,[5] for it carried the whole of Romagna (the northern Papal provinces) with it, and most of the upper districts of the Marches as well. In fact they liked to take a line of their own; and the northern portion of the Papal State would usually follow Bologna rather than Rome.

Over these and some others of its subjects the Papal

[4] All the above grievances are admitted, even by Metternich, v, 325.

[5] In 1815 the Bolognese sent a memorial to the Congress of Vienna asking for one lay government for all the Legations, with its seat in Bologna, and at one time it was almost settled to turn Romagna into a separate duchy. But the Congress of Vienna gave Bologna and the Legations to the Pope. They were thus forced, unwillingly, to become part of the Papal State. Concerning Bolognese local patriotism, v. Vicini's Manifesto in 1831, quoted by Farini, Lo Stato Romano dall' anno 1815-50, I, 42; also Tivaroni, Italia durante il dominio Austriaco, II, 113, and others.

government had never obtained any real hold since its return in 1814. This was not altogether surprising. It was entirely unrepresentative, being merely imposed upon the people from above.

The Papal administration was arranged as follows: the state was mapped out into twenty-one divisions, which correspond almost exactly with the territories already named—each administered by an ecclesiastic, assisted by a committee of four laymen. The four[6] most important of these divisions—Bologna, Ferrara, Ravenna and Forlì, were called Legations and each administered by a Legate, who was always a Cardinal; the rest were called Delegations and were administered by a Delegate who was usually a Bishop.[7]

Rome was the centre of organisation. Each of these Legates and Delegates was appointed by, and responsible to, the government at Rome, that is to say, the Secretary of State. These ecclesiastics directed the police, commanded the forces, presided over the administration, overlooked the municipalities, and condemned prisoners or pardoned them (Farini, I, 134). Thus the supreme power was in the hands of

[6] Later increased to six by the addition of Urbino-Pesaro and Velletri. For a short account of the Papal territories, v. Rosi, Storia contemporanea d' Italia, p. 68; also the Catholic Encyclopedia, etc.

[7] The number of the Legations and Delegations was changed several times: the full list consists of six Legations, fourteen Delegations and Rome with the Comarca. Thus: Rome, The Comarca. The Legations, namely, Bologna, Ferrara, Ravenna, Forlì; Velletri, Urbino-Pesaro. The Delegations, namely, Viterbo, Civita Vecchia, Orvieto, Ancona, Macerata, Fermo, Ascoli, Camerino, Perugia, Spoleto, Rieti, Frosinone, Benevento, Loreto. But they were often altered. In 1815 there were seventeen divisions—four Legations and thirteen Delegations; these were reduced to thirteen in 1824 by Leo XII; but, later, they were increased to twenty; of these twenty territories, "the Legations", i.e. Bologna, Ferrara, Ravenna and Forlì, remained unchanged; but to their number were added two new Legations, namely Urbino-Pesaro and Velletri. But the term "The Legations" is always, I think, used of the first four northern Legations. V.Pelczar, Pio IX e il suo pontificato sullo sfondo delle vicende della chiesa nel sécolo XIX, I, 33, 91.

clerics; but each of them was assisted by his "congregazione governativa" or committee of four laymen who acted in a consultative capacity. They too were appointed by the Pope.

At Rome the Cardinal Secretary of State was the head and centre of everything; and around him were the great governmental offices, about eight or nine in number, all directed by ecclesiastics appointed by the sovereign.

So much for the Central Government. In local matters the laymen had more say. Each Legation or Delegation was divided into Governi or Circondarii under a governor or lay stipendiary magistrate with very wide powers; and each Governo was divided into communes. Each commune had its council consisting of property-owners, men of letters, or tradesmen, originally chosen by the Delegate, but renewable by co-option with his approval.

The Central State Government at Rome was thus entirely unrepresentative and the heads of departments were all priests advised by lawyers (*uditori*). This accusation was hurled at it thousands of times, with perfect truth. But one might add that in this respect it was merely on a par with all the other governments in Italy. They were all unrepresentative. Even Piedmont was mapped out into divisions administered by military governors. The only difference—but it was one that aroused great resentment—was that in the Pope's states they were priests advised by lawyers, whereas in conservative, aristocratic Piedmont they were retired officers,[8] and nominated officials called Intendenti; and similar conditions, I think, existed in Tuscany.

[8] *V.* Fabris, *Gli avvenimenti militari del* 1848 *e* 1849, I, 60, or Bersezio, *Il regno di Vittorio Emanuele*, I, 84, for a short description of the Piedmontese administration: of course there are many longer accounts of it.

II. PIEDMONT (THE KINGDOM OF SARDINIA)

Of all the conflicting ambitions during this period, the most dangerous to the Holy See in reality was to be found, not among the Great Powers, but in the small nation of Piedmont, or as it was officially termed, the Kingdom of Sardinia; for here we come to the state which was destined to a great mission: in due time to unite the whole of Italy beneath its crown.

By the settlement of 1815 it included Savoy, the wild alpine country originally granted by the Emperor Conrad to Count Humbert of the White Hands in the early years of the eleventh century, and erected into a duchy in 1416; secondly Nice, a town of 20,000 inhabitants in 1815, and its comté, both of which, originally, had been part of ancient Provence, but had adhered voluntarily to the Count of Savoy in the year 1388; thirdly, Piedmont, the sub-alpine land where Emmanuel Philibert established his capital in the sixteenth century when the Dukes of Savoy began to turn their eyes southwards—and since then that capital had grown into the thriving city of Turin with 80,000 inhabitants; fourthly[9] Sardinia ceded by Austria in 1720 and carrying with it the title of King: and finally, to these there had been added, under the Treaty of 1815, the busy city of Genoa (76,000 inhabitants) with all the Genoese Riviera, about forty-five leagues by ten, a long narrow strip of indescribably beautiful shore land between the mountains and the Mediterranean.

In this little nation there lived about three and a half million people in 1815, but before the war of 1848 their total had increased to 4,368,972 without counting the Island of Sardinia with 547,112. Historically, the astonishing point about these populations is the degree of unity which they exhibited under the House of Savoy. It redounds greatly to the honour of the rulers,[10] because in reality these peoples

[9] I omit the smaller divisions of Monferrato (Acqui) and the Milanese Sardo (Alessandria).

[10] "The difference of language seems to keep us separate but none the less it is true that for eight centuries we have fought under the

were entirely different from one another, as has since been proved. In Savoy there were half a million people and they spoke French; so did most of the citizens of the then small town of Nice, though a majority of its surrounding peasants must have spoken Provençal; in Piedmont every one used the curious Piedmontese dialect—to which the educated people added Italian or French. In Genoa—where at first most people hated the Piedmontese connection—and along the Riviera, almost every little town had a slightly different variation of the Genoese dialect which sometimes contains traces of Moorish or Provençal; in Sardinia the half-million of inhabitants had their own form of neo-Latin in which Spanish[11] words occur. And these places were much farther apart then than now; in the time before steam and electricity it often took four days to cross the Alps, and any period between two days and a week to reach Sardinia. Nevertheless for forty years to come the dominions of the House of Savoy

same standards and that hand in hand we have won fame for our Alpine rocks, while founding and aggrandising the power of that noble race which was born among us." Words of the revolutionary leader Count Santarosa in his proclamation to the soldiers of the Savoy Brigade, April 1821 (*v.* Santarosa, *De la révolution pié-montaise,* II, 181). The officers of the Savoy Brigade joined the revolution, but their men remained loyal to the King.

The only important instances of real separatist feeling were found in the town of Genoa which naturally could not at once forget its glorious individual history.

The rest of the kingdom was wonderfully united in sentiment. Its loyalty to the king was genuine, because he was not, like the other princelings, a scion of some foreign royal family imposed on them during the eighteenth century; he was one of their own glorious line of Savoy. Thus the aristocracy could be loyal to him without ever becoming disloyal to the nation: the private soldier regarded the king as his national leader and the feudal gentry as his national officers. Gualterio, *Gli ultimi rivolgimenti italiani. Memorie storiche,* vol. I, pt I, 494 *et seq.*

[11] In 1831 there were 374 feudal fiefs in Sardinia, of which 188 belonged to Spanish barons. Cibrario, p. 51. The Piedmontese dialect was an official military language; French was permitted for the Savoyards and Valdostani, Genoese for the Ligurians, and Sardinian for the Sards. *V.* Gori, p. 24.

remained a nation, and the only real nation in the peninsula:[12] but when it gave birth to United Italy its work was accomplished and it died.

In reality, during this period after 1815, the Kingdom of Piedmont was still in the process of becoming Italianised. In former days—as long as the dukes had possessed only Savoy, Nice and Piedmont—the French influence had predominated over the Italian throughout their state. But during the eighteenth century these northern Savoyard rulers had begun to enter into the circle of Italian politics; and, after 1815, the greater portion of their realm actually lay south of the Alps. Henceforward a new life and a new field of ambition had begun to open out in front of their eyes. They and their people were to be Italian not only in politics, but also in culture; and they were becoming conscious of this change;[13] for it had been proclaimed by Alfieri and by other writers and soon was to be preached by Gioberti. At the same time there had arisen an honourable sentiment of duty to the rest of Italy: a feeling that the House of Savoy, which held the northern roads and the fortified Alpine passes, must close

[12] The government was entirely unrepresentative. The supreme courts were known as the Senate. It was their duty to examine each new law and see that it did not contravene the rights either of the crown or of the people. They registered it; but they also had the right of refusing it. This right was only exercised in extreme cases: the crown could override it, but naturally hesitated to do so. V. Bersezio, I, 55, for a fairly short account of these institutions.

[13] "Il s'était fait en Piémont une grande révolution dans les esprits. Emmanuel Philibert, en transportant le siège de son gouvernement à Turin; Charles Emmanuel II par ses mœurs avaient dès longtemps annoncé que leur maison et leur royaume devaient cesser d'être français; mais les Piémontais ne reconnurent entièrement cette vérité que sous le règne de Victor-Emmanuel. Une jeunesse nourrie des écrits d'Alfieri, et une foule de braves militaires sortis des rangs des armées de Napoléon concoururent à donner ce mouvement à l'opinion...." Another Italianising influence, he says, was hatred of the Austrians. This was written in 1821 by the revolutionist Count Santarosa, De la révolution piémontaise, p. 34.

them against invaders and prevent the peninsula from ever again becoming a thoroughfare for all the armies in Europe as it had been during seventeen long years under Napoleon. The House of Savoy was to "hold the keys" and not to forget that it was the defender of the northern gates of Italy.

This feeling was right; but if the House of Savoy was to defend the Alpine gates, it was necessary to increase the strength of Piedmont; and indeed this was necessary even to secure diplomatic independence for the small kingdom. Now, obviously, Piedmont could not hope to extend her territories northwards into France; but after 1815, very possibly she might extend them southwards into Italy. And this—so people had already begun to say—would be the mission of the younger branch of the House of Savoy. Henceforward the traditional ambition of that house was to coincide with the hopes of the unfortunate Lombards and Venetians who had been handed over to Austria; the next achievement in its wonderful history was destined to be the liberation of the subject Italians; the formation of a strong kingdom right across the north of Italy, for the defence of the whole peninsula; and some day, perhaps, this great enterprise would culminate in the founding of the new Italian nation.

The most accurate existing description of Piedmontese policy is—strange to say—one which was written before that policy ever took shape. It is in fact a prophecy, and one of the most remarkable prophecies recorded.

In 1814 when, at Vienna, the question was under discussion of handing over Genoa to the rulers of Piedmont, a certain Genoese patrician, Count Antonio Brignole-Sale, presented to Lord Castlereagh a note in which he strongly opposed this union. The following quotation is part of this note of October 11th, 1814, and it is certainly one of the most accurate forecasts to be found in history.

What will happen to the Kingdom of Sardinia when it is increased by the addition of Liguria? It will be more powerful than it was, but nevertheless it will remain only a secondary state, neither weak enough to rely for safety on the preservation of the general equilibrium of Europe, nor strong enough to stand independent and enjoy a quiet existence, content with its own boundaries; but being situated at the foot of the Alps and in contact with regions which are the most fertile in Italy, and in reality form a continuation of Piedmont, will it not inevitably conceive the idea of self-aggrandisement and independence, and feel itself confident of being able to achieve these aims? Confident, in fact, of re-constituting that kingdom of which it is the kernel. Such a re-constitution is intended by nature and is already the design of a numerous party which at this very moment looks on the House of Savoy as its support and its hope. Are we not led to believe that these will be the aims of the Cabinet of Turin and that, encouraged by the prospect of such self-aggrandisement, it will form and carry out the plan of bargaining with its alliance (as it always has, throughout all history) for the purpose of getting help from France and thus gradually making itself master of the whole of Italy? Such a course is merely in accordance with human nature.[14]

[14] This prophecy is quoted in Rosi, p. 62.

Chapter V

PIEDMONT AND CHARLES ALBERT
1815 TO 1830

In 1814, after Napoleon's departure, the last two descendants of the ancient male line of Savoy were restored to Piedmont: they were two old brothers, namely:

<blockquote>
Victor Emmanuel I (1814–1821)
Charles Felix   (1821–1831).
</blockquote>

Neither of these old men has any direct influence on the Risorgimento; but they brought back to Turin with them the next heir to the throne, a young man, who is one of its principal and most interesting figures, namely:

<blockquote>
Charles Albert (1831–1849).
</blockquote>

I. THE MUTINY OF 1821

From the first Charles Albert's position must have been rather curious. He was heir to the throne but he could hardly be called a member of the royal family, for he was merely a distant cousin—related to them only in the eleventh degree. He was the head of the junior branch—that of the princes of Carignano—but his ancestors had not been sovereigns for some two and a half centuries.[1]

Moreover he can have known nothing of Piedmont. Born in 1798 he was of the generation which was scattered by

---

[1] Charles Albert, Prince of Carignano; afterwards King of Sardinia. Born, October 2nd, 1798; succeeded Charles Felix, April 27th, 1831; abdicated after the battle of Novara, March 23rd, 1849; died at Oporto, July 28th, 1849. The princes of Carignano descend from Thomas (born 1596), younger son of Duke Charles Emmanuel (1580). They took their title from the fief of Carignano, about 25 miles from Turin, and they lived at the castle of Raconigi. Costa de Beauregard, *La jeunesse du roi Charles Albert*, pp. 2–4.

the Revolution: a boy of no very special importance, sent to
school in Paris, and finally placed in the charge of a Swiss
Protestant pastor at Geneva. But the main line of Savoy
was without male issue, and presently people began to realise
that some day he would be its heir. Napoleon created him
a Count of the Empire and gave him a hundred thousand
francs a year to live in Paris, a brand-new coat of arms and
a lieutenancy in the 6th Dragoons.[2] The Empire fell; and
Charles Albert, aged only sixteen, was taken to Turin, as
second in succession to the throne, by the kindly old head of
his clan, King Victor Emmanuel I.

In his life there are three main crises: the rising of 1821,
the troubles between 1831 and 1834, and the war of 1848
and 1849.

From 1815 to 1821 he was living in Turin, befriended by
the old king, Victor Emmanuel I. At that time he was a tall,
slim, laughing young officer with dark hair, full of martial
ardour and much attached to his cousin. He was described by
both the king and the queen, as a brilliant, high-spirited
youth, rather too much given to making fun of people;[3] and
according to his equerry, Silvano Costa, he seemed to be
less addicted to work than to amusements or sport, such as
hunting, fishing and riding. Indeed for the first three years
he was regarded as an idler, but in 1817 he married, and from
that time onwards seems to have taken the world more
seriously. It is evident that already the guiding principles of

---

[2] Predari calls it the 8th Dragoons. Napoleon evidently intended
to expropriate Charles Albert on fairly generous terms; but the gift
of a new coat of arms to the House of Savoy showed a lack of
humour. *V.* Rodolico, *Carlo Alberto, Principe di Carignano*, p. 13.

[3] Gino Capponi says that when Charles Albert went to Florence
in 1817 to be married to the daughter of the Grand Duke of Tuscany,
he (Capponi) reproved him on one occasion for the light manner in
which he spoke of religion. Charles Albert was only nineteen then;
in reality there was a very deep vein of religious feeling in his
nature. This marriage, one may note, was with an Austrian. Yet
even on this occasion Charles Albert spoke to Capponi of helping
to drive out the Austrians.

his thoughts were Piedmontese patriotism and a belief in the future of the House of Savoy. One of his finest qualities was physical courage, and even in these early years the dream of his life was that some day he might lead Piedmont in a war of Italian liberation against Austria.[4]

In 1821 his misfortune came upon him.

It was a period of great discontent both in Piedmont and elsewhere in Europe. The Restoration of 1815 had been, not an equitable settlement, but merely the triumph of a returning faction; the re-establishment of privileges, of exceptional tribunals and other pre-war ideas. It has been said of the Piedmontese nobles that they travelled back to Turin still in their powdered wigs and queux, and that they proposed to ignore the great Napoleonic era and its servitors by the simple process of going back to the Palma verde or calendar for 1798, "comme en novantott", the last year before their king had gone into exile. But these attempts at putting back the clock involved a great deal of injustice, and for years to come were a cause of irritation to many of the younger men who had never known the glories of the eighteenth-century régime; especially to those who were Liberals—such as Massimo d'Azeglio, his brother Roberto d'Azeglio, Cesare Balbo, Cavour and others who afterwards became leaders of Italy.

The fatal defect in the Piedmontese state was that there existed no assemblies or other institutions through which people could make their feelings known to one another[5] (Santarosa, p. 37).

---

[4] This sentiment was certainly tinged with "municipalism". What he hoped for was a Piedmontese advance led by himself as chief of the House of Savoy; but its goal was to be the liberation of Lombardo-Venetia and ultimately the union of all Italy.

[5] The following were the chief causes of discontent in Piedmont: the reaction with its family privileges; the remembrance of the more democratic days of Napoleon; the fact that many of the Napoleonic officers and N.C.O.'s had been deprived of a step in rank, and many officials dismissed; a hatred of Austrian domination, and a dawning feeling of Italian nationality. *V.* Gualterio, vol. i, pt i, p. 514.

This Piedmontese mutiny of 1821[6] was part of the general European movement against reaction. In 1820 Spain rose against her absolutist king. This news aroused Italy. Lombardy was soon filled with conspiracy against Austria, and a Carbonari rising took place in Naples; early in 1821 the Neapolitan army marched northwards under the celebrated General Pepe. It seemed as though the moment were come to strike at Austria; and when in February, Metternich sent a strong force southwards to crush the Neapolitans, many of the young Piedmontese officers felt as if they must support Pepe or die. It resulted in a widespread army-plot whose actual working organiser was an officer in the footguards, Count Santorre di Santarosa.

Santarosa's conspiracy is a landmark in the period. At first it found its principal supporters among the officers; it

[6] The Piedmontese movement of 1821; the principal original authorities are:

Santarosa, *De la révolution piémontaise*. The narrative of the revolutionary leader. (Bound in the same book there are three other works on the subject, namely, *Les trente jours de la révolution piémontaise*, by Un Savoyard (De Maistre, but probably inspired by Charles Albert, so Manno says); *Histoire de la révolution de Piémont*, by De Beauchamps; and an Italian essay by a Piedmontese officer.)

Manno, *Informazioni sul ventuno in Piemonte*. This gives three narratives written in self-defence by Charles Albert: the *Memoriale* (April 1821); the *Détails sur ma régence*; and *Ad majorem Dei gloriam* (1839). Also the narratives of Balbo, Gifflenga and others.

Scritti varj di Carlo Alberto, collected by Fiorini. This contains the three narratives published by Manno; also the *Simple récit des événemens (sic) arrivés en Piémont*. (This was not written by Charles Albert but by some of his party. It was inspired by the Marchese Michele di Cavour, by Rodolfo de Maistre and by Conte Luigi d'Auzers, who gave the data to a French journalist (Luzio, *Profili biografici*, p. 7). It was more or less as an answer to Santarosa.) Also 94 letters written by Charles Albert between 1821 and 1823.

Bianchi, in *Curiosità e ricerche*, vol. III, mentions another *Memoriale* written by Charles Albert, but apparently it is not in print: *Détails sur la manière dont j'ai su la révolution qui allait éclater et sur ce que je fis pour l'empêcher*. And there are very probably other documents in existence not yet available for the public.

was a curious semi-loyal mutiny. But then the officers saw
that to achieve any success they must have civilian assistance,
so they made overtures to the Carbonari. This was rather a
surprising step on their part. The Carbonari programme included the "Spanish constitution", an extremely democratic
form of government which virtually excluded the aristocracy.
One wonders whether Charles Albert was ever informed of
this. However, the conspiracy developed with two main ends
in view, namely a Liberal constitution and a war of liberation
against Austria. The young officers hoped to march on Milan.

In reality it always remained more an armed demonstration
than a rising. Victor Emmanuel I was very popular: he was
a kindly old gentleman and he hated the Austrians; and the
officers thought—so Count De la Tour afterwards told
Mr Hill,[7] the British Minister in Turin—that they might
place their old king at the head of the army and then cut off
the retreat of the Austrians from Naples, and become masters,
temporarily at all events, of the whole peninsula. They
counted on getting 60,000 soldiers and 20,000 volunteers from
Piedmont, and perhaps another 70,000 from Lombardo-
Venetia and elsewhere. And it is very remarkable that De la
Tour, although he agreed with Mr Hill that this plan had
been "unpromising if not absurd" yet "had no doubt as to
its temporary success". If the king, as was hoped, had agreed
to lead the movement, De la Tour and the army would have
gone with him; but, in reality, there was no likelihood of his
doing so. Failing him, the conspirators counted on getting
Charles Albert.

It is impossible to write with absolute finality about the
episode of 1821, because various reasons lead one to believe

[7] General Count De la Tour was G.O.C. of the army which
remained loyal to Charles Felix. He was a Conservative, but not
averse from constitutional ideas. Mr Hill had been some fourteen
years in Turin, and his conversations with De la Tour, with Charles
Felix and Victor Emmanuel are interesting. He seems to have been
on very friendly terms with all three, especially Victor Emmanuel.
V. F.O. 168, vol. 4.

that there may be documents in existence which have not yet been made accessible to students: but one can give the main points of importance.

The Santarosa conspiracy nearly ruined Charles Albert. Undoubtedly he was implicated in it, but the question is: how far? Its leaders used to come to his house and were among his best friends,[8] and when they spoke of their ideals, of a war of liberation and of freeing Italy, he sympathised with them. He was an enthusiastic young anti-Austrian, but temperamentally he was not a strong Liberal; in fact, throughout his life he was very definitely a Conservative. His guiding motive according to his own account[9] was a patriotic desire, natural in an officer of only twenty-three, to seize the moment and march against Austria under command of his old kinsman. He did not want the crown, and as for a constitution one feels that never, during his life, did such an idea make any great appeal to him. He only wanted the advancement of the House of Savoy and the independence of Italy.

Thus he was neither a revolutionist nor even a strong Liberal, but unfortunately he had earned the reputation of being both. He was ready enough to accept some of the Liberal ideas, and the methods of the Reaction irritated him so sometimes he opposed them. Coming from the heir-presumptive this was unfortunate because it spread the belief that he was a Liberal, as were many of his companions, and even a sympathiser with revolution. Of course the Liberals exaggerated his views, exploited every word of his and wrote panegyrics about him until he was regarded all over Italy as the coming[10] Liberal "messiah". Manifestly the name of the heir-presumptive as leader would be the making of any such movement as this. He himself does not seem to have realised

[8] Gualterio, pp. 538, 553.

[9] *Ad majorem Dei gloriam*, written by Charles Albert in 1839.

[10] "Prince of Carignano...has been held up as a sort of idol by the Liberal party and as the proper prince to be put at the head of the Italian government they proposed to erect." Mr Percy's despatch, March 6th, 1821. F.O. 168, vol. 3.

that loyal people would be induced to join it if they were told that one of its leaders was the Prince of Carignano.

The first sign of the coming trouble occurred on the night of March 2nd, 1821. Some conspirators' letters were captured by the police in the false bottom of a carriage belonging to Prince Della Cisterna. These letters implicated various people in the plot and, among others, Charles Albert.

He was informed immediately of what had occurred by Count Saluzzo, the Minister of War, apparently by order of the king; but he was not deeply compromised and the king pardoned him for these earlier doings.[11]

This Cisterna episode was unimportant in itself but it probably had the effect of hastening matters. None of the conspirators could tell whether or not they were compromised in the letters. Evidently Santarosa and his friends thought that it was time to act.

The tragedy of poor Santarosa will never be forgotten, because he was a single-hearted man who offered his life and all his possessions for the cause of a free and united Italy. He had begun his career as an ensign of thirteen serving against Napoleon, and though small in stature he retained the hard and vigorous body of a man trained to arms. His high forehead, however, and spectacles suggested rather a plain-looking student. It is generally agreed that he was gifted with an active brain and also with charming manners of the best

[11] Later on, about May 9th, 1821, Count Revel, Governor of Turin, told Mr Hill that on being informed by Count Saluzzo as to the Cisterna letters, Charles Albert "went out at once to the king at his country seat and, it is said, disclosed whatever he knew of this plot, and in doing so compromised all his young friends. On this account from being the idol of popularity, his name ever since has been only pronounced with execration and contempt by all parties". It may be true that Charles Albert went out to the king at Moncalieri, but there is no reason to suppose that he compromised any of his friends. Mr Hill proceeds to say that the old king did not divulge what passed between himself and Charles Albert, but said that he immediately granted his royal pardon; and that goes far to excuse Charles Albert. *V.* F.O. 168, vol. 4.

Italian type; but at the same time he was evidently over-emotional,[12] and astonishingly optimistic for a man of thirty-eight.

The following is the story which he has left us, and it is very different from that of Charles Albert.

On March 6th, 1821, at about 6 p.m., he says that he went with four[13] friends to wait upon Charles Albert and told him in stirring terms that the movement was completely prepared for March 8th, two days later. "Prince, all is ready. Nothing more is required but your consent. Our friends are assembled. When we return to them they expect either the signal to save their country or the disastrous news which would destroy all their hopes."

It must have been a terrible moment for Charles Albert. He was the heir to the throne and at the same time he was the rallying-point of those who wanted to attack Austria. Should he agree to head Santarosa's movement, most probably he would lose his royal inheritance and, on the other hand, if he refused, he would lose all credit with those who hoped to free Italy; they would regard him as a turn-coat. Either determination might lead to civil war. He was only twenty-three, and as we know, this decision was destined to cast a shadow, year after year, over all the remainder of his life.

He gave his consent—at least so Santarosa says. But

[12] In his own diaries and letters he seems to be rather given to writing poetic soliloquies; a better testimony to his worth than his own writing is the opinion of his friends. Cesare Balbo, for instance, though he did not agree with Santarosa, says that he was a man of really pure heart and disinterested beyond all saying, "whose mind was high, imaginative and cultivated".

[13] Carlo di San Marzano, the Cavaliere di Collegno, and the Conte di Lisio. These, with Santarosa, were the leaders. They were all Piedmontese nobles, officers and friends of Charles Albert; enthusiasts for the liberation of Italy; and all except Charles Albert were members of the secret Federati society. The name of the fifth was kept secret, but now he is identified as the Marquis Roberto d'Azeglio, elder brother of Massimo d'Azeglio. *V*. Rodolico, p. 133; Tivaroni, *Domin. Austr.* I, 53.

Charles Albert says that he refused it; that he tried to dissuade them from the enterprise; and that later in the day he informed the Minister of War, Count Saluzzo, that a conspiracy was in progress, but apparently without revealing any names. It is generally believed, however, that he did accept their proposals[14] on the 6th.[15]

On the following day, March 7th, Santarosa continues, they found Charles Albert in a state of great agitation and he countermanded the movement. Charles Albert's version is that again he refused to have anything to say to it. Between these two statements one fact remains certain; the movement undoubtedly was countermanded and did not take place on the 8th as previously arranged.

On the 8th Santarosa says that they heard (he does tell us how) that the prince was again disposed to favour their plot, so they fixed it for the 10th. In the evening they called upon

[14] The question is: What was the exact rôle that Charles Albert was asked to carry out? The latest writers on the subject, Luzio and Rodolico, say that he was only to be Mediator: that the Mutineers and Carbonari were to ask for a constitution and for war against Austria, and he was to carry their demands to Victor Emmanuel I and act as mediator.

[15] The king told Mr Hill that Charles Albert had only been slightly compromised in the Cisterna letters, and that he had pardoned him: but that "the moment he returned to Turin he involved himself again in the plots of the conspirators". His denials seem to me rather of the nature of traverses. In his position as a royal prince it was a difficult matter for him to admit any impertant points; there was every prospect of his having to stand a trial. *V*. F.O. 168, vol. 4. Did he really reveal the plot to Saluzzo on the 6th? Saluzzo says that Charles Albert told him with joy that the plot was over; that he had succeeded in stopping it. Saluzzo, of course, already knew that plots had been brewing, so that this information would not have made him much the wiser. This story of Saluzzo's is curious. Most writers believe that on March 6th Charles Albert agreed to the movement; that on the 7th he countermanded it: so that Saluzzo's story would fit in far better on the 7th. (Rodolico's view is that Saluzzo meant the 7th and not the 6th.) If Charles Albert really refused point-blank on the 6th (as he says), how is it that his lifelong friend Roberto d'Azeglio never wrote a line to clear his character?

him and informed him that the movement was to take place, but, in spite of his questions, they refused to tell him the exact date. Charles Albert's version is that he again refused to have anything to say to it.

On this occasion Charles Albert certainly seems to have tried to edge away from them. They admit that he would no longer agree to play so prominent a part as heretofore. Most probably he did not want a plot, and most certainly he did not want his friends to suffer. It looks as if he wished to know what they were doing without definitely joining them. Apparently he let them talk in his presence—which was wrong of a prince because his name naturally carries great weight with loyal men. On the other hand one feels that the conspirators were not dealing quite fairly with him. They were keeping him in the movement by not telling him its date. Had they told him that it was due to break out within about thirty-six hours from that moment, he would have countermanded it at once.

That evening Cesare Balbo, a Liberal, but one opposed to the plot, told Charles Albert (owing to a misapprehension) that it was to come off next day, on the 9th. Charles Albert at once sent him and several other officers to find Santarosa, Collegno and the other leaders, and say that he would oppose it with arms. They went, but it was dawn on the 9th before they could find anyone.

On the morning of the 9th they found them. The plot was countermanded.[16] Charles Albert was immensely relieved.

---

[16] According to one account, when Charles Albert believed that the plot was at an end he spoke openly (to Saluzzo, I think), on the understanding that all concerned in it should be pardoned in consideration of his own good work. This would have been an unwise thing to do, even though he had received a definite promise from the conspirators. It seems very hard to believe that Charles Albert intentionally turned informer. If he did so, how could Roberto and Costanza d'Azeglio remain his friends for life? Roberto had been one of Santarosa's four chief colleagues, one of those exiled; a Carbonaro. He and his wife were people of the highest character, and they remained devoted to Charles

He embraced Cesare Balbo again and again; he believed that he had staved off this outbreak and all its suffering. But—and it seems tragic—they were now too late. It was no longer possible to stop it.

The actual revolt has little interest. On March 10th several garrisons mutinied, and Alessandria, a town of 30,000 inhabitants, became the centre of resistance; the rebel troops there proclaimed the constitution, and raised the tricolour flag of red, green and blue, which was "beloved by the Lombards" because these had been the colours of Eugène Beauharnais' kingdom in northern Italy. On receipt of this news Santarosa and the three other leaders of revolt realised that their friends had now committed themselves, and—honourable gentlemen as they were—went out to join them. On March 11th, Turin, the capital, began to move; some 1200 men seized the Citadel and raised the Neapolitan or Carbonari tricolour of black, red and blue. During all these troubled days Charles Albert remained in constant attendance on the king and queen, and won the lasting gratitude of the latter by his coolness and evident determination to shield them against the crowd. On March 12th he went out and, in spite of the risks, rode up to the Citadel to enquire about the mutineers' demands. He was soon surrounded by an immense concourse shouting for the "Spanish" constitution, so he told them he would try and get it for them.

But there was no longer any question of winning constitutions or of making war on Austria. The Holy Alliance had decided to intervene. The Marquis di San Marzano had returned only the day before from the meeting of Austria, Prussia and Russia at Laybach, and he brought news of their determination to suppress any Liberal movement within their reach.[17] The Austrian army was marching, and at

Albert. The same consideration also applies to others less closely concerned; to Balbo, for instance.

[17] *V*. Victor Emmanuel's proclamation of March 12th, published in De Beauchamp, *Histoire de la révolution de Piédmont*, p. 149. Also

Metternich's word Russia was ready to mobilise 100,000 men to prevent the setting up of progressive constitutions in Italy. Poor old Victor Emmanuel, who had behaved with a good deal of sangfroid and dignity, now found himself between two fires; to grant the constitution meant an overwhelming invasion, but to refuse it meant repression and shooting down his own people: so he decided to abdicate in favour of Charles Felix, and at the same time he asked Charles Albert to act as regent until the new king should arrive back from Modena where he was staying. "Je demande à Dieu que vous soyez plus heureux que moi", he said, and during the night of the 12th he and his queen departed for Nice.

One tiny episode during these days brings tears to the eyes. At times the mob seemed threatening and some of the old loyal *émigrés* who had followed their king into exile heard that he was again in danger, so they rode round to the palace with their swords and pistols to defend him, although several of them had to be lifted onto their horses.

Charles Albert thus found himself face to face with a rebellion of which at first he had been considered the leader. The ministers all hastily resigned; he was left almost alone; so he appointed a Junta of Liberals to carry on the government. By that time he was quite aware that there was no

La Tour's proclamation of March 23rd, *ibid.* p. 161. Also the declaration of Austria, Russia and Prussia at the Congress of Laybach May 12th which refers with especial bitterness to Piedmont and to Naples; published *ibid.* p. 194. "...fidèle à ses promesses, la Russie sur la demande de l'Autriche et du Souverain légitime du royaume de Sardaigne, avait fait marcher une armée de cent mille hommes afin de prévenir les funestes et trop probables effets de la révolution militaire qui venait d'éclater dans le Piémont...." Nesselrode's (Russian ambassador) despatch to all Russian embassies abroad. Dated Laybach, April 28th (May 10th), 1821. De Beauchamp, p. 198, gives this document. "...elles (the troops) auraient traversé paisiblement les immenses espaces qui les séparent de l'Italie, et dès que le but pour lequel les deux princes les avaient appelées eut été atteint, l'empereur leur aurait donné l'ordre de rentrer dans ses états." *Ibid.* p. 200.

longer the slightest hope of any Liberal success.[18] But the
people were calling for the "Spanish Constitution". To refuse
it meant bloodshed and possibly a civil war; so Charles Albert
granted the Spanish constitution, but at the same time he
pointed out that any such grant must necessarily be subject
to the approval of the new king, Charles Felix. By this concession he was able to maintain order in Turin. But on
March 16th there arrived from Charles Felix a proclamation
in such terms that Charles Albert could no longer stay in
Turin without becoming a rebel. His friends now had him
watched, for he was their last remnant of legality. Finally
after appointing Santarosa to the Ministry of War in place
of the Marchese Pes di Villamarina,[19] on the night of March
21st he left Turin with the loyal troops to march to Novara
according to the orders of the new king.

The old Reactionist champion, Charles Felix, was absolutely
furious. When he heard that his beloved brother had been
obliged to abdicate, that his young heir had flown in the face
of the Holy Alliance, had granted a very democratic constitution, and had left to him the unpopular task of revoking
it, he threw the letter in the messenger's face, refused even
to see Charles Albert, and exiled him to Florence. Although
more than half of the army had remained loyal, he applied
for reinforcements from the Austrians and with this joint
force on May 8th he defeated the mutineers, only about
4000 strong, outside Novara.

----

[18] The king had abdicated; the leading officials had resigned; the
people were apathetic; more than half the army were against the
movement; and there was not sufficient material to declare war on
Austria, which had been the chief dream of Charles Albert. Moreover, the Holy Alliance was moving. Before the mutiny ended the
Austrians had crushed Pepe. "I found him very much depressed
in his spirits", adds the British Minister, Percy, who was a friend
of his. F.O. 168, vol. 3.
[19] The Cavaliere Ludovico Sauli d'Iglano was Foreign Minister;
Santarosa was Minister of War and of the Navy.

Thus the mutiny of 1821 was over; but its results were very far from being over.[20] Two young officers were condemned to be shot, and many others were imprisoned or exiled.

The fate of Santarosa has always aroused great sympathy. He was a man of thirty-eight with a wife and family; a genuine self-sacrificing patriot though rather a slave to his own ideas. Of course his mutiny of 1821 was a rash undertaking, but there was some truth in his own verdict on it:[21] "The emancipation of Italy will be an event of the 19th century; the impulse has been given". More truth in fact, than he suspected; for it was the sight of those sad and silent exiles on the quays of Genoa which first inspired the boyish enthusiasm of Mazzini.[22] And, in Milan, the fearful sufferings of Silvio Pellico, Count Confalonieri and their fellow-prisoners did more than any propaganda to turn the culte of Italian nationality into a holy cause.

[20] 142 were tried: 2 officers condemned to death, 5 to the galleys, 16 to prison, and 54 acquitted. Of the "contumacious" who had made their escape 54 were condemned to death and 11 to the galleys. A commission inquired into the conduct of 565 officers and 123 N.C.O.'s: of these 243 officers and 75 N.C.O.'s were dismissed, pensioned, or reduced in rank, the rest were acquitted (Manno, p. 25, note). But Gualterio gives a list of 119 names, of whom 84 were condemned to death, but apparently only 1 executed; 34 to imprisonment, and one acquitted (Gualterio, vol. 1, Doc. 1, p. 175).

[21] Santarosa, p. 177.

[22] Mazzini was a boy of sixteen (1821), walking with his mother on the quay, when she gave some money to a collection for the exiles. He says: "I could guess which they were (among the other people) by the look of profound but silent suffering in their faces....That day was the first upon which there appeared confusedly before my mind the conception—I will not say of Fatherland and of Liberty—but the conception that it was possible and therefore that it was a duty to strive for the freedom of our native land. The image of these proscribed prisoners followed me everywhere throughout the day and haunted my dreams—if every man had done his duty they might have been victorious". When speaking of his decision (1827) to go into politics he says: "The ideas of 1821 flamed up again within me and determined my vocation", to give up literature and to enter upon "political action". He joined the Carbonari. Mazzini, *Scritti* (A.E.), 1, pp. 14, 15, 19.

Santarosa's place in the story of the Risorgimento is plain. In Piedmont he was the first man to put into practice the prophecy of Count Antonio Brignole-Sale; he forms as it were a connection between Brignole-Sale and Charles Albert. He was the first to offer his life in the cause of a Piedmontese advance linked with the idea of freeing and uniting Italy. Since then, of course, history has proved that this was the true line of progress.

His end was sad. He sought refuge in Switzerland but was soon driven from there: in 1822 he was arrested in Paris; in October of that year he went to London to try and earn his livelihood by teaching. In November 1824 he volunteered to fight for the freedom of Greece and died gallantly, arquebus in hand, defending the island of Sphacteria against a Turkish landing.

II. RESULTS OF THE MUTINY FOR CHARLES ALBERT

Historically, the most important results of this movement of 1821 were those which affected Charles Albert. For the time being he was ruined. The royalists called him a traitor and the revolutionists called him an informer, and every compromised man used the royal heir's name as a shield.[23]

On the one hand Charles Felix, who had been on bad terms with him for two years, seized this opportunity to keep him out of the state. For nearly two years to come Charles Albert was compelled to remain in Florence, living near the Grand-duke, his father-in-law.[24] During his absence the royalists pursued him with secret agents and slanders until hardly any of his old friends would have anything to say to him. He was a young man and sensitive, and in January 1822 it was feared

---

[23] Charles Albert's letter to Barbania, July 17th, 1821. *V.* Fiorini, p. 175.

[24] During that period he wrote two defences of his conduct: the *Memoriale* (or *Rapport et détails de la révolution*, etc.) and *Détails sur ma régence*. Many years afterwards, in 1839, he wrote *Ad majorem Dei gloriam*, another defence.

that he might shoot himself: a disastrous day that would have been for Italy!

On the other hand, far worse than the machinations of the royalists were the jibes of the revolutionists. The people whose friends and relations had gone to the galleys or to exile had no words bitter enough for the prince whom they believed to have turned informer. Even after seven years had passed the poet Berchet held him up to the obloquy of future generations in the well-known lines:

> Esecrato o Carignano,
> Va il tuo nome in ogni gente
> Non v' ha clima si lontano
> Ove il tedio, lo squallor,
> La bestemmia d' un fuggente
> Non t' annunzi traditor!

Like many another moderate man he had become the scapegoat for both sides at once. A royalist would say: Carignano is a traitor to his king. A Carbonaro would say: Carignano is a traitor to his country; whereas in reality each of them was thinking of his own party. And, of course, there exists no vindictiveness so spiteful as that of a small clique in a small nation because it can aim at ruining isolated individuals, such as Charles Albert.

It may be that these years of suffering inspired him with a hatred of revolutionists which accounts for some of his later actions—as, for instance, the Repression of 1833.

In reality the most definite political result of the whole episode of 1821 is that Metternich seems to have succeeded in using it to place Charles Albert morally "in chains". About this question one hesitates to write positively because of the possibility that some day fresh documents will become available; but there appears to be no doubt that Charles Albert was compelled to make a promise which tied him for nearly all the rest of his life, and that he made it under threat of disinheritance. It came about as follows.

By this time Charles Felix hated him, and this was not altogether surprising. After fifteen years in exile he had come home at last to enjoy his rights and had now, as he believed, been turned out again into the wilderness by a boy who ought to have been his devoted supporter. The Piedmontese nobles, too, regarded him with the "greatest distrust, contempt and abhorrence".[25] He had signed the Spanish constitution, the most fatal of all to aristocratic privileges; he was a danger which must be kept out at all costs. This perhaps explains some of the stories which reached the king's ears—that his cousin was still plotting against him, that he had bribed witnesses at trials, and the like. At one period it seemed doubtful whether Charles Albert would ever again be able to show his face in Piedmont. Charles Felix determined to disinherit him.

The difficulty was: how to oust Charles Albert and yet retain the true line of inheritance in the House of Savoy. Charles Felix decided to pass over this unworthy scion in favour of his (Charles Albert's) infant son, now two or three years old, and to get this arrangement approved by the five Great Powers in congress.

In 1821 at the Congress of Laybach this scheme was pushed for him with great enthusiasm by the Duke of Modena, who hoped to be regent for the infant son, but without success.

In 1822 Charles Felix went himself to the Congress of Verona with the intention of getting it passed; but he, too, found that his project received no support. To break the legitimist succession to a throne was considered a very strong measure, and one that was impossible without definite proofs of felony; and in spite of all the trials in Lombardy and Piedmont no sufficient proofs had been obtained against Charles Albert. On the other hand Louis XVIII and the Czar were disposed to be sorry for this young prince; and Metternich, in spite of his early threats, had decided that the most advantageous course would be, not to shut out Charles

---

[25] Hill's despatch, March 3rd, 1822, F.O. 168, vol. 5.

Albert, but to let him reign on condition of his first giving a written guarantee not to have anything further to do with Liberalism. By this means Europe would have, for Piedmont, an heir who was bound not to alter the fundamental laws of the kingdom; that is to say, not to grant a constitution. This idea of a guarantee was taken up at once by Charles Felix, and he formed the following plan which is of considerable importance in the history of the period. He decided[26]

(1) To send Charles Albert to serve in the French army which was invading Spain under command of the Duc d'Angoulême. By shooting down Spanish Liberals he was to compromise himself in the eyes of all Liberals.

(2) On his return he was to sign a solemn oath binding himself not to make innovations in the bases or fundamental laws of the monarchy.

Thus Charles Albert was to have a chance of clearing his name by service on the field of battle. He accepted with great joy and there is this to be said in his favour, that whatever may have been his early Liberal leanings, he hated the Revolution, and Spain was now in revolution. In any case Charles Felix was quite definite on this point. "Either he'll get his head broken and that will end the whole matter as far as he is concerned, or else he can put himself in a position to make some reparation for all the wrong that he has done: for there is nothing in the world that is such a bother to me as this man."

He did extremely well. He was under fire on thirteen different occasions. In June, in an engagement at the Sierra Morena he won the Legion of Honour, and at the final night-assault on the Trocadero he led the 6th Regiment with such courage and success that on September 2nd he was decorated before the whole army by the Duc d'Angoulême with the Cross of St Louis, and—which was perhaps a more precious honour—also by his own men with the corporal's stripe. "Carignan marches into action just as if he were going to a wedding", they said; and strangely enough this was exactly

[26] Rodolico, p. 341, quoting a note of Pralormo's.

the same honour which some twenty-six years later was conferred on his son, Victor Emmanuel, by the French Zouaves at Palestro. It is sad to have to relate that at home, in Piedmont, the *Gazzetta di Torino* which reported these engagements, carefully omitted the part played by Charles Albert until the French ambassador protested against this affront to a volunteer in the service of France; and then the omission had to be rectified.

On his return Charles Albert spent several months in Paris where he was received as a hero and treated with supreme kindness by the great royalist families, and especially by Louis XVIII himself. In Piedmont Charles Felix was not equally enthusiastic, but he adhered to his plan of receiving him back on stated conditions. After several months he sent him the proposed declaration to sign.

This document is no longer extant; but there is no doubt that it did once exist. From statements in several contemporary letters there seems to be no doubt that, before being re-admitted to Piedmont, Charles Albert had to swear solemnly that when he became king he would not alter the fundamental laws of the monarchy; and that he would set up a council of state composed of certain dignitaries, high ecclesiastics and other named members as a safeguard against innovations. Of course, the exact terms of the document are not known, but it seems evident that, taken as a whole, it was drawn so as to prevent his ever granting a Liberal constitution, even if he should want to do so.[27]

[27] So Bianchi asserted: and Berti (*Cesare Alfieri*, pp. 77–8). I see that M. Vidal says that no document now known permits one to assert the existence of such an agreement. Masi, however (*Il segreto del re Carlo Alberto*, pp. 144 *et seq.*), says that the document in question does not now exist, but that there is no doubt that such a document did once exist. Signor Rodolico, the latest authority, also takes this view, and has more or less re-constructed the document from several contemporary letters. Metternich always claimed that Charles Albert only regained his throne through the help of the Emperor of Austria, to whom therefore he owed gratitude. *V.* Metternich to Buol, May 9th, 1846, Metternich, VIII, 232. But

This arrangement was confirmed in 1825 by a meeting between Metternich, the Austrian Emperor, Charles Felix and Charles Albert at Genoa, where—if we are to believe Metternich—Charles Albert "said his pater peccavi" and entirely abjured Liberalism. Metternich of course made the most of the situation and, in later years, always claimed that Charles Albert owed his throne to the intercession of Austria.

These years of trial left a permanent impression on Charles Albert. He had entered upon the period a laughing careless young man, but he emerged from it old for his age and rather as one who has a mark against him; tall and pale and sad; of charming affectionate manners when with a friend, but often suspicious and unable to look people in the face; constantly on his guard as to what he said and did. He is one of the strangest figures in the Risorgimento—the Hamlet of Savoy as Mazzini called him. During the remainder of his life he still cherishes secretly the same ambitions as heretofore—that of fulfilling the destiny of the House of Savoy and of leading a war of Italian liberation—but always with the shadow of 1821 hanging over him; the memory of Santarosa.

Even in 1839, some eighteen years after the outbreak, he published another defence of his actions in 1821, and it bears the mark of a grief still unforgotten.

Ad majorem Dei gloriam—it has a religious title, for henceforward the guiding influence of his life is religion. In proof of the ever-enduring presence of this influence, Bianchi gives eleven extracts from letters[28] written after the rising of 1821, of which the following are specimens.

M. Vidal has shown that the question was re-opened in 1828 and that the situation was saved by Charles X of France. On all these points *vide* Masi, *Il segreto*, p. 123; Vidal, p. 37 and also p. 17; Vidal, *Charles Albert, Louis Philippe*, etc. p. 21; Rinieri, *v.* documents in Appendix; Gualterio; Cibrario, p. 34; Rodolico, pp. 384 *et seq.*; also general historians, especially Tivaroni, who quotes documents, *Domin. Austr.* I, 101–12.

[28] *Curiosità e ricerche di storia subalpina*, III, 718, Article by

I. "This has been a bad year and has ended in a bad and melancholy way, especially for me. But as you know, my dear Barbania, I am not complaining; I submit myself to the Will of God." (Letter of January 1st, 1822.)

II. "You mention the slanderers; I know only too well that they are pointing their venomed darts against me. But they cannot change the Will of Our Lord and will merely condemn their own souls." (April 29th, 1822.)

Thus the two guiding influences of his life were religion and the great work of the monarchy of Savoy: and the combination of these two led him in future years to regard life as a mission.[29] In this connection a story worthy of the days of chivalry is told of a meeting after his return from Spain between Charles Albert and the Marchesa Costanza d'Azeglio in Paris at a ball given by the Duchess of Clermont-Tonnerre. They had been looking together at a book which contained knightly devices and mottoes, and he asked her to give him an emblem. As we have seen, "this brave lady" and her husband, the Marquis Roberto d'Azeglio, had been implicated together with Charles Albert in the movement of 1821, so he and she decided to give their prince an emblem which should suggest to him how to restore his dignity before the nation. D'Azeglio had already selected a design, and he made two different drawings of it, both conveying the same thought. It was a knight in full armour, cap-à-pie, with his face covered by the lowered vizor, and the motto *Je me ferai connaître*. It is from this design that Charles Albert has been called "the Knight of the closed vizor", a name which is strangely descriptive of his life. When he saw these drawings he was greatly pleased and kept one of them. The other one he returned to the Marchesa, after writing on the back of it *Patrie et Victoire, Sincérité et Persévérance*, and told her to

Bianchi. Bianchi gives eleven extracts from his letters between 1822 and 1840 to prove the deeply religious turn of his mind: and, of course, many others could be quoted.

[29] Cf. Rodolico, p. xiii.

present it to him if ever in the future she should require any favour.[30]

[30] *Curiosità e ricerche*, etc. III, 720, note, Article by Bianchi. Bianchi says that he was shown the design by the Marchese Emanuele, son of Roberto d'Azeglio. The story was originally printed in Briano's biography of Roberto d'Azeglio. Roberto was the elder brother of the better-known Massimo d'Azeglio. He (Roberto) had been a Carbonaro, and one of Santarosa's four principal associates; after the rising of 1821 he was sent out of the state by the Marquis, his father, one of the steadfast old nobles who had stood for the king. In 1826 Roberto returned; he was still a Liberal but would have nothing more to say to revolution. His wife, the Marchesa Costanza d'Azeglio (*née* Alfieri), is described as a wise, courageous and loving adviser of her husband, brother and brother-in-law; and as an angel of kindness to the poor people. *V.* d'Azeglio, *Ricordi*, II, 333, quoted by Bersezio, I, 244. The motto *Je me ferai connaître* means "I will make myself known".

Chapter VI

CHARLES ALBERT'S REIGN. FIRST PERIOD 1831 TO 1834

I. CHARLES ALBERT'S CHARACTER AND POLICY

In July 1830 another convulsion of Europe took place. A revolution broke out in Paris; Charles X was driven into exile and Louis Philippe became king of the French. This re-hoisting of the tricolour in France sent a thrill through all the surrounding nations, but its most serious results occurred in Italy.

In order to keep Metternich busy the French revolutionists had proclaimed the doctrine of non-intervention: each state in Italy was to have the right of settling its own form of government, and if the Austrians should interfere they would find themselves face to face with the French army. This announcement set the whole peninsula in a turmoil. Before many months were past Modena and the Papal State were in rebellion, and Piedmont was filled with conspiracies.

In April 1831 Charles Felix died and Charles Albert succeeded to the throne of Piedmont. He was now a man of thirty-three, hardened and developed by ten years of bitter experience; a king upon whose name there lay a stain.

Evidently he realised the unusual difficulty of his position and had decided on the definite line of policy which he followed during the rest of his life. He was between two fires: on the one side he stood in danger of losing his throne through the machinations of the reactionists and of Metternich; on the other side he was in peril even of death by the hand of the Revolution which was soon to resume its activities under the direction of the Giovine Italia (1831) and the new leader Mazzini. In both camps he was regarded as a traitor.

His policy was twofold. He was weak, therefore he must

bide his time. *Vis-à-vis* of Metternich and the Holy Alliance he must show himself compliant and conservative until the great opportunity should arrive. *Vis-à-vis* of the Revolution he must show himself strong, and refuse to have his hand forced. While he remained King of Piedmont he could be of great service to Italy, but, if he were dethroned, he would become merely "another heart and sword" in the service of his country.[1]

Secretly his early ambitions were still unaltered;[2] he was perfecting his army for a war of Italian liberation. To those around him this seemed only a dream, and one may add, remained only a dream until the writings of Gioberti (1843) initiated a new phase and sent such a wave of Liberal feeling all over the peninsula, that it actually brought a Liberal Pope[3] to the throne of St Peter.

So much has been written about Charles Albert's mysterious character, that one would hesitate to add any new opinion to those already existing. And surely the simplest version seems to be the truest, namely that he acted as was natural for a man of his training and ideals amid such a conflict of parties and passions.

He was by conviction a Conservative; a legitimist, even an absolutist (Vidal, p. 23), but he had a very severe standard of duty for kings. He was very severe with himself because his convictions were strengthened by a profound sense of

---

[1] Cibrario, p. 22, says that this sentiment had affected Charles Albert in 1821.

[2] "I admit that it would have been more prudent for me to keep silence, in spite of my extreme youth, when I heard people talking about war and about their wish to increase the state of the king, and to contribute to Italian independence; to win at the price of our blood a strength and an extensive territory sufficient to ensure the happiness of our country. These were the impulses of a young soldier, but even now my grey hair does not dispute them. Certainly I do not want to do anything contrary to our holy religion, but I feel that to my last breath my heart will beat for our native land and for its independence." *Ad majorem Dei gloriam*; given in Manno, p. 122.

[3] Pius IX, 1846.

religion. Although from the year 1836 onward he suffered frequently from inflammation of the abdominal veins (Cibrario, p. 184), he would rise at five in the morning. He worked intensely: "he sacrificed not only himself, and his recreations, but even his sleep, his rest, his health and his life itself" (Cibrario, p. 25), imposed macerations on himself, and—even when he was forty years of age—"rough mortifications" and spent long intervals in prayer (Vidal, p. 26).[4] He was the protector of the Church, the ruler whom the ecclesiastical historians love to honour; he authorised the Jesuits to teach in six colleges: "I will protect you as Charles Felix did, and even more".

One of his best qualities as a ruler was his realisation of the value of authority. In this respect he showed to a great advantage as compared with some of the other sovereigns, notably Pius IX. He knew how to keep himself aloof; he disliked ovations and thought little of popularity. "I was born during the revolution", he once said at Villamarina, "I have been through all the phases and I know what

---

[4] Cibrario, a senator of Piedmont who had known Charles Albert since 1820 and was one of the three to be with him when he was dying at Oporto in 1849, describes the fact in the following terms: "As was to be expected with a man of his type, both nature and his previous misfortunes had taught him the art of concealing his sentiments. He had gained a complete mastery over his own feelings, although by nature they were heart-felt and masterful and he knew how to cover his face with a leaden mask of impassibility which contrasted strangely with the flash of his penetrating glance. He knew also the secret of speaking the language most pleasing to each interlocutor, in order to find out his inward intentions. No one surpassed him in courtesy; no one had a voice or bearing more caressing and at the same time more dignified; no one could direct his shafts more effectively into the hearts which he wanted to win". Cibrario, p. 22. But perhaps the most instructive character of Charles Albert is that given by Solaro della Margherita, *Memorandum*, p. 519, a whole chapter. For twelve years they worked together, though never in sympathy with one another: and Della Margherita evidently regarded him as a contradiction in terms. But it is an honest description and confirms most of what has been said here in the text.

popularity is: to-day 'Evviva!' and to-morrow 'Morte!'."
And he hated the speech-making and ceremonies from which
royalty can never escape. "Princes ought to avoid those
comedies—God did not mean them to be comedians."

The weak point in his character seems to have been his
unreadiness in coming to an immediate decision. This was
due perhaps to a slow-moving brain, perhaps to an over-
conscientious temperament, but more certainly, as Cibrario
points out, to his lack of experience in administration. He was
extremely persistent in the long run,[5] but not sufficiently self-
confident at the moment; unendowed with that athletic grasp
of a new situation so necessary for a leader both in war and
peace: better on paper than in immediate action. On the
other hand, however, he preserved throughout all his life a
clear, unchanging view of the main lines to be followed; and
one must admit that, among his contemporaries in Piedmont,
it would be hard to select any other man who would have
played Charles Albert's twofold part as well as he himself
played it during his reign of eighteen years. He held everyone
in leash until the very day for action had arrived.

In spite of his good intentions Charles Albert often failed
to inspire confidence. He had a charm of manner which
captivated both men and women, but did not always win
their trust. This was due partly to his own fault but partly
also to their failure to understand the necessity for constant
watchfulness and caution in all his words and in most of his
actions. He himself perceived this; at the end of his life, when
in exile after Novara, he said to one of his oldest friends, "My
life was a romance. I have not been understood". That saying
at all events is reported in the narrative of the Senator
Cibrario who was with him to the end.

[5] Since writing the above I have read the most interesting
work of Signor F. Lemmi, who has had access to many new
documents. His view of Charles Albert's pertinacity entirely
confirms that in the text (v. Lemmi, *La politica estera di Carlo
Alberto*, p. viii, 1928).

II. HIS REIGN

His reign may be divided into three[6] periods:

The *First* from 1831 to 1834. In spite of several plots Charles Albert succeeds in asserting his authority as opposed to the Revolution. During this period he is compelled, for safety, to ally himself with Austria.

The *Second* from 1835 to 1843. During these years Charles Albert feels that he has successfully repulsed the Revolution, and therefore he parts company with the Austrophils. Under Count Solaro della Margherita his policy remains Conservative—almost as Conservative as that of Austria—but he refuses to be a satellite of Austria. He asserts Piedmontese individuality while pursuing Conservative reforms.

The *Third* from 1843 to the end. After the appearance of Gioberti's writings Charles Albert cautiously but continuously reveals to partisans his anti-Austrian feeling. Between 1843 and 1846 he succeeds in regaining among nationalists his position as the leading prince in Italy.

The First Period. It is remarkable that both Charles Albert and Pope Gregory XVI began their reigns in 1831, in a time of rebellion arising out of the Paris revolution of the previous year. Charles Albert was not long in discovering the threads of a conspiracy known as that of the Cavalieri della Libertà in which several officers, including the afterwards well-known Giovanni Durando, were implicated, together with the historian Brofferio and some other civilians. This plot, however, did not mature into an open outbreak, so Charles Albert satisfied himself with placing the civilians under police supervision and with cashiering the officers.[7] In reality the

---

[6] In this division of Charles Albert's reign I have followed M. Vidal's arrangement in his fine work *Charles Albert et le Risorgimento*. The first period is given above; the second and third periods are in chapters XIV and XVII.

[7] In this plot of 1831 in Piedmont the two best-known of the officers were Giovanni Durando and Ribotti. They spent the next fifteen years or so serving in the armies of Spain and Portugal, and

most serious result of the episode was that it exhausted his patience and caused him to adopt very severe measures against the conspirators of 1833–4.

In July 1831 he signed a military alliance with Austria for defence against the French, who were now regarded as a public danger. Piedmont was to provide 37,000 men and Austria 65,000.[8]

The Revolution, however, was not going to let Charles Albert forget that it claimed him as a Liberal renegade of 1821. Before the end of 1831 Mazzini, who had been exiled by Charles Felix, addressed to the new king, publicly, the letter already mentioned, a powerful but rather insulting harangue urging him to lead the Italian revolutionary movement, and ending with the words: "Sire...whatever your reply may be, rest assured that posterity will proclaim you either *the first of the men or the last of the tyrants of Italy— choose!*" This effusion produced no results.[9] Probably Charles Albert was annoyed at being reminded of the episode of 1821, and in any case he hated revolutionists (Luzio, *Carlo Alberto e Mazzini*, p. 189): so the Mazzinians started operations.

In 1833 there resulted a serious army plot fomented by the Giovine Italia. Mazzini was only at the beginning of his career and was making rapid progress. The two previous

Durando rose to be a colonel. His brother, Giacomo Durando, then a lawyer, was also implicated, and he also rose to be a colonel after serving in Spain and Portugal. Brofferio we have already mentioned. In 1831 there was also a rising in Modena, from whence Fanti, Cialdini, Fabrizi and Panizzi were obliged to flee, with various others less known. In the Papal State many were implicated notably Farini and Mamiani.

[8] *V.* Srbik, 1, 675, and in note 2. He gives a short analysis of it.

[9] Mazzini says that he had not the slightest expectation that Charles Albert would do anything for the cause, and wrote this letter merely to make that fact plain to all Italy. Some of Mazzini's friends were urging him to abstain from action in order to see whether Charles Albert would not do something. Mazzini, *Scritti* (A.E.), 1, 52.

years he had devoted to organising the immense network system of the Giovine Italia. Then, in 1833, he decided that his party was so strong and enthusiastic that he must seize the moment to strike.[10] His proposal was accepted by the Congrega Centrale (Central Committee), and the Giovine Italia decided upon a rising which was to begin in Piedmont. Their plan was to corrupt the army, to overthrow Charles Albert if he refused to join them, and then to lead a united national movement against the Austrians. This ambitious scheme had actually been in progress for some time when, owing to a silly accident—two sergeants fighting over a woman—it was discovered (April 20th, 1833) by the Piedmontese government and cut short with great severity; ten soldiers (one subaltern and the rest N.C.O.'s) and two civilians were shot[11] by order of the courts martial and about thirty condemned to the galleys or to other penalties. Among those exiled was the Abbé V. Gioberti, one of the court chaplains, who was then almost unknown, but whose writings were destined, a few years later, to inaugurate a fresh phase in the Italian question.

To tamper with the army which he loved, and which he considered indispensable for the redemption of Italy (Cibrario, p. 53), was a crime that Charles Albert would never forgive. No doubt he felt that it was a matter of life and death. Revolution in Piedmont would probably lead to invasion and annexations by France or Austria. His punitive measures were evidently severe. It is hard to discover for certain exactly what happened, and this leads one to suspect that all the known facts are not yet made public. Masi supports the statement that three of the soldiers were shot merely because they were aware that a conspiracy was in progress and did

---

[10] Mazzini, *Scritti* (A.E.), I, 394.

[11] Almost every single historian gives slightly different figures. Luzio, the latest writer on the point, says that fourteen were shot in all, *v.* Luzio, *Gli inizi del regno di Carlo Alberto*, p. 156. Mazzini said eleven. *V.* also Mazzini, *Scritti* (A.E.), III, 325.

not turn informers. It has been said, too, that torture was used to extract evidence,[12] and that no genuine defence was allowed. Charles Albert's partisans allege that he was obliged to employ agents of the legitimist type to carry out the repression, and that they seized this opportunity to sever him for ever from the Revolution :[13] others add that his subsequent macerations were due to his remorse for the cruelties of these years. Whatever may be the exact truth, the episode has always been regarded with special horror by revolutionary writers, and soon afterwards a plot was laid to stab Charles Albert; it was suggested by a Corsican named Antonio Gallenga who was to act with the consent of Mazzini.[14] The whole story is a sad instance of what occurs in days of revolution. Mazzini was a man so kind-hearted that he spent most of his miserable income on feeding his poorer brothers in exile.

The Repression of 1833 is considered the darkest stain on

[12] Sir Augustus Foster, during his enquiries for the British government, was evidently very uncertain as to the truth. He makes one definite point against Charles Albert: "The King, dreading the length of such a process, has rejected [the charge of High Treason] at the same time desiring the charge of Treason to be omitted and the prisoners...to be proceeded against for attempting to excite Mutiny in the Army; so as to bring them under the articles of war". The courts martial, he says, were not open to the public: the prisoner could not have his own counsel but was obliged to select an officer to defend him. Charles Albert probably remembered all the harm done by the interminable trials of 1821; and very likely there are other answers to these statements of Foster; but in any case this grievance would only apply to the civilian prisoners. *V.* F.O. 168, vol. 11. During the time of the Repression General Della Rocca was Charles Albert's second equerry. His opinion is that excessive severity and cruelties were used by subordinates "which surpassed the intentions of the sovereign"; he does not mention torture. That the royal rewards given to some who had displayed most severity caused a genuine grief at court: that this grief was shared by the king himself, who after reading the despatches would often remain crushed and silent during a whole morning ride. Della Rocca, *Autobiografia d' un veterano*, 1, 87–8.

[13] Predari, *I primi vagiti della libertà in Piemonte*, p. 290, and others.

[14] *V.* Mazzini, *Scritti* (A.E.), 111, p. 342.

the life of Charles Albert. Certainly to shoot three soldiers merely for not reporting their comrades is an extreme measure; and to obtain evidence by torture, either physical or mental, or to countenance or shut one's eyes to such proceedings is horrible. One must remember, however, that the use of torture always had been part of the law of Piedmont until Charles Albert himself had abolished it on his accession. On the other hand, most undoubtedly he did a great service to the Risorgimento by purging the Piedmontese army of sedition. It was the only military force that could be used against the Austrians, and it was ensconced in a country which they could not occupy unless by agreement with France. It was a small but permanent block of trained soldiers of all arms, an invaluable asset as events proved, and both officers and men were animated by a good tradition of discipline and by a hereditary devotion to the House of Savoy. Mazzini's propaganda would have undermined these fundamental qualities without supplying any corresponding advantage. At most he would only have achieved results similar to those of Santarosa, namely the dividing of the Piedmontese army into two hostile camps. Certainly it was a good day for the Risorgimento when Charles Albert made plain to all men that there was no room in his barracks for revolutionary propaganda.

In the following year, 1834, Mazzini[15] found himself strong enough to re-arouse the movement against Charles Albert. His plan was to start a rising in Genoa and to support it from

[15] Mazzini seems to have been fearfully embittered by the death of Ruffini, one of his dearest friends. Ruffini had been imprisoned and questioned: according to one version he had been told that Mazzini had betrayed him. According to another he feared that he himself might reveal the plot under duress. He committed suicide by cutting out one of his veins. Brofferio says that he left his last testament written on the wall in blood: "I hereby bequeath my vengeance" (Brofferio, *Storia del Piemonte,* pt III, vol. I, p. 49), but it is very hard to know the truth. Mazzini undoubtedly exaggerated. For instance, he says: "It was a terrorism...Charles Albert had called for blood and they gave him blood. They shed it at daybreak between the hours of darkness and the dawn".

the north by invading Savoy from Switzerland. General Ramorino, an ex-Napoleonic squadron-leader, who had won some reputation for generalship during the ill-fated Polish rising of 1831, advanced from Geneva at the head of a band of about a thousand Swiss, Poles, Germans and Italians. But the Swiss authorities intervened and, after about twenty-four hours, his expedition came to rather a farcical end. The only point of interest in this venture is that several men, afterwards celebrated, took part in it and were compelled to flee for their lives. Among them were Fanti, the future conqueror of Umbria and the Marches, Giacomo Durando, Melegari and, greatest of all, "Borel", that is to say, Garibaldi, who was condemned to death but made his escape to Monte Video. After their dispersion there followed a period of recrimination during which Ramorino, Mazzini and other leaders exchanged accusations, and their whole movement became discredited for some years to come. From 1834 to 1840 no further risings were attempted by Mazzini. The year 1834 ends the first period of the Giovine Italia.

Thus Charles Albert emerged safely from these years of danger. He had proved that he would have no connection with the Revolution. To all appearances he was as respectable a Conservative as any other Italian princeling: his government was entirely unrepresentative; his attitude was quite satisfactory *vis-à-vis* of Metternich.[16] He was, it is true, rather too much of a Conservative reformer to please some of the reactionary legitimists of Turin society; he was interested in such novelties as gas-lighting and railways. But he was sound about the army. He continued to increase it, and introduced very few new ideas—very few at all events before the campaign of 1848.

[16] Brofferio the revolutionist has described his early régime as: "For foreign politics Rome and Vienna; for home politics the Police and the Jesuits" (Brofferio, pt I, vol. III, p. 63). As to Metternich, *v.* Lemmi, pp. 66, 67, referring to June 14th, 1831.

The Revolution loathed him. To them he was known as the traitor of 1821 and the torturer of 1833. Henceforth he and Mazzini were both working for Italy, but there was a blood-feud between them; and so it came to pass that Charles Albert, who was in reality the most persistent patriot among them all—who was afterwards designated by Radetzky himself as the arch-enemy of Austria—remained for ever condemned to brood[17] over these hopes alone, a man under a cloud, a king whom no one trusted.

The truth was that Charles Albert understood, as no one else did, that these ideals must remain his secret until the right moment should arrive. He still retained his strange semi-mystical faith in the destiny of the House of Savoy and in its motto *J'atans mon astre*, I await my star; and believed that he, Charles Albert, "was fated and called by God to the future redemption of Italy, though at the price of himself becoming its victim".[18]

[17] Charles Albert must have felt deeply the cloud under which he lay, for as late as 1839 he wrote *Ad majorem Dei gloriam*, another justification of his conduct in 1821 some eighteen years before. As to his secret hopes there is plenty of testimony. They were not unmixed with ambition, but it was ambition for the House of Savoy and for Piedmont, rather than for himself: and always tinged with religion. The following is an extract from a letter of his to the Marquis Pes di Villamarina, dated August 6th, 1840: "Twenty battles won is very fine. *For a cause that I know* I should be content to win ten and to be killed in the last. Oh then I could die happy blessing the Lord".

[18] Della Rocca, p. 79. These are General Della Rocca's own words. He was one of Charles Albert's household, both in his early days and after his accession to the throne, and was greatly attached to him, though grieved at some of the shifts to which he was driven to maintain correct appearances *vis-à-vis* of Metternich. V. also Genova di Revel, *Dal 1847 al 1855*, p. 2. Di Revel gives similar testimony and ends up: "Thus Charles Albert vacillated, awaiting the future ...*Je attends mon astre (sic)*; however, he held high the prestige of the sovereign, kept a splendid court, and offered grandiose hospitality to all foreigners of rank who entered the kingdom". *Ibid*. p. 3.

NOTE TO CHAPTER VII

The main thread of importance running through the chapters on the Papal State (chapters IV, VII–IX and XV–XVIII) is the growth of the Moderate or Reform movement which gradually takes the place of Mazzinianism, though without killing the latter.

Gregory XVI's pontificate (1831–46) began amid the fury of revolution: but the more thoughtful and constructive patriots gradually came to see that for many reasons, better results could be obtained by a moderate programme than by violence. And this movement reached its zenith during the first two years of Pius IX (1846–48); it is the most important theme of this volume.

To simplify the reading of these chapters on the growth of the Reform movement in the Papal State we may say that there are three main landmarks, firstly, the *Memorandum* of 1831 (described in this chapter); secondly, Gioberti's book, the *Primato* 1843 (chapter XI); thirdly, the *Manifesto of Rimini* in 1845 (chapter XV).

The *Memorandum* was the first scheme of reform: it was proposed in 1831 by the five Great Powers, as a cure for rebellion: next comes the Moderate movement, heralded by Gioberti; then the *Manifesto of Rimini*, which was the statement of their claim by the Moderates or Reformers in 1845, when they had become a power in the land.

These lead up to the period of Pius IX's movement, which included reform, Liberal advance and the great attempt at Italian federation: 1846–48.

Chapter VII

THE PAPAL STATE: THE
REBELLION OF 1831

After the restoration of 1815 the first four Popes succeeded
one another in the following order:

Pius VII   (restored 1814, died 1823)
Leo XII   (1823–9)
Pius VIII   (1829–30)
Gregory XVI   (1831–46)

None of the above Pontiffs has any important connection
with the Risorgimento until we come to Gregory XVI,
elected in 1831.

I. THE REVOLUTION OF 1831

The flood of revolution in 1830 and 1831, like all forms of
war, very soon tested the soundness of everything around it.
To Charles Albert it was dangerous, but to the Papacy much
more so.

How slight was the grip of the Papal government on its
towns was plainly proved after this Revolution of 1830.[1] In
that year Lafitte[2] (Prime Minister), Soult (War), Sebastiani
(Foreign Affairs), La Fayette and other French politicians

[1] Farini, I, 31; Gualterio, vol. I, pt I, p. 46; Silva, *La Monarchia
di Luglio e l' Italia*, p. 65 *et seq.* and Vatican Arch.

[2] Stern, *Geschichte Europas seit den Verträgen von 1815 bis zum
Frankfurter Frieden von 1871*, IV, 199; Thureau Dangin, *Histoire
de la révolution de juillet*, Paris, 1884–92, I, 197–8, quotes a speech by
Lafitte on December 1st, 1830: "'La France', s'écriait M. Lafitte, le
1ᵉʳ decembre 1830, aux applaudissements de la gauche, 'ne per-
mettra pas que le principe de non intervention soit violé. Sous
très-peu de temps, Messieurs, nous aurons outre nos places fortes
approvisionnées et defendues, cinq cent mille hommes en bataille,
bien armés; un million de gardes nationaux les appuieront, et le
Roi s'il en était besoin, se mettrait à la tête de la nation'". Other
similar speeches by Lafitte, Soult and Sebastiani are quoted.

had declared themselves ready to defend Italy from any intervention by outside powers; and they intimated to the Italian exiles in Paris that the Italian states were to be free to select their own form of government. The effect of this declaration was electrifying. Rebellion broke out all over the peninsula (February 3rd, 1831).

In Piedmont, Mazzini started upon the abortive movement already described; in the small states of Parma and Modena (Menotti's rebellion) the governments were temporarily overthrown and their rulers fled: then the Revolution spread into the Papal State; Bologna rose (February 3rd), headed by some of its rich men and nobles, and was soon followed by Forlì, Ravenna, Imola, Ferrara and Ancona. On February 5th the Bolognese set up a provisional government under a president; on February 8th they declared the Temporal Power of the Pope at an end, *de jure* and *de facto*. Having thus burnt their boats they proceeded to appoint various Napoleonic veterans to command their volunteers, namely General Armandi,[3] and under him Generals Sercognani,[4] Grabinsky (a Pole), Olini, Guidotti and, later on, General Zucchi,[5] the leader of the Modenese revolutionary troops. They had two main forces; one, under Sercognani, marching southward on Rome, the other, organised later on, under Zucchi, about 5000 strong. But there was no opposition. When the tricolour was raised most of the Papal Delegates gave in; their troops joined the

---

[3] Armandi, born 1778, in Romagna: a retired Napoleonic artillery colonel (1813). Tutor to the sons of Jérôme and Louis Bonaparte. After this rebellion of 1831 he retired to France, where he produced some military and literary works. In 1848 and 1849, though seventy years of age, he joined the Italian revolutionists in Venetia. In 1851 his former pupil, Louis, became the Emperor Napoleon III, and conferred high honours upon him. In 1855 Armandi died.

[4] Sercognani, born in 1780: from 1797 to 1814 served in Napoleon's army, retiring with the rank of Lieut.-Colonel. After this rebellion of 1831 he emigrated to France, and died there a poor man in 1844.

[5] Zucchi. For a sketch of his life, *v.* pp. 95–7.

people amid festivities, balls and rejoicings, and the whole
Revolution was carried out with the ease and gaiety of a flower-
show.[6] On February 13th Spoleto adhered to the movement;
on the 14th Perugia, Urbino and Pesaro followed suit; on the
15th Osimo, Foligno, Todi and Assisi; on the 17th Macerata;
on the 18th Loreto and Recanati; on the 19th Tolentino; on
the 21st Camerino; and on that day Sercognani took Fermo;
and on the 23rd he emerged at Ascoli at the southern end of
the Marches. On the 25th the assembly at Bologna proclaimed the union of all the insurgent provinces under one
government, to be called the United Provinces of Italy. They
sent a deputation to Paris and raised a flag. Bologna was to
be their capital.

Thus, with the exception of Rome, Rieti, Orvieto, and
probably a few smaller places, the Pope had lost all his towns
within three weeks. But this was not in reality a universal
rising of the people, but rather a successful achievement of
the active political organisations working upon the municipal
directing classes of each town.[7] The poor people were not
directly stirred and not unanimous; and even these richer
people themselves had no definite constructive scheme. They
included every type of politician from a Voltairean philosopher
to a federalist. Some few were pan-Italian nationalists, but
the great majority confined their aspirations to their own
Papal State and were agreed only in wanting the reform of

[6] *V.* account given by Lanove, French minister at Florence
(Silva, p. 55).
[7] This seems to be one reason for the astonishingly rapid changes
that occurred with very little bloodshed. Masi says: "Though one
notes a numerous participation of all social classes in the revolution
(but in both town and country districts the populace even when
not entirely adverse is represented only by a minority), it is none
the less true that it proved the inability of the secret societies,
however strong numerically, to organise a sufficiently effectual
action". Tivaroni says: "the sentiment of nationality and independence, though widespread ever since 1814, inspired only a
minority which was not strong enough to fight against Austria".
Tivaroni, *Domin. Austr.* II, 198.

their priestly government and the right to have a share in it. What these Liberals ought to have done was to open negotiations with Gregory XVI at once,[8] because their movement was fundamentally unsound, inasmuch as it relied entirely on French support against Austria:[9] and in reality the French were not in a position to interfere, whereas the Austrians were perfectly ready to do so.

By an exceedingly unfortunate chance this period of turmoil had begun on the very day of the election of the new Pope, Gregory XVI. For no fewer than fifty days, previously, the cardinals had sat in Conclave unable to make their choice. At last they had fixed on Cardinal Capellari, a man of 65, of "learning and of high character" (Seymour's despatch, F.O. 171, vol. 2), a Camaldolese monk, with some experience of outside work, but mainly a theologian and a philosopher:[10] "very remarkable both for innocence and gravity of manners and for being most learned especially in ecclesiastical matters; and for protracted labours endured on behalf of the Apostolic See"[11]—so he had been described by Leo XII. He was elected Pope on February 2nd, 1831, and began his reign by ordering an enquiry into the grievances of the Legations; but on the very next morning, February 3rd, news arrived that the rebellion had already broken out. On February 9th a plot

---

[8] When rather too late they signed a treaty with Cardinal Benvenuti whom they had made prisoner, but the Papal government refused to ratify it. As to their diversity of opinions, v. Seymour's despatch February 19th, F.O. 171, vol. 2.

[9] Bianchi, III, 44, and others.

[10] V. Catholic Encyclopedia. An interesting first impression of him was that of Sir Brook Taylor, after their interview on April 20th, 1831: "One of the principal qualities, however, of the Pope is said to consist in great firmness of mind. He is a man of profound learning and research and accustomed to business, but with little confidence in his own judgment upon political affairs. His age is about sixty-five years; stoutly built and of healthy constitution with very mild, quiet and engaging manners". F.O. 43, vol. 24, letter of April 20th, 1831.

[11] Wiseman, Four last Popes, p. 269.

to take the Castle of St Angelo was discovered. On the 12th we are told by Cardinal Wiseman, who was then in Rome, "some sharp reports of firearms reached our ears" and information of an attack on the post-office, during which several people were wounded. "As for ourselves, not knowing what might happen or in what direction the blind fury of the rebellion might direct itself, ignorant also of the extent and resources of the aggressors, we took every precaution against nocturnal surprise. Our doors were solid, our windows well-barred, our walls well-nigh impregnable....Watch and ward were also kept up, till morning dawned on our untried defences and nodding sentinels."

In his younger days Gregory XVI had been credited with Liberal sympathies, but this hostile reception produced a profound impression upon him: "It is a crown of thorns not a tiara that they have set on my head", he said to Bunsen; and unfortunately it provided him with an excellent reason for believing that without Austrian help he could never retain possession of the Papal State.[12] Within Rome itself, however, the rebellion proved a complete failure. He was welcomed not only with loyalty but with the greatest enthusiasm. On Rome the Popes could nearly always rely. When Gregory began to raise troops, even the sons of the noble families flocked to his standard under Prince Altieri, and when he drove out in his carriage he was soon surrounded by thousands of the poor people, especially the Trasteverines, the laughing, ignorant, loyal, warm-hearted men from across the river, shouting "Courage, Holy Father! Courage; we'll defend you!" In some of the outlying towns, too, the revolutionists found themselves checked, notably at Orvieto, and also at Rieti, where the Bishop, Monsignor Gabriele Ferretti, armed

[12] F.O. 43, vol. 24. When Gregory XVI heard that the rebels were marching on Rome he wrote in despairing terms to Vienna asking for intervention by their troops. He feared that Rome would fall, and after Rome perhaps Naples and Tuscany. The Austrian Emperor had already offered him a refuge in Venice. Vatican Arch., Austria Ambasciatore Bernetti's letter of March 15th.

his people and repulsed the rebels from his walls. One rather suspects that if all the southern Delegates had shown similar determination, some of them at all events would have achieved similar results. The towns within the circle of Roman attraction were divided in sentiment and it was the strong hand that carried the day.

The influence of these events on the new Pope soon became apparent. He called, in the most urgent terms, for the intervention of Austria, and as soon as the Austrian army intervened the end of his difficulties was near.[13] The rebels possessed no forces able to hold out for any length of time against it. They had relied entirely on the French politicians' guarantee of non-intervention, and the French had failed them. Nevertheless some fighting took place.

In the beginning of March the Austrians re-occupied the states of Parma and Modena, and then crossed the Papal frontier and entered Bologna[14] (March 21st). The Bolognese revolutionary government at once appointed General Zucchi to command all the volunteers that they could raise, about 5000 men with four guns; and Count Terenzio Mamiani offered to organise a house to house defence of the town. But Zucchi, who was an experienced officer with a fine record— promoted to be brigadier-general after the battle of Raab in 1809; named divisional general and publicly complimented before his Italian brigade[15] by Napoleon himself in 1813—

---

[13] Vatican Arch., Austria Ambasciatore, March 15th, 1831; *v.* also Bianchi, III, 57. Metternich had informed the Papal government that he would not intervene unless he received a formal request, as he had from the Duke of Modena, *v.* despatch of February 18th, 1831, from the Nunzio in Vienna. Vatican Arch., Nunzio at Vienna, 1831.

[14] *Rassegna storica del Risorgimento*, Article by Gamberale.

[15] "The enemy, who was always close behind us, gave us no respite; we had to fight every day. On September 22nd at midday the Marshal [Macdonald] had ordered the whole army to stand to arms, on account of the great movements of troops which were visible all around us among the Russians and Prussians. At that moment the Emperor arrived; he came and stood in front of my

saw that with his young volunteers the best chance of successful resistance was to retire into Ancona, the only fortified town in the Papal State. Towards Ancona, therefore, he directed his march, followed, very shortly, by the Austrians.

On March 25th the Austrian advance-guard caught up Zucchi's columns at the bridge of Rimini, and a rear-guard action ensued. The whole Austrian force on the spot was about 5000 strong, with cavalry and four guns, and the Italians only about 4000, with two squadrons and six guns. At first there was a temporary alarm in the ranks of the volunteers, but then under Generals Zucchi and Olini a rear-guard was formed of 1200 stalwarts, and, although many of them carried only pikes and shot guns, they succeeded in repulsing the enemy with some loss, and in delaying him for an hour while the rest retired.[16] Their own losses numbered only thirty; but they had achieved their object, and their leaders were greatly encouraged, in fact rather pathetically happy, because these untrained boys had stood well. In his

brigade. The following is the actual conversation which the Great Captain held with me:
'Zucchi, I am pleased with you, I have appointed you general of division. And I am pleased with the Italians; wherever they are they always distinguish themselves. How many strong were you when you left Italy?'
'Eight thousand five hundred, Sir.'
'And what is your strength now?'
'About six thousand.'
'What has happened to the others?'
'The others, your Majesty, are dead, wounded or prisoners.'
'Yes; I know', returned the Emperor. 'You have always had to stand the roughest affairs throughout the whole campaign. In his reports Macdonald has constantly praised your zeal, your courage and the bravery of your troops.'
Anyone in the world can imagine my joy at that instant. And the compliments which I was paid by everyone including the King of Naples [Murat] were also very pleasant indeed to hear. In fact I was at the very zenith of happiness." Zucchi, *Memorie del generale Carlo Zucchi*, p. 63.
[16] This description is taken from the writings of Zucchi, Armandi, Farini and Gualterio.

Memoirs Zucchi speaks of the episode in the following terms: "This resistance to a large and powerful hostile force by young soldiers unaccustomed to war, remained to us as a far-distant hope: a hope that some day the united Italians might show to Europe that they have bold and generous blood in their veins...".[17] On the 27th, however, news arrived that the revolutionary government had come to terms, and had surrendered Ancona, so that no course remained open but to lay down their arms.

Meanwhile Sercognani's advance on Rome also had proved a failure—and in his case this was not due to the Austrian intervention, but to lack of popular support. On March 5th

[17] Zucchi, p. 109. Zucchi's own fate was profoundly sad. He set sail from Ancona in the belief that he was safely covered by the terms of the capitulation; but he and a shipful of his companions were betrayed to the Austrians. In spite of a protest by France and England they were taken to Venice as prisoners. At the outbreak of the rebellion he had been in Austrian service, so that he was naturally regarded as a deserter, and on being captured he gave up all hope of life. After a trial which dragged on for two years, most of which time he spent in a stone cell and weighed down with iron chains, he was at length condemned to death, but the Emperor commuted his sentence to twenty years' imprisonment. The first two years were spent in solitary confinement in a dim cell, on insufficient food, until his health broke down. In 1840, by the efforts of his wife, he was allowed to serve the rest of his sentence living with her in the fortress of Josephstadt. In 1848 he was liberated by the new revolution. Though seventy-one years of age he instantly offered his services to the Italian revolutionists and defended the fortress of Palmanova against Austria, until finally it was obliged to surrender. His next year was spent in the service of Pius IX. In one sense only he was fortunate: he lived to see the triumph of his cause. In 1859, when Piedmont was arming for the campaign of Solferino, he volunteered again, at the age of eighty-two, and was accepted with the rank of lieut.-general and witnessed the defeat of the Austrians. He died in 1861. His was a truly remarkable life. The above-mentioned betrayal of Zucchi and his shipful of companions offers a strange instance of "poetic" justice. The captain who betrayed them died untimely. The Austrian officer to whom they were betrayed was Post-captain Baron Bandiera, an Italian: he lived to see his two sons executed as rebels in 1844, the celebrated Bandiera brothers. Masi, I, 487; also Zucchi, p. 113.

one of his columns under General Guidotti had won a small engagement, inflicting, so it was claimed, a loss of forty-three on the Papal troops at the cost of only one man on their own side; and Sercognani himself had progressed successfully as far as Terni and Ponte Felice on the Tiber. But from thence onwards he found that the people were not with him. In the province of Lazio alone there had been collected as many as 2100 volunteers to fight against him, and many others in Rome itself. From Terni he detached a force to attack Rieti, but it was repulsed by Bishop Gabriele Ferretti and Colonel Bentivoglio, as already mentioned. He sent another force of a thousand men to take Orvieto, but they were surprised and defeated at San Lorenzo Nuovo, near the Lake of Bolsena. Several other skirmishes took place, and finally, when he heard of the surrender of Ancona, he started at once to retire to Spoleto.

It was near Spoleto that finally he surrendered to the Archbishop Mastai Ferretti (afterwards Pius IX). This surrender was considered a good piece of work on the part of Mastai Ferretti. He made matters as easy as possible for the rebels and provided them with a sum of 12,000 scudi to take them home; but unfortunately, near Terni the disarmed men were set upon by hordes of infuriated peasants, and—it is said—some of them were killed.

The rebellion of 1831 had taken only three weeks to reach its zenith and four more to wane; but in that short time it had proved that the municipalities alone could achieve nothing,[18] and this, at all events, was a step onward in experience. In reviewing the whole history of the Italian Risorgimento one can divide it, quite roughly, according to its risings, each of which seems to be an advance on its predecessor. Thus the movement of 1821 was the work of the secret societies; that of 1831 worked through the municipalities; in that of 1848

[18] It had also convinced most people of the uselessness of trusting France. Yet Cavour was destined to achieve his final success by means of France.

the units were the small states; and that of 1859 and 1860 was an appeal, at all events, to a united Italy.

When order was restored the Papal government granted an amnesty to the rebels. There were thirty-eight exceptions made, and among those to whom pardon was refused were Count Terenzio Mamiani della Rovere and Count Pietro Ferretti, cousin of the Archbishop Mastai Ferretti (Pius IX), Professor Orioli and one or two more who will reappear in the story of this period. Mamiani had been the only man who refused to sign the capitulation of Ancona; and three years later, in 1834, he joined in Mazzini's plot against Piedmont, and spent the next thirteen years in exile, living in Paris, but still working for his cause. Apart from his inherited position he was a distinguished man well known for his writings on philosophy, so his case aroused a good deal of sympathy.

This rebellion of 1831 marks the end of the Carbonari, and the rise of the Giovine Italia under Mazzini.

During these months there occurred a curious little episode of paramount importance, later on, in the history of the Papacy and of Italy. One of the main actors in the drama, in fact a future emperor, makes his first appearance on the scene. In Rome the rebellion had been preceded (December 11th, 1830) by an attempted rising, headed by Napoleon and Louis Bonaparte (afterwards the Emperor Napoleon III), the two sons of Louis Bonaparte, ex-king of Holland. It need hardly be said that all the Napoleonidae were born adventurers; they had it in the blood. And so the two brothers rode gallantly through the town with tricolour ribbons on their horses, but hardly anyone joined them and very soon they were arrested and escorted to the frontier of the state. From thence they joined the rebels and, during their early successes, the elder brother, Napoleon, wrote a private letter to the Pope, apparently of a boyish type, saying that no one wanted His Holiness to give up the spiritual power, but asking him "to resign the temporal power which is incompatible with his

sacred ministry ".[19] To this suggestion, dated Sunday, March
27th, 1831, no answer was returned, but afterwards, when
communicating with the powers, Cardinal Bernetti referred
to a letter received "from a certain Napoleon Bonaparte",
and observed that the preserving and handing on of the Papal
dominions was for him (the Pope) a sacred duty, and that he
had no means of doing so except by help of the Austrian
troops. Here then we have the whole crux of the Papal
question stated in a nutshell; exactly as it was afterwards
repeated again and again between Pope Pius IX and
Napoleon III, younger brother of the writer of the letter,
until its final settlement in 1870. On the one side Napoleon III
saw that the continuance of the Papal State was impossible in
a united Italy. On the other side the Pope felt it a sacred duty
to hand on the states of the Church intact to his successor.

As a matter of fact the two young brothers had very little
success during this insurrection. Their assistance was not
much appreciated by their own friends, because it afforded
Metternich a splendid chance of representing to Louis
Philippe that the whole rising was in reality a Bonapartist
intrigue; and he did so most circumstantially.[20] So the two

---

[19] Bunsen's despatch of March 3rd, 1831. This young Napoleon
asked the Pope to pardon his addressing him: "de ce que je me
permets de m'adresser à Lui, moi qui ne suis rien". The most
sensible remark in the letter was that the purpose of the movement
was "to obtain civil liberty such as that which makes the happiness
of France and England".

[20] Metternich played the Bonapartes as his trump-card against the
newly established Louis Philippe. For instance, in his confidential
letter to Count Apponyi in Paris he says sarcastically: "Is the
French government still quite firmly decided not to have a Bonaparte
as a neighbour? I think it is right: for otherwise...danger for the
Orleans dynasty. Has it never occurred to anyone in Paris that they
owe us a debt of gratitude for our correct attitude as regards
Napoleon II? [The Duke of Reichstadt: he lived in Austria.] We
surely deserve praise on that head....Let them keep propaganda
in check and start no movements in Italy; that is what we are
demanding on this 18th of January 1831, and it is not an exaggerated
demand". In another letter dated February 15th, 1831 (Metternich,

young men were ordered by their friends to retire to Forlì, where shortly afterwards Napoleon died; he was the elder and the more popular of the two. Thus Louis[21] was left head of the family: and one remembers with a kind of wonder that it was during this short rising of 1831 that he made his first start on that strange career of ups and downs, which included exile to America, six years' imprisonment in the fortress of Ham, a daring escape from that place, and finally culminated in his ruling France for twenty years as the Emperor Napoleon III, the most brilliant sovereign in Europe. He had his first actual experience of fighting during this rising of 1831, at the skirmish of San Lorenzino,[22] where, pistol in hand, he attacked one of the local volunteers of the Papacy and made him drop his blunderbuss. If we are to believe the story usually told, he merely said "I give you your life", and passed on; whereupon another of the defenders picked up the blunderbuss and would have shot him in the back but for a comrade named Martelli, who cut the man down with his sword. If this anecdote is true Martelli certainly did better work, that day, than he knew, for the unity of Italy. Thus Louis Napoleon began life as a revolutionist—indeed, formerly he

v, 155), he says: "We know that the movement in Italy is Bonapartist and we are determined to fight it". He then goes on to say that Louis Philippe did not relish the idea of a Napoleon II on the throne of Belgium but that he would be far more dangerous on the throne of a united Italy. "Yet this is the end to which the party of anarchy [i.e. the revolutionists] are making a direct path, and it is this same end that we are resisting". On October 9th, 1830, he enclosed documents showing that old Joseph Bonaparte had designs for setting his nephew Napoleon II, son of the Great Emperor, on the throne of France. Metternich, v, 159. Louis Philippe believed or pretended to believe this story that the Italian revolution was a Bonapartist plot. Vatican Arch., 1831, No. 165, Paris, Nunzio's despatch of March 4th, 1831.

[21] Louis was the third son of Louis Bonaparte, brother of Napoleon I: his mother was Hortense de Beauharnais; he was born in 1808. His eldest brother died a child in 1807; his next brother, Napoleon, died as described in the text (1831).

[22] Masi, *Nell' Ottocento*, p. 122.

was credited with having been a Carbonaro; and, as is well known, he was never able entirely to shake off his past. When twenty years later he made an end of the French republic and laid hands on the imperial throne, there was one section of the European population, and that a very dangerous section, which never forgave him, namely the Italian and republican circles. They regarded him as a double-dyed traitor. And before he had been on that throne for six years, all Europe rang with the celebrated attempt to assassinate him, planned by one of the iniziati in revolution, Felice Orsini.[23]

[23] The story is told by Bishop Pelczar (1, 75), but without giving his authority, that it was Felice Orsini's father who had first initiated Napoleon III into the revolutionary society. If this were true, it would explain in a singularly dramatic way Napoleon's profound unwillingness to condemn him to death, as being the son of his old friend. It is said that he only agreed to do so when his Council threatened to resign. But it is not believed now that Napoleon was ever actually initiated a Carbonaro. *V.* also The O'Clery, *The making of Italy*, and Vidal, *Louis Philippe, Metternich, etc.* p. 65.

Chapter VIII

THE PAPAL STATE, 1831 TO 1834: THE MEMORANDUM

I. THE MEMORANDUM[1]

By appealing for the intervention of Austrian troops the Pontifical government had succeeded in emerging intact from the period of danger, but it had turned its own short-comings into a European question.[2] Before the year was out various schemes were under consideration for reforming and strengthening it. The first of these was the Memorandum.

At the close of the rising there must have been many people in France who felt that their nation was gravely responsible for the sufferings of the Italian Liberals. Lafitte had said "France will not allow the principle of non-intervention to be violated...we shall soon have five hundred thousand men in battle order".[3] But when the Italian revolution began, the French government not only left it unaided, but actually intercepted some of the volunteers and arms on their way to Italy.[4] Such deceptions "come home to roost": on the one hand the Papal government was bitterly incensed because the French had caused revolution. On the other hand the Italian exiles in Paris, naturally enough, were furious, and Mazzini wrote a description of the fight at Rimini, pouring out his

[1] General histories: Tivaroni, Masi, Rosi, Raulich, Stern, Hillebrand, and others. Special histories: Bianchi, Thureau Dangin, Silva, De Guichen, Vidal, Bastgen, *Rassegna storica*, 1927 (Article by Gamberale). Contemporary sources: Metternich, Farini, Gualterio, Bunsen's *Memoirs*, etc. Clerical: Hergenröther, Gams, Pelczar. Also Vatican Arch., British Record Office, Gamberale Collection of unpublished documents, etc.

[2] That was realised at the time.

[3] *Moniteur*, December 2nd, 1830, and January 7th and 9th, 1831: quoted by Silva, pp. 38, 39.

[4] *V.* Lemmi, pp. 53, 54; also Mazzini, *Scritti* (A.E.), vol. II.

whole soul in taunts of unparalleled bitterness against France: it is considered one of the most scathing and powerful pieces of propaganda ever written.[5]

The new French ministers of Louis Philippe very soon showed that, although they wanted peace, they had no intention of permitting an Austrian occupation of the Papal State. On March 27th, 1831,[6] their ambassador in Rome, the Comte de Sainte-Aulaire, sent a formal protest to Cardinal Bernetti, Papal Secretary of State, demanding evacuation by Austria. But soon it became evident that the Roman question was one of European interest. On April 13th a formal conference was opened between the representatives of the five Great Powers. For this meeting Austria (Count Lützow) had appealed to Russia (Prince Gagarin) and Prussia (Baron Bunsen) to support her; and France (Comte de Sainte-Aulaire) and Austria had invited England (Sir Brook Taylor, who arrived on April 16th, as unofficial agent of H.M.'s government). Soon afterwards the Sardinian (Piedmontese) ambassador, Conte Croza, was also invited to be present, in a consultative capacity.[7]

The French ambassador, Sainte-Aulaire, was faced by the now impossible task of reconciling the angry Italian Liberals; and he was none the more popular for being, in spite of his official views, a noble of the old type and a sympathiser with the Holy See. However, he opened the conference with a bright and conciliatory speech,[8] admitting the original necessity of

[5] Quoted almost in full in chapter IX.

[6] Bunsen's despatch of March 26th, 1831 (Gamberale documents).

[7] Piedmont was thus already regarded as in some measure representing Italy, a position which, afterwards, was won for her, gradually, by Cavour. Cf. Bunsen's despatch of July 5th, 1831 (Gamberale docts.). The English account of all this year is to be found in the letters of Sir Brook Taylor (F.O. 43, vol. 24) and of Mr Seymour (F.O. 171, vol. 2).

[8] "Je n'ai aucune hésitation à déclarer que pour le bien du pays et du gouvernement considérés isolément, j'aurais désiré que les troupes Autrichiennes fussent restées dans les provinces insurgées. Mais en considérant l'affaire du point de vue européen, la retraite

intervention, but claiming three main points: evacuation by the Austrians as soon as practicable; a thorough reform and reorganisation of the Papal State; and thirdly a wide amnesty for the unfortunate rebels. It was only in connection with this third subject, the amnesty, that he succeeded in obtaining any concessions, namely a Papal edict of April 30th modifying the previous order of April 14th: as to the other two points he found himself at once opposed by Cardinal Bernetti and Count Lützow (the Austrian representative) whose interests coincided. Bernetti dreaded the evacuation of the Austrian troops, and Metternich saw that it would mean a fresh rebellion; and they both were opposed to fundamental Liberal reforms: especially Metternich, because he perceived that if free institutions were set up in the Papal State, free institutions would also be demanded by his subjects in Lombardo-Venetia.

It is evident, however, that the incompatibility between the Austrian and the French views was not yet fully realised, for about ten days later Baron Bunsen (Prussia) tried to settle the whole problem before the conference by drawing up a Memorandum expressing the wishes of all the powers as to reform within the Papal State. On May 21st, 1831,[9] the Memorandum was issued by the five Powers; and in it they addressed the Pope, urging him to carry out a drastic scheme of re-organisation.

The Memorandum[10] is a turning point in the history of the Papal question, because it starts a new idea, namely that of Reform within the Papal State instead of Revolution. This is

de ces troupes me paraît d'une immense importance et d'une nécessité si impérieuse que je considère comme un bienfait de la providence, et que je sens mon âme remplis de reconnaissance que le gouvernement ait si parfaitement compris la situation de l'Europe...." He had great difficulty over the Amnesty question (v. Bunsen's despatches), but was strongly supported by Sir Brook Taylor. V. F.O. 43, vol. 24.

[9] Farini and Tivaroni give this date as the 10th: this is a mistake.

[10] The full text is given by Farini. V. Lo Stato Romano, p. 55. It was principally the work of Baron Bunsen.

the first important scheme of reform on popular lines; the first attempt to satisfy the people. In reality it constitutes the true beginning of this book, but for the present, we need only say that, summarised quite shortly, the Memorandum recommended:

I. Reforms of:

(a) The judicial side, the laws, law-courts and legal system. (Cap. iv.)

(b) The local administration, by introducing the *representative* principle as far as possible into communal and municipal affairs. Also the setting up of *provincial councils*[11] to help the Papal governors in matters of administration and finance; and these provincial councils were to consist preferably of members chosen from the new municipal councils. (Cap. iv.)

(c) The erection of a *permanent central Junta* to regulate finance; to be composed (1) of members chosen by the municipal councils, and (2) of the government's advisers; and this Junta was perhaps to form part of the proposed Council of State.

(d) The erection of a *Council of State* which was to consist of members nominated by the Pope; and perhaps also to include the Junta as already suggested.

II. Laymen to be admitted to the judicial and administrative posts. (Cap. ii.)

This Memorandum (which rather suggests a devolution scheme) is significant in two opposite ways. Firstly it shows that the Great Powers recognised the justice of many of the popular complaints; but secondly it also shows that they did

---

[11] During the eighteenth century the Papal towns had possessed important local rights which were abolished during the centralising régime of Napoleon; and the centralising principle was continued by Cardinal Consalvi in 1815. But Baron Bunsen and others thought that much of the discontent in the Papal State could be met by reviving provincial liberties, and thus focussing interest on to them rather than on to the central government.

not consider the people yet fit for more than a slight degree of self-government.

It is not a very definite document, but it works out more or less as follows:

1. The lesser (communal and municipal) councils are to be *elected* by the people; it does not specify the electors.

2. The new central *Junta for finance* is to be composed partly of members chosen by the communal and municipal councils, and partly of the government's advisers. Now the communal councils, as we said, are to be elected by the people; it follows therefore that the Junta is to be partly elective—but only secondarily elective. Still this is an immense step forward, for it means that the people partly control the finance of the State.[12]

3. The Junta may perhaps be united with the Council of State to form a consultative national assembly. If so most probably it would be swamped by the nominated (government) members—for the Council of State consists entirely of nominated members. This clause was inserted to give the whole scheme a conservative character.

---

[12] Baron Bunsen, the actual composer of the Memorandum, says that the provision for popular election to the communal and municipal councils was vetoed by the Austrian Emperor, who said that if such municipalities were brought into existence in the Papal State he would not be able to refuse them to Lombardy. Bunsen claims that the Memorandum of 1831 was killed by Austria and its remains were betrayed (*trahi*) by the Cardinals and prelates: that this same Memorandum, in all its plenitude, was proclaimed by Pius IX as being the basis of his reforms, but in 1848 he was compelled to grant more than would have sufficed in 1831: that nevertheless this basis remained in existence even after the end of the revolution of 1849, as is proved by the electoral law of Pius IX in 1852. Bunsen, *Memoirs*, II, 536. Incidentally, Bunsen says that four-fifths of the Papal population lived in towns (*villes*). He probably includes villages important enough to have a council. As a matter of fact, at least five-sixths of the Papal population was country-bred. Corsi gives a list of the towns in 1860 and shows that their population was not more than one-sixth or one-seventh of the whole state; he includes those down to a thousand inhabitants.

4. Add to the above reforms that *laymen* are to be admitted to all administrative or judicial offices. Their exclusion had always been a crying injustice; it was complained that even rich men who paid a large quota of taxation were not allowed to hold any of the highest offices of state. This reform, however, would mean that the Memorandum, taken as a whole, implied an immense, almost a revolutionary change in the Papal organisation.

The three most important points in the Memorandum are undoubtedly the above-named: the introduction of the elective principle into the lesser councils; the Junta; and the secularisation of the government offices.[13]

Some popular reform was necessary, and this was a good scheme, but it went rather too far for the safety of the Church's interests. At this moment it behoved the Holy See to measure each step by inches. The Church stood in danger of being plundered.

II. BERNETTI'S SUBSTITUTE FOR THE MEMO-RANDUM

At this point we had better pass over five weeks and proceed at once to the next landmark in the story, namely the Papal edict of July 5th, 1831; it was Cardinal Bernetti's reply to the Memorandum.[14]

The conference of the five Great Powers affords—one cannot help thinking—rather a sad instance of inefficiency. They met in conference every few days during three months (April 13th to July 10th), and spent about another year in interminable discussions, and at the end of that time, although they could command all the resources of the civilised world,

---

[13] The reform of the Council of State would also have been an immense change, but there was never any real chance of its acceptance, so it need not be considered.

[14] During those five weeks there took place a good deal of diplomatic bickering; but, for the history of the Risorgimento, there are only two important landmarks, namely the Memorandum and Bernetti's Edict of July 5th.

they had failed to deal with the difficulties of a very small province; and the main reason for their failure was that they spent too much of their time in trying to thwart one another: in this respect the diplomats were not so bitter as their governments.[15]

France was genuinely anxious to help the Italian Liberals to get reforms, and wanted to pose as their protector, but her primary preoccupation was to assert herself in Italy as opposed to Austria, and especially to make the Austrians evacuate the Papal State. Austria genuinely—and very naturally—wanted to restore law-and-order; to figure as the predominant power; to discredit France throughout the peninsula; and to prevent the granting of any Liberal concessions in the Papal State, lest she should be called upon to make similar concessions in Lombardy and Venetia.[16] Russia apparently was ready to support Metternich blindly. The British government showed both tact and good sense. As a Protestant power it decided not to be diplomatically represented, and its "confidential agents", Sir Brook Taylor and after him Mr Seymour, were directed primarily to concern themselves with preserving peace in Europe; in the matter of reforms both they and the French took a Liberal view but did not believe in setting up a representative government in the Papal State.[17] Baron Bunsen was equally moderate; he was the first constructive reformer. He pressed his Memorandum on the Pope. But these representatives were Protestants and did not entirely realise the difficulties of the case. And before the end of this period Bunsen was ordered by his government to vote with Austria

[15] For this portion of the narrative, *v*. *Rass. stor*. 1927 (Article by Gamberale); also Barante, *Souvenirs*, p. 236.

[16] Bunsen said afterwards that Austria was more hostile, for the reason above-named, to the Memorandum and to reform than were the Pope or Bernetti. *V*. Erster Bericht Bunsen's April 29th, 1832 (Austria Amb. Sect. 1, Rep. 1, Italien; Gamberale docts.): from the Berlin Archives.

[17] F.O. 43, vol. 24; Bunsen's letter of March 3rd, 1831 (Gamberale docts.).

rather than quarrel with Metternich over so unimportant an affair. This was a pity; for he was a very able man and it was he who had written the Memorandum.

One notices that Metternich had placed himself in a very sound position. He had not occupied the Papal State until after receiving the most urgent appeals from the Pope; and—a shrewd move—on Sainte-Aulaire's arrival Metternich had placed his Austrian troops at the disposal of the conference. He knew, of course, that it could not keep order without them.

Thus France, England and, at first, Prussia, were more or less in agreement; opposed to them were Austria, Russia and Piedmont.

Between these two huge opposing masses Cardinal Bernetti threaded his way with a remarkable degree of independence. He was probably the ablest of the negotiators in Rome at that time—a good-tempered, polished, charming, dextrous man-of-the-world, and not altogether devoted to Austria; in fact, one of the few capable servitors whom the Holy See found to its hand during this period, and one of the last who was a cardinal without being a priest. He had no intention of accepting the Memorandum; he realised that, at that moment of revolution, it would have endangered the whole existing order of the Temporal Power.[18]

Vis-à-vis of the rebels his policy[19] consisted in refusing any concession of Liberal political institutions and in offering to them judicial and administrative reforms instead. Consequently he did not intend to grant the three main concessions which we have noted in the Memorandum, namely:

[18] "The Memorandum, in short, wanted to transform the Pontifical government from ecclesiastical to lay; from being absolute to being—if not actually representative—at least consultative, a first step which might, and in fact would, lead to many others. All this represented a radical upheaval which the government of the Pope could not accept without starting on the way of its own destruction." *Rass. stor.* 1927 (Article by Gamberale), p. 672.

[19] Bernetti's letter of June 5th, 1831 (Gamberale docts.).

(*a*) The elective principle in the lesser councils; undoubtedly in the northern provinces it would have filled those councils with rebels.

(*b*) The central Junta, which most probably would have become a rival of the existing assembly, the "College of Cardinals".

(*c*) The secularisation of the offices of state.

But he was perfectly ready to reform the existing judicial and administrative institutions; and he seized at once upon Bunsen's idea of setting up provincial councils.

Vis-à-vis of the people, in fact, in order to avoid granting self-government he proposed to grant non-elective county councils.

Vis-à-vis of France: he would get French agreement to these limited concessions by obtaining for her, eventually, the evacuation of his state by the Austrian troops:[20] but he meant to stave off as long as possible her three-fold demand for amnesty, reforms, and Austrian evacuation.

Vis-à-vis of Austria: at first he needed close union with Metternich because he regarded the Austrian troops as the only means of saving the Papal State; and he wanted the support of Metternich to stave off reforms. The opinion has been expressed that he had some project for using Austria at first to ensure his own safety, and then, later on, appealing to the French as a counter-balancing power to Austrian occupation; but his letters, I think, show a genuine reliance on the Austrian army and an equally genuine dislike of the French reforms.

In justice to Bernetti one must admit that to grant the Memorandum in full just then would have been very difficult for any sovereign in Italy and almost impossible for the Papacy: in the first place because the northern part of the state was

---

[20] *V.* his note to Lützow of April 29th, 1831, F.O. 43, vol. 24. It is hard to say how far Bernetti had planned his policy beforehand; later on he is certainly believed to have agreed, at all events, to the French occupation of Ancona; and when he retired in 1836 his fall was considered an Austrian victory over the French interest.

almost split in two; during these troubles the four Legations
had summoned an assembly in the north and—as has been
described—Bologna was trending towards becoming a separate
capital. But, apart from that difficulty, the Memorandum
meant transferring an indefinite portion of the Pontifical
administration from clerics to laymen—an immense innovation; and turning its government from absolute to consultative—which is the beginning of representation. In
themselves these reforms would be good; but with revolution
in progress all over Europe the year 1831 was no moment for
changing authorities. The regrettable point is, of course, that
Bernetti did not propose ever to make real political concessions.[21] One cannot help feeling that the Memorandum
was an honest scheme, and that, as soon as possible, some
portion of it ought to have been tried.

The Edict of July 5th, 1831, was Bernetti's answer to the
conference and his alternative to the Memorandum. In this
edict none of the hoped-for political reforms were included;[22]
the elective communal councils, the Junta, and the laicising
of the offices of state were not even mentioned. The following
are its chief provisions. He restored two old Delegations
(administrative areas) and created a new one (Orvieto); to
the four existing Legations he added two more, namely
Urbino-Pesaro and Velletri. By this means he had divided
the State into eighteen or twenty provinces. Each of these
provinces—Legations and Delegations—was to be governed
as heretofore by a Legate (cardinal) or Delegate (bishop)
but henceforth he was to be assisted by a Congregazione
Governativa or committee of four laymen belonging to the
district. The duties of these committees were deliberative as
regards finance, but only consultative as regards other
matters.[23] Attached to them there was to be a Legal Assessor.

---

[21] V. Bernetti's private letter of July 12th, 1832, to Mgr Brignole
(Rass. stor. 1927, p. 712).

[22] V. The Edict of July 5th, 1831, Vatican Arch.

[23] Titolo I, 11: All these officials, of course, were to be appointed
by the government, but the Congregazioni (Committees) were

The establishment of these committees of four laymen was not, in reality, a step forward, but merely a return to Pius VII's laws which had been almost abolished by Leo XII. At the same time Bernetti increased the independence of the committees as opposed to the Delegates.

The communal councils (sixteen to forty-eight members according to population) were, as heretofore, to be nominated—not elected. In the first instance they were to be nominated by the Legate. After that they were to fill their own vacancies by co-option;[24] one-third to be co-opted every second year from among property-owners, clergy, literary men, shop-keepers or heads of professions or arts. In towns they were under the Gonfaloniere and Anziani (elders), and elsewhere under the Priori. By this edict their powers were slightly increased.

But the creation of *provincial councils* was the only real innovation in the edict; in each province, under its Legate or Delegate, there was to be a council.[25] It was not to be

renewable every three years. Titolo I, 12: Each Legation and Delegation was divided into "governi" or administrative units under a "Governor", an executive official with very wide powers, under the orders of the Legate or Delegate.

[24] Thureau Dangin says that the communal councils were elective, but this is a mistake; they were co-opted. Their co-option was subject to the approval of the Legate or Delegate, who, however, could not veto the choice without giving his reasons (Titolo II, 4).

[25] *The President* was to be the Legate or Delegate. *The Members* were to be in the proportion of one to every 20,000 inhabitants and to include also eight property-owners (Titolo III, 2). They were to be chosen on the following system. Each Communal council chooses four, three, two or one deputy according to the population of the commune. These are the electors. They meet in the chief town of the district and, by secret ballot, elect Terne—one Terna (a list of three people) for every Provincial Councillor claimable by their district. From these Terne the Pope selects the members of the Provincial Council. One notices that the electors of the Terne could nominate any man they liked, but two of the three had to be landowners and the third a prominent industrial or commercial man of the district (Titolo III, 2 and 3). One-third of them retired

elected by the people but on the following system. The communal councils were to choose electors; the electors were to draw up lists of names; from these lists of names the Papal government was to select the members of the provincial council. This system must have seemed rather derisory to Liberals. But one must remember that real democracy was not feasible in those days. There was no real democracy even in England or France.

In an accompanying circular it was added that the provincial councils might *express the wishes of the people* and add their own observations upon the various parts of the new reform, as the Holy Father was anxious to accept any demands of these councils that were not prejudicial to his sovereignty. This was an important concession; nevertheless the edict was obviously a grant of unrepresentative county councils offered to the people instead of a beginning of self-government. These provincial councils, even if they developed a will of their own, which was likely enough, could never have any authority over national matters, such as the budget, the army or the central machinery of state.

every second year. *Duties.* To deliberate on public works, finances, estimates and the amounts allotted between commune and commune throughout the province. Its acts were to be approved by the Secretary of State, and the government could dissolve it. *Session.* It sat for fifteen days in each year, during which it got through its work, and appointed a *permanent committee of three* to work with the approval of the Congregazione Governativa (four Councillors) of the Legate, on finance (Titolo III, 13). It must be remembered that the Governors (already mentioned, p. 50) had very wide powers. Farini says that they presided over the municipal councils in their districts and decided what they might discuss. "They are also directors of the police in their own district, they spy, arrest, inquire: they are criminal judges in cases of crimes carrying penalties up to three years' hard labour; in cases of theft can sentence up to ten years in the galleys. They are judges in civil cases up to 200 scudi. They carry on the administrative correspondence between the municipalities and the capital of the province."

III. RECEPTION OF BERNETTI'S EDICT

Bernetti had therefore succeeded in evading the Memorandum, but only to find himself face to face with rebellion. He had completed some administrative reforms, but from the first it was evident that the people did not mean to accept them. The northern part of the state—Bologna and the other Legations—would have to be re-conquered. The Liberals of these four Legations in the north felt themselves deceived. Their hopes had been raised by the interference of the Great Powers, but Bernetti's reforms did not touch the points which they wanted: in Bologna the people would not allow his edict even to be read.

During this crisis there are so many cross-currents that it is very difficult to discover what the majority of the people really wanted. It was probably a period of flux. Throughout the country in general the Liberals were determined not to live any longer under an unrepresentative bureaucracy directed entirely by priests, and reputed, rightly or wrongly, to be very corrupt. But the Liberals were divided. The majority probably wanted to reform their own small state; to introduce secular and representative institutions, and to turn the Pope into a constitutional monarch. The difficulty was that complete constitutionalism was impossible, most probably, for a Pope. But there were many different types of Liberals. Others looked outside their own state and dreamt of a united Italy: some of these were Carbonari republicans; and some were members of Mazzini's new republican society the Giovine Italia, which was beginning to send its propaganda speeding along the network of secret agents all over Italy. On the other hand about five-sixths of the population consisted of peasants or poor townsmen who were either loyal to the Pope or else indifferent. Strange as it now seems hardly anyone thought of Charles Albert.

In the north the problem was rather different from that elsewhere, and far more acute. The Liberals were determined to have a modern government and to be done with the priestly régime. But some of them were separatists and wanted the Legations to be parted from Rome. Just a very few—no doubt encouraged by Metternich—had formed the Ferdinandea Society, headed by Baron Baratelli of Ferrara, and wanted the Legations to be joined to Austria. In reality, however, Metternich was probably right when he said (Letter, May 3rd, 1832) that the most important revolutionary influence in the Legations was the hatred of the richer classes for the rule of the priests. And within this hatred there dwelt an element of municipal jealousy; many citizens of Bologna bitterly resented being secondary to Rome and wanted to make their town an independent capital.[26]

The Legations, then, were in revolt, and the question was arising before Bernetti: what would the powers do?

IV. THE ENDING OF THE CONGRESS

We have begun by dealing with the schemes of reform—the Memorandum and Bernetti's edict of July 5th. Our next enquiry leads us to the ending of the congress.

In France, by the beginning of June the departure of the Austrian troops had become a necessity for Casimir Perrier, because he required some success to show at the rapidly approaching general election.[27] Bunsen[28] says that Sainte-

---

[26] Gualterio, though himself a Liberal, admits this fact when speaking of the rising of 1831: "Bologna bears unwillingly her dependence on far-off Rome...and desires to be something more than a provincial city. I do not mean to say that this was the principal cause of the movement of the Bolognese, but, owing to it, many of the most distinguished citizens compromised themselves in the revolution, men whose convictions were certainly retrograde and strongly aristocratic". Gualterio, vol. I, pt I, p. 50, note.

[27] V. Barante, p. 168, letter to Sebastiani, March 28th, 1832. Metternich and Bernetti intended to help Casimir Perrier through his elections, lest he should be re-placed by someone more extreme; but they evidently meant to make him pay for this help.

[28] V. F.O. 43, vol. 24; also Bunsen's despatches of May 5th, May 27th and June 2nd, 1831.

Aulaire actually referred to it in a despatch as "a question of life and death".

Already, even in April 1831, both Lützow and Bernetti had pointed out to Sainte-Aulaire that an Austrian evacuation would be followed at once by a fresh rising in the Legations, and on June 1st Lützow had added that, before calling upon the Austrians to retire, Bernetti must have the integrity of his Papal State formally guaranteed by the powers; if the Austrians departed he would have no other security for its continued existence. To this Sainte-Aulaire replied (June 3rd) that France refused to guarantee the Papal State until its government had been drastically reformed; that no one would guarantee it in its existing condition; and Sir Brook Taylor supported him. Thus one may sum up the situation as follows: France had claimed evacuation by Austria. Austria and Bernetti replied: No evacuation unless you guarantee us. France and England rejoined: No guarantee without reforms. Austria was supported by Russia and Prussia.

At the end of May a French squadron arrived off Ancona and the relations of the hitherto most friendly ambassadors became rather embittered; at the same time this step brought matters to a head.

On June 1st, in a nebulous note, Bernetti agreed that the Pope should let the Austrians retire; but first the French must give the guarantee; and he promised further reforms, but in vague terms.

The situation therefore was that as soon as the Pope should give satisfactory reforms the French would give the guarantee; and in return, if the French gave the guarantee, then the Austrians would retire.

In this brief summary it is impossible to go into detail. The next month was spent by Sainte-Aulaire mainly in trying to pin Bernetti to definite reforms[29] on the lines of the Memorandum, and by Bernetti in refusing to bind himself.

[29] Ste-Aulaire claimed three definite genuine reforms, those in the Memorandum (v. his note of June 7th, 1831): (1) Administrative

Finally on July 3rd Bernetti wrote to Sainte-Aulaire rather
a clever and defiant note in which he (1) agreed to call upon
the Austrians to evacuate the state, but (2) said that he would
not bind himself to the reforms demanded by the French,
and (3) that consequently he no longer asked the French for
their guarantee.[30]

Bernetti had had the best of it—and, of course, the situation
had been in his favour. As to reform, he had retained a free
hand; as to evacuation he had been compelled to let the
Austrian troops go—as a sop to Casimir Perrier, in order to
help him through his elections; but in reality this concession
was farcical, because he foresaw immediate rebellion, and
intended to recall them whenever required.[31] As to the
guarantee, he had given in to France; he had resigned his
claim; but he was aware that he could get a fairly satisfactory
guarantee for his state from the other Powers.

and judicial posts were to be thrown open to laymen in a fair
proportion with ecclesiastics. (2) The municipal councils were to be
based on free election. (3) Provincial councils and the Central
Junta as mentioned in the Memorandum. Without these reforms he
would not give the French guarantee.

    [30] Bernetti's despatch ends up as follows: "As to the reforms, the
Undersigned declares that if the Holy Father were to accept the
conditions imposed he would be doing himself an injustice. Better
than anyone else he knows what he should do for his people, to
promote their real good. He has already given the clearest proofs of
that fact. His honour requires no stimulus and his goodwill no
guarantee: if his agreement to the evacuation, if his amnesty and his
promise not to confiscate are not enough to persuade the Royal
Government to join the other Powers in guaranteeing the integrity
and independence of his state, then His Holiness, though he would
be grateful for such assistance, will in the contrary event, resign
himself to await a better future, relying upon the justice of his cause
and on the help of Heaven". This is a translation of Bunsen's copy
(in the Gamberale docts.). It differs from the copy sent by Sir
Brook Taylor. F.O. 43, vol. 24.

    [31] In writing to Lützow Bernetti even said that he resigned himself
to the departure of the Austrian troops, because they would be back
again so soon. Vatican Arch., Austria Amb. Bernetti to Lützow,
July 3rd, 1831.

On July 5th he issued his edict, already described. During the French elections this might stand for "reforms", although of course it did not satisfy Sainte-Aulaire's claims under that heading; nor even those of England.

On July 10th the conference of the five Powers came to an end. What happened finally was as follows: as to the question of the guarantee they could not act jointly. France refused to sign it at all until the reforms should be completed; England expressed the most friendly sentiments but would not sign a formal guarantee; Prussia gave a guarded undertaking; but Austria gave an unconditional guarantee of the Papal State and Russia followed her lead; so the Temporal Power remained in a fairly safe position.

On July 15th, 1831, the last of the Austrian troops evacuated Bologna. Bernetti had kept his word to France and England. "The Holy Father", he wrote, "resigns Himself to the fate which awaits this unhappy country where new commotions will follow the retirement of the troops" (F.O. 43, vol. 24).

V. THE REBELLION; AND THE FRENCH OCCUPATION OF ANCONA

The Legations promptly rose in rebellion; but Bernetti was not entirely without troops. It had been his ambition— with the approval of the five Powers—that the Papal State should have enough armed force to stand independent of all outside help, and with this end in view he had been recruiting for some time.

But he did not move at once: his policy, approved by Metternich, consisted in completing his reforms and then, with the expressed consent of the Great Powers, enforcing them upon the people (Metternich, v. Letter, July 31st, 1831). He was working away on the judicial and financial side. Between October 1831 and September 1832 he published regulations re-ordering the civil and criminal courts, and also promulgated a penal code. It is impossible now to say how far these reforms were beneficial, but they have been warmly praised as being the most important work of Gregory XVI's pontificate. In finance he was less successful.[32] His Congregazione or Commission of Revision was directed to reorganise the revenues of the state (cap. 6); to see that a Budget and Estimates were properly presented each year and to attend to the National Debt, but this excellent order unfortunately remained a dead letter.

By November 22nd, 1831, Bernetti was able to notify the Nunzio in Paris that he had duly fulfilled his promise to the Great Powers of introducing reforms.[33]

By that time the crisis was very near. In so short a summary as the present it is impossible to record each step of the negotiation: the final episode took place when on January 3rd, 1832, an assembly of deputies from the Legations was summoned to meet in Bologna. On January 10th Bernetti, who was determined to put his edict into practice, consulted the five Great Powers as to his position.[34] Great Britain took no part in the matter, but the other four signified their agreement as to the necessity for an immediate submission of the Legations to the Papal government, and for assuring the re-establishment of the authority of the Holy See in the Legations, so Bernetti felt that he was free to act.

On January 19th, 1832, the Papal troops began their advance under the orders of Colonel Bentivoglio, with Cardinal Albani in command as Commissary Extraordinary. In case of serious resistance he intended to appeal to the Austrians for a fresh occupation (v. F.O. 170, vol. 22).

This rebellion was mainly a mutiny of civic guards; the local columns of insurgents marched out from Cesena, Forlì, Faenza, Imola and Bologna to concentrate near Cesena, about 1800 men in all. They are described as ill-armed and ill-trained—the best of them being, apparently, 300 civic guards

[32] Edict of November 21st, 1831.
[33] Vatican Arch., Segr. di Stato, 120.
[34] Diario di Roma, 1832, No. 4. Bunsen, January 12th, 1832 (Gamberale docts.).

from Forlì with a gun, and 100 students from Bologna with a gun. On the Pontifical side the attacking force consisted of nearly 5000 men, including 300 cavalry and six guns, but many of the men were recruits enlisted by Bernetti and not yet fully disciplined.

On January 20th the rebels took up their position on the hill of Madonna del Monte near Cesena, and soon afterwards the Papal troops advanced against them. For six hours[35] (says Masi) the defence continued, but then the rebels broke and scattered. Thereupon the victorious Pontifical troops forced the gate of the town; street-fighting ensued and many of the citizens including some women and children were killed and their houses sacked. On this day, however, Cardinal Albani evidently decided that the undertaking was too big for him, for he sent off a fresh appeal to the Austrians for another intervention. They promptly re-crossed the Po and the rebellion came to an end; against such overwhelming strength the insurgents were obliged to give in. On the following evening the Papal troops entered Forlì. There was no defence, but during a night of rioting, some twenty citizens were killed and others wounded. On the 24th the soldiers entered Faenza, on the 25th they entered Imola, and on the 26th Bologna. On the 28th the Austrians arrived in Bologna and were received by the population as liberators from the Papalini.

The rebellion was at an end; but hopeless though it had been, the armed resistance had produced its effect in compelling Cardinal Albani to apply again for the Austrian army of occupation; and this was an important result. It aroused France to action. On February 23rd, 1832—after Bernetti's tacit acquiescence had been obtained[36]—the French fleet

[35] For the fighting I have followed the figures stated by Masi in *Nell' Ottocento*, p. 138, published in 1922. But I note that Tivaroni, who is of course very impartial, gives a different story; he says there were 2500 rebels, badly armed, and over 4000 Papalini; and that the fight lasted for two hours, after which the rebels retired to Forlì. Farini says the struggle was short.

[36] Whether Bernetti agreed or not is a good deal disputed. At the British Record Office there are various documents which throw light

sailed up the Adriatic to the port of Ancona, and landed a force of infantry to garrison both the forts and the town.

This French retort to Austria was received with loud protests throughout Europe. The Germanic courts complained that public right had ceased to exist; Russia ordered her ambassador to leave Paris if the Austrian ambassador should be recalled; the Pope issued a formal demand for withdrawal.[37] In England—so Talleyrand informs us—the episode was regarded as a foolish blunder[38] (*une bêtise*). But the British government, though quite correct (Metternich), had been warned beforehand, and maintained its good relations with France. And the French intended to remain in Ancona as long as the Austrians remained in Bologna. In

on the matter. On December 29th, 1831, the British ambassador in Paris, Lord Granville, was invited to a conference of the five Powers. At that conference M. Casimir Perrier said that the Papal government had already decided to order its troops to advance against the rebels of Bologna. If this advance resulted in a fresh occupation of Bologna by Austrian troops, he wanted the Powers to agree to French troops occupying Ancona. This suggestion was opposed by Count Apponyi, the Austrian ambassador; but the idea had been started. *V.* F.O. 170, vol. 22, Granville's despatch of December 30th, 1831. On February 13th, 1832, Lord Granville wrote that Sainte-Aulaire "at Rome, reports that upon entrance of the Austrian troops into the Papal States he had communicated to Cardinal Bernetti the intention of the French government to send a small force to Ancona. M. Casimir Perrier tells me that a doubtful answer was returned to this communication, but he had no expectation that any opposition will be made to the landing of French troops, by the Papal government...". He added that if the Austrians anticipated the French in Ancona his troops would occupy Civita Vecchia. For further information and documents, *v.* Silva, p. 187; Srbik, p. 678; Vidal, *Louis Philippe*, pp. 201, 234, etc.

[37] Bernetti had been previously warned. But it has been suggested that Gregory XVI had not been fully informed of the situation, *v.* Silva, p. 186 *et seq.*

[38] It was not the actual occupation of Ancona which was a blunder, but the manner in which it was carried out. The French officers who seized the forts did so by a *coup-de-main* which looked very like an act of filibustering, and this set all Europe against France. The forts might have held out for days, if not for weeks, against a bombardment. *V.* Thureau Dangin, I, 536.

reality the position was absurd: in 1815 the five Great Powers had guaranteed the Papal State, and in 1832 all five of them were engaged in violating its neutrality, either directly or indirectly; and at the same time their diplomats were crying out. Metternich—so says his biographer—had shaken French credit in Italy. But for all that the French were in a very strong position. They had only to raise a tricolour on top of the hill fort at Ancona, and it might easily send a flame of revolution running northwards to the Alps and southwards to the Gulf of Taranto: and already their officers were all afire for the adventure.

The net results of the European conference had been a second rebellion, a consequent deficit, and the occupation of Ancona. And again the Legations and some parts of the Marches were entirely out of hand: various assassinations and numerous trials for rebellion were taking place, with sentences of imprisonment for five, ten or even twenty years. Many people, including the afterwards notorious Pietro Sterbini, were flying from their native land. Fresh wrangles were beginning between France and Austria (supported by Russia and Prussia). And Bernetti was enlisting Centurioni (police).

It was at this moment that there appeared a protest which has remained rather like a milestone on the road of Liberal development in Italy. In the spring of 1832 by a concerted arrangement, the French and British governments had each presented a programme of reforms for the Papal government; among other suggestions the French demanded a separate lay administration in Bologna for the four Legations; and the English demanded ten definite points, including the organisation of a municipal police, the introduction of the elective principle, the secularisation of the offices in the Legations, and various other measures of good English Liberalism.[39] Obviously they were both asking too much. One sees that

---

[39] *V.* F.O. 170, vol. 22, Palmerston to Seymour March 22nd, 1832.

Seymour's sympathies were Liberal to the point of being anti-Papal. At that moment these reforms would not have been accepted by any Italian ruler so that it was useless suggesting them to the Pope who had to keep in existence the Temporal Power, as desired and guaranteed by all Europe in 1815. On their refusal, however, Palmerston wisely decided to withdraw his representative; and he did so with a resounding protest. It was delivered by Seymour and couched in the plainest terms, as will be seen from the following extract.[40]

More than fourteen months have now elapsed since the *Memorandum* was given in, and not one of the recommendations which it contains has been fully adopted and carried into execution by the Papal Government. For even the Edicts which have been either prepared or published and which profess to carry some of those recommendations into effect, differ essentially from the measures recommended in the Memorandum.

The consequence of this state of things has been that which it was natural to expect. The Papal Government having taken no effectual steps to remedy the defects which had created the discontent, that discontent has been increased by the disappointment of hopes which the negotiations at Rome were calculated to excite; and thus after the Five Powers have, for more than a year been occupied in endeavours to restore tranquillity in the Roman States, the prospect of voluntary obedience by the population to the authority of the sovereign, seems not to be nearer than it was when the negotiations first commenced.

And he goes on to say that for maintaining order the Court of Rome relies entirely on the presence of foreign troops, or on raising a Swiss force of its own. That keeping order by means of foreign soldiers cannot be a permanent arrangement, and "certainly is not the kind of pacification which the British government intended to be a party in endeavouring to bring about". That consequently he has received orders to leave the conference and return to his post in Florence.

Seymour's home-truths were good; it was well to remind everyone that the Pontifical government ought not per-

[40] F.O. 170, vol. 22, Seymour's note to the representatives of the five Powers, September 8th, 1832.

manently to rely on an un-Liberal administration supported
by foreign bayonets, and that Metternich and Bernetti were
merely pretending to consider suggestions. But why single
out the Papal State? Metternich retorted that this criticism
would have applied equally well to almost every ruler in
Italy; and, he might have added, immense territories of the
five Powers as well. In any case the Papal State was admittedly
an abnormal institution, guaranteed in 1815, in order to
safeguard the Church; it was international in character.

In reality the situation was an inextricable deadlock. Most
of the town populations in the state did not want to be ruled
by the old ecclesiastics. They were Liberals; educated but
often rather vociferous Liberals, of many different types and
descriptions. On the other hand a goodly portion of the
country people was ready to break the head of anyone who
tried to separate them from their Pope. Meanwhile the Papal
government was quite aware that the introduction of modern
elective councils would soon endanger the existing régime.
Already even the nominated councils in Romagna contained
many strong Liberals—not to say rebels.[41]

On this arena the five Powers had presented themselves,
each, of course, working primarily for its own hand. France
and Austria had faced each other sparring like boxers—
France seconded by England and Austria by Russia. Only
one thoughtful, studied suggestion had been made, namely
the Memorandum, by Bunsen; and even he had been disapproved eventually by his own government. The result had
been success for those who aimed at doing nothing really
remedial, namely, Bernetti supported by Metternich. One
can sympathise with Bernetti in not wanting to enter, at the
moment, upon the reforms of the Memorandum; but unfortunately we know from his own letters that he had no
intention of ever adopting a more progressive attitude. So

[41] V. the formal notification sent out by the Papal government to
the ambassadors on September 4th, 1831. Vatican Arch., 1831,
Austria Amb.

that, even though Seymour's suggestions were impracticable, one is glad that he pointed out that the existing state of affairs could not possibly continue for ever.

Meanwhile the net result of all these long discussions was that Bernetti proceeded quietly to force upon his state the erection of his reformed communal and provincial councils. The presence of the Papal and the Austrian troops enabled him to carry out these proceedings, and by the end of July 1832 a great deal had been achieved towards restoring law-and-order.

Chapter IX

THE PAPAL STATE, 1834 TO 1840

I. THE SITUATION REVEALED BY THE MEMO-RANDUM

This conference of ambassadors over the Memorandum has one feature of value for us students; it affords us our earliest bird's-eye view of the difficulties which beset the Papal question throughout the whole of this period: firstly, that in Italy the settlement of 1815 could not co-exist with political progress, because, so long as the Austrians were holding down Lombardo-Venetia by force, Metternich would veto representative institutions in any other Italian state; secondly, it reveals the attitude of each of the Great Powers—more especially the interminable rivalry between France and Austria; thirdly, it shows that as yet Mazzini's unitarian-republican scheme was unrealisable; lastly, and most important of all, it exposes, for the first time, the difficulty of maintaining in existence the Temporal Power of the Papacy. We are faced with the permanent dilemma that owing to his religious ties the Pope would never be able to concede a representative government in the full sense; but that on the other hand, as the nineteenth century wore on, he would not be able to govern without making some political concessions.

This last item leads one to perceive that on broad general theory there is a certain amount of justification for the policy pursued during fifteen years by Gregory XVI. On this point he made a very significant observation in the year 1831. When the Prussian minister, Baron Bunsen, urged him to grant the Junta, Gregory XVI replied "that he saw in the establishment of a Central Junta the beginning of a representative system, and this is incompatible with the Pontifical government". In other words he held that to be a constitutional Pope was not possible, and he regarded Liberal institutions—

however moderate—as merely the beginning of such constitutionalism. He meant to rule as a Conservative; and
undoubtedly this was a tenable point of view in 1831. And
these were Metternich's[1] directions; but nevertheless, one
feels that the existing conditions could not be permanent.
Some change was inevitable, and between extreme Conservatism and extreme democracy there was room for a middle
policy; a policy which undoubtedly would be difficult and
hazardous for a Pope, but the only one which could find
practical suggestions for the future. We are in fact coming
to the Moderates' scheme for introducing freer institutions
gradually: it could only be carried out by a Liberal Pope.

As yet there was no practical school of thought among the
Liberals, and no Moderate party in existence. It was necessary
to create one.

It was this *juste milieu* which Bunsen had tried to touch in
his Memorandum—the first scheme suggested by a moderate
statesman. He felt the absolute necessity, for a modern
government, of relying on the support and confidence of its
people, and he had planned the Junta in order to obtain that
confidence without setting up a national assembly. He tells
us that "I predicted to the Pope that at this period of the
world's history either the Papal government will disappear
from the face of Italy, or Gregory XVI, or his successors if
they still have time, will adopt the system that has been
recommended to them".

Gregory XVI, however, regarded a Liberal Pope as impossible. His reign may be called the last stand of the *non-
possumus* ideas. Unfortunately he failed to perceive that an
ultra-Conservative Pope would soon become equally impossible: that if he could not accept representative institutions

---

[1] When Bunsen had been in Rome about two years he wrote to
his government that the power behind the scenes, and the preventer
of all Liberal advance, was undoubtedly Metternich. F.O. 43, vol. 24.
Sir Brook Taylor says that Gregory XVI's refusal of the Junta was
made, not to Bunsen, but to Lützow: but that it was "indirectly
encouraged" by Austria.

he must at all events keep himself in touch and in sympathy
with his people. In reality there existed only one chance
of success for a Conservative ruler, namely that he should
be a Conservative reformer; a modern, progressive promoter
of railways, telegraphs and commercial treaties, more up-to-
date than his own subjects. This fact was realised by younger
men such as Charles Albert—a genuine Conservative who
tabooed Liberal advance, but in its place devoted himself to
reforming existing institutions and to promoting the latest
material developments of every type. Gregory XVI, it is
true, was responsible for certain reforms, especially during
his first years. Between 1833 and 1836 Bernetti produced
various edicts too lengthy to be analysed here, but evidently
good work for which he has received little credit. But
Gregory was too old and too weary to throw himself into the
whirl of the new century.

The result was that ever since then his government has
been made the target for every imaginable accusation, both
true and false.

The whole pontificate of Gregory XVI has been so often
an object of abuse that one is unwilling to criticise it fully
until the specialists in this period have given their verdict
after reading the original documents thrown open to them
during the last few years. And one point should be remembered, namely, that the rising of 1831 to 1832 was certainly
not due to Gregory's misgovernment—as is sometimes stated
—for it had already begun before his exaltation to the throne.
Still there is no doubt that his administration was actually
bad in practice, besides being antiquated in principle. When
stating this view one need not rely for confirmation on the
opinions of revolutionists such as Mazzini, or of Piedmontese
Albertists such as d'Azeglio,[2] or of Protestants such as Crud,
Bunsen and Seymour;[3] or of interested parties such as

[2] *V.* chapter xvi of this book.
[3] Crud's account of the Papal administration is published in the
Rassegna storica, Anno xi, April–June 1924; it was annotated and

Metternich;[4] or of free-thinking Liberals such as Pellegrino Rossi.[5] The facts speak for themselves; a government which issues no Budget for ten years stands self-condemned. Manifestly its reform was an absolute necessity.

But the amount of discontent during his pontificate has been exaggerated—except perhaps in the Legations. In reality after the first period of agitation had ended in 1834, most of the Papal State remained in a fairly peaceful condition until 1840. Incidentally one notices that these were the years during which Mazzini was inactive in Italy: he was temporarily under a cloud. But after that period from 1840 to 1846 Mazzini was again the leader of the Young Italy Society and these last years of Gregory XVI were a period of violence and strife which left the bitterest memories.

As to the general situation throughout Italy in 1832 Baron Bunsen's opinions are very interesting.[6] He did not believe that the united Italy movement could be a danger to the *status quo*, unless it were supported by the French army. If war should break out, he said (between France and Austria), the first French victory would complete in Italy what the

approved by Bunsen and is edited by Bastgen. Seymour's protest is given, p. 124. His correspondence was published in the English papers.

[4] Metternich said, in June 1831, that during the sixteen years since 1815 the Papal government had not put its administration into proper working order (Metternich, v, 175). He also said that the Papal government is among the most incapable; that the disaster is mainly its fault, and due still more to the incapacity of its agents; and that the revolutionists are no better. (It has been suggested that he wanted, with his Ferdinandea Society, to take over the government of the Legations himself.) Metternich, v, 314. On another occasion, when speaking to Monsignor Cappaccini, he characterised the Papal administration as "both detested and detestable".

[5] Pellegrino Rossi wrote to Guizot, July 28th, 1847: "Gregory XVI left to his successor a state which could not have been worse governed: finances in disorder; justice decried; police odious; crying abuses; general discontent and irritation which threatened each moment 'to break out into revolt'". Paris A.E., Rome, 1846, 1847.

[6] Bunsen despatch of March 3rd, 1831 (Gamberale docts.).

Revolution has already begun. But he sees no reason for war: and if there is no war the four principal governments of Italy will defeat the Revolution. In Tuscany there will be no movement because its government is too kindly: Naples will not move because it has had enough of revolutions, and because it has a powerful army which is loyal to the king. In Piedmont there might be some danger if the army should be tampered[7] with: the Papal State will remain unchanged because it is required by the Catholic Church.

II. THE CENTURIONI

The Pontifical government was certainly in a parlous condition: the Austrian troops were protecting it against rebellion, and simultaneously the French troops were protecting it against Austrian encroachments. From this time onward Bernetti's chief aim is to raise enough armed forces to enable the Pope to keep order himself, and consequently to obtain the withdrawal of both Austria and France. With this end in view he set to work to enlist a force of regular troops nominally about 18,500 but actually only about 13,500 strong, of whom the best were probably a Swiss brigade, and the regiment of Roman dragoons.[8] This was the army which fought in 1848.

This regular army was small and expensive; so he decided to support it by enrolling large numbers of volunteers mainly enlisted for the purpose of keeping order—the afterwards infamous Centurioni. It is this force which left a permanent stain on his memory. What happened was more or less as follows.

Bernetti had evolved the very practical scheme of raising armed volunteers from among the loyal section of the population, not only for protection against the internal revolutionists but also, in time of need, against outside interference. It was to consist of country-bred men of good

[7] It will be remembered that this was the very point attacked by Mazzini in 1833.

[8] Tivaroni, *Domin. Austr.* II, 225.

character. A large proportion of the country people were loyal to the Pope: he would use them. In the year 1832 the enrolments totalled no less than 50,000, which was a far greater number than ever had been raised by the Liberals.

The organisation was simple: ten or twelve men to a decuria; ten or twelve decurias to a centuria; ten centurias to a comando; and ten comandos to a division. But it was a scheme which worked out very badly in practice: it meant arming one section of the civilian population against the other, and inevitably placing physical force in the hands of men who had received insufficient training in police-work. This was a fatal mistake, especially throughout the Legations where political feeling was fearfully bitter and the parties were more evenly balanced than elsewhere.

During the more peaceful years matters were not serious, but in troubled times—such as those of 1833 and 1834, and especially during the last four years, from 1843 to 1846—the results became fearful. It is, I think, these last four years—long after Bernetti had resigned—which have left such bitter memories about the pontificate of Gregory XVI.

The Centurioni were so virulently hated that it is hard to discover the truth about them. They have the odious reputation of having been a secretly armed police which gradually came to be used for political ends by the government.

The following account is given of their origin by Tivaroni, the great historian, a republican, but extraordinarily impartial:

One must not forget that by now there had been numerous assassinations due to party strife: amongst others those of Canon Montevecchi, Santo Bertazzoli, Francesco Querzola, Antonio Cellini, Paolo Guardigli, Michele della Ravaldina, Giovanni Galli, Marino Ballanti, Moretto Ravajoli, a man named Morbietto, Zauli Maltazza, a man called Casante di S. Giorgio, others called Numai, Boluga, Trivella, Columbino. Then permission to carry arms was given to the faithful, and the Pontifical volunteers and Centurioni came spontaneously into being, after the example of the Modenese volunteers.... [9]

[9] Tivaroni, *Domin. Austr.* II, 225.

That they were a reply to the assassinations committed by revolutionary societies is not denied by the Liberal writers. Farini, for instance, admits it. And on January 1st, 1833, when Cardinal Spinola published their regulations, it was laid down that "they were to be natives of the state, free of any criminal sentence and commended for their good conduct, whether religious, moral or political".

This is a good instance of what may easily occur when a government arms its civilian followers. Their iniquities were overlooked by the authorities. The conspirators, of course, can find no words bad enough for them. "How abject and cowardly were the Centurioni", writes Zellide Fattiboni, "no words can describe. One had to see for oneself their cowardly bragging, their acts of violence, their abuse of authority in every possible way; how they, being armed, would irritate the unarmed citizens who simply fled before them whenever they could". Farini says they were "Party assassins". Vesi tells us that in Faenza alone over 800 people were killed or wounded, and "modest girls were violated, and honourable women raped because they belonged to families believed to be Liberal". These last statements are extremely hard to believe; but a moderate historian, such as Professor Masi for instance, refers to the force as "A true society of sedentary assassins, collected place by place and assured of impunity for any crime",[10] and Count Pasolini,[11] a most moderate writer,

[10] Masi, *Nell' Ottocento*, p. 139.
[11] Pasolini, *Memorie raccolte dal suo figlio*, 1815–76, 1, p. 63, speaks of them as follows: "Cardinal Bernetti, secretary of state, was of opinion that the popular movement of 1831 was attributable to the bourgeoisie and the middle-class, and that most of the nobles had stood aloof from it, as mere spectators. He purposed therefore to arm and order the people against the bourgeoisie and against the landowners. Such was the origin of the Centurioni, a set of armed partisans, overbearing and insolent because they were guaranteed against the rigours of the ordinary law". And he quotes at some length the opinions of Massimo d'Azeglio, who of course was very bitter against the Centurioni. The following is a specimen: "There exists among the population of Romagna a certain low and obscure

calls them "armed partisans, overbearing and insolent because they were guaranteed against the rigours of the ordinary law".

How often has this occurred when a government has tried to repress political crime by enlisting its own partisans. Out of good recruits it creates a police composed of politicians. They are constantly at handgrips with people of the opposite faction and soon get to look upon their political opponents as criminals. Thus, very shortly, the Centurioni themselves were no better than a "Setta" or factious association. At the same time there existed, of course, Liberal "Sette", so that in the towns of Romagna, especially Faenza, men often fought with dagger against dagger along the back streets, even in the light of day.

On January 12th, 1836, Cardinal Bernetti resigned. Stern gives good reasons for attributing his fall to a court intrigue, but other writers believe that it was mainly due to Metternich who, they say, suspected Bernetti of being secretly pro-French. Both opinions may be true. He was succeeded by Cardinal Lambruschini, an able determined man, Genoese by birth, a believer in "strong" government, very Conservative and reputed to be pro-Austrian. His appointment was considered a success for Austria.

In the following year, 1838, both the Austrians and the French withdrew their troops from the Papal State. It must have been a relief for Lambruschini to see the French embark.

breed of men of unsettled and scoundrelly life, accustomed to idleness, rioting and tavern brawls, which boasts loudly of its devotion to the Pope....This evil race, taking advantage of the unceasing terror in which the governors live, holds meetings in secret conventicles, and prepares imaginary conspiracies, and evidence, or even worse, plans of revenge or assassination". On the other hand the Papal writers insist that the revolutionary societies had spread a network of branches all over the whole country, preaching revolution and irreligion among the people, and threatening to reduce the whole state to a condition of anarchy. There is a great deal of truth in this, but in such cases it surely behoves the government not to imitate the methods of the revolutionists. For the Papal view, *v. Pio IX*, by Bishop Pelczar, vol. I, chap. IX.

But a worse trouble was at hand: during the year 1837 there was an outbreak of cholera which carried off thousands of people; in Rome alone there were 5000 dead. It was by his good work during this epidemic that Angelo Brunetti, better known as Ciceruacchio, first made his name as an organiser and leader of the populace.

III. A SPECIMEN OF MAZZINI'S PROPAGANDA

For five or six years after the failures of 1833 and 1834 Mazzini remained discredited throughout Italy as a man of action; in reality it was always as a propagandist that he was at his best. And as we are now approaching the period of the literary movement perhaps it may be as well to give a specimen of his work, because, of the literary men, he stands first of all. For stirring up passion there is no other writer of the time gifted with power even approaching that of Mazzini.

The following sketch[12] is a description of the fighting at Rimini in 1831. It was written to taunt France with having left the Italian Liberals to their fate, and it has been considered one of the most powerful pieces of propaganda that he penned.[13]

He begins by describing the scene on the night after the battle:

C'était la nuit du 26 mars—une nuit belle, calme, et sereine; et la lune éclairait de son demi-jour la campagne de Rimini. Il y avait une beauté indéfinissable dans ces lignes et dans ces contours suaves qui forment l'horizon romain. Il y avait un sourire dans ce ciel azuré, et dans ces étoiles groupées comme de jeunes filles. Il y avait un souffle, une voix d'amour dans les airs, dans le bruit du feuillage, dans le murmure de l'eau qui s'écoulait doucement à travers la verdure. C'était une nuit faite pour rappeler Francesca, et le Dante, le Génie, et l'Amour, Dieu, et la Liberté.

Mais il y avait là,—sous ce ciel calme et pur—sur cette terre

---

[12] This sketch is barely mentioned by Mazzini in his memoirs, he felt perhaps that it was not a historical description so much as a propagandist piece.

[13] Mazzini, *Scritti* (E.N.), II, 3.

riante et parée—des hommes dont la destinée était un blasphème à la Providence, une protestation énergique contre cette belle Nature, qui se plaît à broder le paradis sur l'enfer, et pare de ses rayons les souffrances humaines, comme le Paganisme couronnait de fleurs ses victimes. C'était un spectacle terrible: des mousquets brisés, des sabres dont le tranchant s'était émoussé à force de frapper, des tronçons d'épées,—puis des lambeaux de chair, des mains gisantes, des crânes fendus; ça et là des cadavres. Il y avait un drapeau tricolore. La lune y donnait en plein, et on aurait pu y lire les deux mots: *Indipendenza Italiana*. C'était un drapeau noirci de fumée, et troué de balles comme un vieux drapeau d'Austerlitz, ou de Wagram; et cependant, il n'y avait pas un mois que la jeune fille qui l'avait brodé—l'avait remis avec son dernier baiser au jeune étudiant Bolonais. Le bras qui l'avait soutenu y était attaché. La mort l'avait glacé qu'il n'avait pas voulu s'en dessaisir: il s'était roidi contre la mort, et le sabre autrichien n'avait pu que le séparer de son tronc.

Ils étaient cent: cent jeunes héros, l'orgueil de leurs familles, l'espoir de leur pays. Le plus âgé comptait vingt-cinq printemps; mais dans cette terre d'oppression, de malheurs, et de souvenirs, les fortes pensées germent vite, les idées coulent brulantes comme de la lave—les années valent des siècles;...

En avant, en avant! enfants de l'Italie!—le signal est donné: le cri s'est fait entendre—et ils s'élancèrent au combat comme à une course d'honneur. Quatre-vingt-neuf mères étaient là pour les retenir; mais la patrie n'est-elle pas la première des mères? La voix de l'honneur parlait haut dans ces jeunes cœurs; une sainte indignation soulevait leur poitrine. Derrière eux se pressaient dix siècles d'esclavage et de honte: une éternité de gloire et de bonheur se déroulait devant leurs yeux; et l'étendard tricolore flottait au vent. Ils partirent. Des larmes amères coulaient le long de leurs joues brûlantes, à l'instant du départ; et en embrassant les mères tremblantes, quelque chose leur disait, que c'était pour la dernière fois. Pourtant, ils n'hésitèrent pas. La vertu, c'est le sacrifice, disaient-ils: consolez-vous. Espérez! l'ennemi est nombreux; mais nous avons pour nous la liberté, Dieu, et la France!

La France!

Elle vous renie: elle renie ses promesses: elle calomnie votre insurrection nationale dans les colonnes des journaux salariés: elle envoie un ambassadeur fêter Grégoire, et lui garantir l'intégrité des états usurpés.

La France!

Ah! elle n'est plus cette France qui s'était portée solidaire pour toutes les libertés de l'Europe, qui s'était engagée à vous défendre de toute agression étrangère. Elle est muette cette belle et glorieuse France! Hier encore le canon tonnait dans ses rues: son cri de '89 glaçait d'épouvante les tyrans de l'Europe; et déjà, les trois journées ne sont pour elle qu'un souvenir. Quelques hommes ont exploité à leur profit l'œuvre de juillet. Ils n'ont vu dans le soulèvement héroïque de tout un peuple qu'une chance de domination. Dix milles victimes, c'était au juste ce qu'il leur fallait pour y asseoir un escabeau de ministre. Ils ont des secrets pour vendre trois millions d'hommes avec une phrase, et pour faire tomber la balance des peuples avec un sophisme. Et maintenant, ils entassent dans les prisons les hommes qui auraient pu vous défendre: ils décrètent la mort de tout un peuple avec une signature de protocole: ils jouent à la diplomatie l'honneur de leur pays, et le sang des nations.—Les secours de la France! pauvres déçus! l'abîme qu'ils ont creusé sous vos pas ne se comblera que par vos cadavres. L'inertie—l'improbation—la défense à vos concitoyens de voler à votre aide—voilà les secours de la France!...

En avant, en avant! enfants de l'Italie! les voilà les barbares! les voilà les tyrans! les geôliers! les bourreaux de la belle Italie! Il y a de l'or sur la garde de leurs épées; c'est l'or de vos frères! Il y a du sang sur la lame: c'est le sang de vos frères! Depuis mille ans, ils ravagent une terre innocente, qui n'a d'autre crime que sa beauté, comme un pays de conquête. Depuis mille ans, ils boivent le sang d'un peuple qui ne leur a rien fait, et torturent vingt millions d'hommes qu'ils ont avilis, corrompus, dégradés. Ils ont proscrit la pensée, interdit le soupir, banni le sourire. Ils vous ont donné à choisir entre le morne esclavage, et le Spielberg; entre le silence de la terreur, et les grincements de dents du *carcere duro*—En avant! en avant! voilà les barbares, et les Français sont loin. Vous êtes seuls, abandonnés, trahis, vendus; et que pourront faire vos jeunes recrues, vos gardes nationaux, vos troupes inexpérimentées, à moitié désarmées, sans munitions, sans canons, sans chefs?—Vous ne pouvez sauver la patrie: sauvez au moins son honneur!

Ils combattirent—ils combattirent jusqu'au dernier soupir. Pendant cinq heures, ils soutinrent eux cent le choc des bataillons, la charge impétueuse de la cavalerie Hongroise, et les décharges de la mitraille. Bien de fois, les barbares reculèrent épouvantés devant cette poignée d'hommes; mais toujours, ils revenaient à la charge grossis de nouveaux bataillons. Pour les pauvres Italiens, point de secours, point d'espoir de secours. À chaque minute, il en tombait un, et personne n'était là pour le remplacer. Les chefs étaient loin, éperdus de se voir abandonnés par la France, et occupés à sauver leur tête en souscrivant des conditions honteuses. Ils combattirent jusqu'à ce que leur bras faibli refusât de soutenir les armes: puis ils tombèrent sur des monceaux de cadavres. Ils étaient là couchés sur la dure et froide pierre pour déposer en faveur de l'Italie, et de la liberté comme ces fragments de colonnes éparses dans le désert déposent de la puissance de Palmyre et de Balbek. Leurs visages étaient tournés vers le ciel, comme pour en appeler à Dieu de la tyrannie des hommes. Un dernier souffle de vie circulait peut-être encore dans leurs veines: peut-être un soupir errait encore sur ces lèvres qui s'étaient fermées au milieu d'un chant de guerre et de liberté: mais il n'y avait personne pour voir s'exhaler ce reste de vie: pas une amante pour recueillir ce dernier souffle avec un baiser; pas un ami pour accepter le legs de vengeance. Les mères étaient loin, pleurant, se tordant les mains, et lisant leur malheur sur les sombres visages des autrichiens, qui menaçaient de leur faire coûter cher les larmes données à des rebelles.

Pauvres mères—ne pleurez pas; ne savez-vous pas que pleurer est un crime sous le code de la tyrannie? Vos enfants sont morts de la mort des braves; c'est du sang qu'il faut à leurs ombres. Mais, lorsque l'heure sonnera, nous leur ferons un monument tel que l'Europe entière en frémira d'épouvante. Il y a un ossuaire à Morat; il y en aura un à chaque ville d'Italie; car, désormais la pitié serait crime; et on n'a laissé aux pauvres esclaves qu'une seule vertu—celle de la vengeance.

Chapter X

THE MODERATE MOVEMENT
AND ITS WRITERS

I. THE MODERATE MOVEMENT

Mazzini's propaganda is magnificent—but it is merely war. For that reason his movement was no longer on the up-grade; in fact he himself remained considerably discredited, partly owing to his failures in Piedmont and Savoy in 1833 and 1834[1] and partly owing to the impracticable nature of his programme. From the year 1834 onwards, some of the Liberals began to realise that Reform was a possible alternative policy to Revolution. Consequently, although the Giovine Italia continued to work in Romagna (the north of the Papal State), in reality—so Farini tells us—it won more sympathisers than actual members, whereas the reformers constantly gained adherents, and their gospel of peaceful work was gradually shaping itself into a policy.

This brings us to the Moderate or Reform movement.

The creed of the Moderates may be summed up as follows: they believed that small risings were useless and that large risings were impossible for the time being; that such sporadic outbursts merely resulted in bloodshed and suffering; that it was better to work peacefully and try to convert the princes to their views; to agitate if necessary for Liberal institutions, and thus to capture and use the Italian governments—instead of following Mazzini's impracticable plan of trying to destroy

---

[1] The leaders accused one another alternately: Ramorino, it was said, had delayed his arrival in Switzerland and had appropriated the money of the Society; Mazzini was said to have lost his head at the critical moment; each accused the other; hence abuse, reproaches, many slanders and "great scandal and discredit". Farini, I, 79. As to Mazzini's programme, v. Farini, I, 77; and Montanelli, I, Preface, and p. 40.

them all simultaneously. Once that each of the small states should be under the rule of a sympathetic prince, or else governed by the people, they could all band themselves together by means either of a league or of a confederation; and then Austria's first moment of difficulty might become their golden opportunity. The Abbé Gioberti, as befitted a priest, hoped that the Pope would be President of this Italian Confederation and that Rome would be its capital; that was his method of settling the Papal difficulty. But Count Balbo, as was natural for a Piedmontese noble, turned rather to Charles Albert to be the "knight and shield" of the movement against Austria.

Of course this scheme of reform had its weak points and they were painfully evident to Mazzini: he saw that it stereo-typed the existing divisions of Italy and that in time of stress or danger, each little nation would think mainly of its own interests. This was true enough; but still, before 1848, no other form of unity was possible, and the reformers felt that without some kind of union Italy would not have the slightest chance of success against the Austrian Empire.

And surely these men were right—according to their knowledge and possibilities.

Looking back on the scene now, some eighty years later, one knows, of course, that no league or federation of Italian states could be as satisfactory an arrangement as their fusion into one people; the united states of Italy could never have functioned as efficiently as the United States of America, or as the Swiss Confederation. But to say this now is merely to be wise after the event: in 1840, fusion was not possible.

Obviously one cannot judge the men of 1840 according to our present knowledge. One must put oneself back to the stage of possibilities in which they were living; and it was an extremely limited stage.

The truth is that when Italy was finally liberated, this was accomplished by the very one device which almost every good judge of her case believed to be futile: namely, by calling in a French despot—not a French republic—to fight the Austrian despot.[2] If any Italian patriot in 1840 had been told that this was the right way to free Italy, he would have replied that all history proved it to be absurd, and especially Italian history. And he would have been right.[3] We must therefore rule out what eventually happened in 1859 as being an impossible contingency in 1840.

When Cavour achieved independence and unity, he achieved a miracle. And even he could not have been successful but for the extraordinary chain of circumstances which actually brought round two complete revolutions within four years and set an ex-captain of anti-Papal rebels upon the throne of France as the Emperor Napoleon III; and kept him in so uncertain a position that he was ready to make great sacrifices in order to obtain the two provinces of Savoy and Nice, which finally clinched his hold on the French people.

[2] I quite realise, of course, the fine work of the Piedmontese army; and also the subsequent assembling of the Italian peoples. But no one will deny that without the French they would not have been strong enough for so great a task.

[3] Farini, for instance, and other good judges, did not believe in seeking help even from a French republic. "Among us, the Liberals have always had the habit—and they haven't given it up yet—of founding their Italian enterprises on the help of France; help which has never in reality been promised by any French Government within our memory, and though often promised by malcontents there, never yet sent by them, and never within the possibility of being sent. They accuse France, and rage against her, and then make love once more to the French revolutions and are taken in again. Foolish loves, mad hopes and childish rage!" Farini, 1, 54, written in 1850.

Nor did Gioberti: "There remains that party of those believers in union-by-fusion (*fusionisti*) who desire that our political unity should be given to us by foreigners. And when asked to determine which foreigners are to be our liberators, most of them select the French, though some favour the Germans. The boldness of this hope is undeniable because it has against it both the immutable nature of things and the experience of twenty-five centuries; still, if in some respects it were plausible and innocent, I should not have the heart to snatch it from those who nourish it. But I do not hesitate to call it absurd...". Gioberti, *Primato*, p. 81.

In the year 1840, all this history would have seemed a fantastic fairy-tale. Let us allow therefore that the only practical lines then existing were those on which the reformers were at work.[4] Perhaps, in reality, their aims may be best summarised under three headings: they wanted independence from Austria; they wanted the unification of Italy; and they wanted Liberal institutions within the Italian states. And most of them believed that these three aims could be achieved by introducing Liberal reforms first and then by uniting the states into a confederation.

At the same time they realised how difficult it was for the Pope to grant Liberal institutions, and that it was virtually impossible for him to become a constitutional monarch. And these are points in the situation which are not always brought out by modern writers. Most undoubtedly, for the Pope-King to have undertaken "to reign without governing" would have meant, sooner or later, his being obliged to stultify himself before the whole world. Supposing for instance that his own parliament were to pass a measure secularising all education: a constitutional Pope would be compelled to affix his name and seal to it. How then could he urge his clergy in Poland, for instance, to oppose the enforcement of such a measure by the Czar? It would be very difficult. Or again, suppose that he were negotiating a difficult Concordat with France or Piedmont in order to save some of the monasteries: his position might be made absurd by the fact that he had already been compelled to resign the same rights within his own state. One notes, throughout all these years, that the revolutionists continually claimed that they were attacking only the temporal power, and not the spiritual; but the hard fact remained that, in practice, they could not always separate the two.

Moreover, sooner or later, a constitutional Pope was certain to be forced into war. And for the Pope, every war is a civil war: he has millions of spiritual subjects on either side.

[4] The main difficulty of describing what the Moderates wanted is the fact that they were very far indeed from being of one opinion.

The hope of the Moderates was that, for the Papal Chair, some self-sacrificing hero might be found who would dare to break with all tradition; and perhaps they did not fully realise that this meant breaking with tradition all over the world. It meant deliberately giving up for ever most of the personal authority which the Pope considered necessary to his sacred trust; it meant the recognition of democracy by the head of the Roman Catholic Church, in the teeth of all those governments which had hitherto been his friends: and democracy would soon bring in its train, nationality. But, for Italy, the reformers required a Pope with enlightened modern ideas, a patriot-king in the truest sense; one who would work for progress, who would introduce railways, industries, commerce, reformed administration, and representative institutions; who would make his little nation a model state where all was efficient and prosperous. Over ecclesiastical questions and Church government he should retain supreme power—probably a final right to veto. This would create a very delicate situation between him and the democracy, requiring a tactful spirit of give-and-take on either side. *But if he made these sacrifices and gave his life to working for the people, in justice he might expect consideration from those whom he had served.*

And then, apart from the Liberal reforms, he would be called upon to create the federation of the Italian states.

II. THE PRINCIPAL WRITERS

The three greatest works produced by the writers of the Moderate School were undoubtedly the following: *Del primato morale e civile degli Italiani* (Of the moral and civil primacy of the Italians), by Gioberti (1843); *Delle speranze d' Italia* (The hopes of Italy), by Balbo (1844); and *Degli ultimi casi di Romagna* (The recent events in Romagna), by d'Azeglio (1846). Presently these will be described in detail.

The growth and development of the Moderate Party was marked and accompanied, after 1842, by a movement of that literary and intellectual type which usually precedes a national advance. In this instance it included a singularly attractive group of men, of whom the best known were the Abbé Vincenzo Gioberti, Count Cesare Balbo, the Marquis Massimo d'Azeglio, General Giacomo Durando (brother of the better known General Giovanni Durando who had been cashiered by Charles Felix in 1821 and became commander of the Papal forces in 1848), Luigi Torelli, Leopoldo Galleotti and the Marquis Gino Capponi; and, a year or two later, Dr Luigi Carlo Farini, Marco Minghetti, the Marchese Gualterio—to say nothing of sympathisers such as Count Pasolini, the friend of Pius IX. Nearly all these were men who had already proved their patriotism and most of whom were destined to rise to high offices of state.[5] Their names show a remarkable array of talent, and it is with this group of exceptionally able patriots that lies the most permanent interest of the Risorgimento; because they turned their brains to a serious analytical study of the problems facing them, and consequently their work is one of consecutive development. Most of them belong to the first years of the re-arising; but the beginning of a national movement is often its most interesting phase; because in those early days there are many good men searching and searching to find the right way, and it is this human effort which deserves our sympathy.

1. GIOBERTI.[6] The first work for us to consider is *Del primato morale e civile degli Italiani*, concerning the moral and civil supremacy of the Italians, by the Abbé Gioberti. In 1843, when he published it, he was already considered to be

---

[5] Gioberti rose to be Prime Minister of Piedmont for several months in 1848. Balbo was Prime Minister of Piedmont in 1848. D'Azeglio was Prime Minister of Piedmont from 1849 to 1851. Count Gino Capponi, though blind, became Prime Minister of Tuscany. Dr Farini, Marco Minghetti and Count Pasolini were Ministers of Pius IX and, afterwards, of United Italy under Victor Emmanuel II. General Giacomo Durando became Lieut.-General, Minister and Ambassador of Piedmont. He was not a Moderate, but is always included in the group of literary men.

[6] *V.* works of Massari, Anzilotti, and others.

one of the two most distinguished Italian philosophers of his day—the other being the Abbé Rosmini.

Gioberti was a Piedmontese, born in Turin in 1801, of lower middle class, very poor and, from his early years, fatherless. But before long he had shown exceptional powers as a student, especially in the fields of philosophy and history. In 1831, he was a chaplain at the court of Charles Albert, and already was known for his immense learning. But he was one of those men who have within them a flame of patriotism which constantly breaks out into truthful sayings, often to their own detriment. In 1833, he was exiled without a trial, and retired to Paris; and then the great Vincenzo Gioberti, endowed with a mind which would have been an honour to any university in Europe, spent his next ten years[7] in Brussels, teaching at the Gaggia College for a salary of about £60 a year. From being the best known of the king's chaplains he had sunk to being a poverty-stricken schoolmaster, tall in stature but somewhat corpulent in appearance and irascible in temper. It was during this period, however, that he published the works which made his fame. He was henceforth in touch with all the most distinguished Italian exiles, including such men as Mamiani, Pellegrino Rossi and others of European reputation, and also with some of the well-known Liberals living in Italy, such as Balbo.

It was not until 1843 that he published *Del primato morale e civile degli Italiani*.

By this time he had broken with Mazzini; but he remained

[7] For a short analysis of the life of Gioberti, *v*. chapter XI. During these years he became head of the Veri Italiani. The Italian emigration due to the rising of 1821 had divided itself into two main streams: the majority, which was republican, went to Spain, and the minority (monarchical) went to England, Flanders and Paris: it was the latter which founded the Veri Italiani, a society of monarchical exiles of comparatively moderate views. The emigrants after the risings of 1831–4 were in most cases monarchists; they found refuge in Paris, from whence they were able to keep in touch with those in Brussels. The Mazzinians, of course, viewed all monarchists and Moderates with great disapproval. *Archivio triennale*, I, 43.

a good Italian patriot. He wrote the *Primato* to catch as many people as possible for a fresh national movement, to form a moderate public opinion, and if possible to reach the ear of the princes and of the great ecclesiastics: to him as an abbé and a distinguished philosopher, most probably they would listen. And he wrote a great and genuine work: in spite of its unnecessary diffuseness it is the book which leaves the most permanent impression of all.

The *Primato* will be analysed in the next chapter; here we need only say that it touched the main problem as follows.

The aims of the Italian nationalists of that period might be classified under three headings: firstly, the independence of Italy; secondly, her unification; and thirdly, the introduction of Liberal institutions into the small states. And many people believed that if they began by securing Liberal institutions, these would enable them to achieve unity and independence.

But, as against these aims, there were two main difficulties for which as yet no solution had been found. Firstly, the position of the Pope; in a united Italy, the Pope could not be king and could not be a subject, and he could not be deprived of his state; yet as long as the Papal State remained in being, extended right across the peninsula, there seemed to be no possibility of unifying Italy, and consequently very little hope of winning independence, or of free institutions. Secondly, another great difficulty lay in the existence of the princes and of the individual state patriotisms,[8] both of which seemed to make unity impossible.

Gioberti solved these problems in the following manner: as to the first two aims, he said, Italy has the right to be

[8] The patriotic love of the Italian for the old historic state in which he was born was naturally very strong and romantic. Manzoni, for instance, could spend his years in peopling the lake-land of his beloved province of Lombardy with picturesque men and women of the Spanish period. To a Venetian the city on the lagoons was everything; to a Neapolitan, the Bay of Naples; and so forth. Each state had its own dialect: there were only two, namely, Florence and Rome, in which Italian was really established.

independent; and her political union is necessary. And the Pope is not in reality the bane or the divider of our country. On the contrary, nearly always he has been her leader during her greatest moments, and her chief glory throughout the ages. The problem, therefore, can be solved by forming a confederation of Italian states—so that neither the princes nor the state patriotism need suffer—and by inviting the Pope to be its president.

In support of this scheme, he urged the immense world influence of the Pope as head of the Roman Catholic Church. That influence would make him the fitting president of the Italian Confederation. At the same time Gioberti also addressed Charles Albert and urged him to become the defender of the confederation; but the main appeal of his book was to the Pope.

As to the third aim, namely the spreading of Liberal institutions, he was very cautious, but he went so far as to suggest that each prince would do well to have a consultative assembly—a council to be consulted only when he himself decided to do so. It might be composed "chiefly of elected members". But he was opposed to anything of the nature of a republican government or popular franchise, at all events for some time to come.

Gioberti's work created a great sensation: it was a new departure; as a rule, no one dared to write a patriotic work, but he had broken the ice and others soon began to follow. In fact he inaugurated a phase of general discussion which developed, later on, into agitation against Austria.

2. BALBO. The next writer on our list, Count Cesare Balbo, was, like Gioberti, a Piedmontese, but of a different type. He was the son of Count Prospero Balbo, Sardinian Ambassador in Paris, and his name is one of the oldest in the provinces around Turin.[9] Count Cesare himself, born in

---

[9] D'Azeglio, who was his first cousin, tells us that the Balbo family was one of the "three B's", namely, Benso di Cavour (of which the great Camillo Cavour was a member), Bertone di Sambuy,

1789, had had some varied experience of the world—like many other people during the Napoleonic era. He had twice accompanied his relatives into exile before he was twelve years old.

At the age of nineteen he had been appointed secretary of the Junta nominated under the Napoleonic régime to re-organise Tuscany on the French model. Then a year later (1809) he was sent as secretary of the Consulta similarly nominated to re-organise Rome. He was at the beginning of a successful career under the Empire. But the work of Napoleonising the Eternal City aroused his Italian sentiment. He was so much impressed by the calm fortitude of Pius VII and his clergy in resisting Napoleon, that he retained for life a great respect for the Papacy, and a realisation of its permanent value to the Italian people.[10] On leaving Rome he occupied various other posts—in Paris, in Illyria and elsewhere—but he was destined also to see the underside of all this splendour. In 1812 he learned that his well-beloved brother had died in the snows of Russia; and in 1813 he saw with his own eyes the downfall of the great régime. He happened to be sent with a message to G.H.Q. just after the

which in the sixteenth century had given birth to the "brave Crillon", and thirdly, Balbo. D'Azeglio, *Ricordi*, II, 321. *V*. also Balbo's *Autobiography* and Ricotti's work on him.

[10] Balbo was in the service of Napoleon. He says: "I was more than ever ashamed before the fortitude of these priests which, for me, was a silent reproof. I began to suspect that they who had been so contemptuously treated were, in reality, the strongest, in fact, the only strong men in Italy. Perhaps if I had had their good example before me sooner, I too might have followed it; at all events, it remained impressed upon my mind and became a well-spring of opinions different from those usually held. When the Pope had departed, his place was taken by one of the Cardinals, with full powers; this was discovered, and the Cardinal was removed. But his place was immediately filled by another, and presently, he too was taken away; then another, and another, until at last either the secret was better kept or the arrogance of the authorities grew tired of a struggle that was useless because they could not take them all away". Ricotti, p. 16, quoting Balbo's *Autobiography*.

battle of Leipzig. The sight of that human flood of hundreds of thousands of men flowing back towards France, with its immense accompaniment of wreckage—there were 104,000 casualties at Leipzig—was a vision of the vanity of empires which remained with him for the rest of his days.

After the Restoration, he served in diplomacy and then joined the Piedmontese army in which he rose to be a major; but, although his appearance was that of a smart officer, he was a student by nature—a fair classic and a thoughtful, widely-read historian—and in politics a Liberal. Unfortunately this last trait implicated him in the rising of 1821. In 1822 he was exiled to Paris, and after his return, in 1824, was ordered to his villa at Camerano where, henceforward, he lived a life of study. Compulsorily retired from active work at the age of only thirty-five! It was a tragic fate for a man of his temperament.

He was an ardent patriot; not a good speaker—better on paper than in an assembly—but an enthusiastic student, quick-tempered, and active-minded. Predari tells us that when engaged on a serious subject of study he pursued it regardless of meals; and he was one of those men who cannot read a good book without planning another. Balbo not only planned, but must have definitely begun some thirty or more works[11] which he never finished. Nevertheless he was a persistent and thorough writer. Of the books actually published, the best known are *Delle speranze d' Italia*; then his *Storia d' Italia* (History of Italy, A.D. 476–774), *Quattro Novelle* (Four short stories), his translation of Tacitus' *Annals* (1830), his *Life of Dante* (1839), *Meditazioni storiche* (Meditations on History) (1842); but these are only a few of the number.

In reality the most useful achievements of this future Prime

[11] Predari, chap. II. In the family archives there are fifty different beginnings of works relating to Italian history alone; of course some of these are little more than preliminary sketches, but others are nearly complete. His friend Predari considers that two of Balbo's minor works are his best, namely, *Pensieri ed esempi* and *Lettere di politica e letteratura*.

Minister were due, not to his books, but to his intellectual influence and civic courage. The results were twofold: firstly, he gradually collected around him a literary coterie of the ablest Liberals in Piedmont—men such as Count Carlo Promis, Count Federico Sclopis, Luig Cibrario, the Marquises Robert and Massimo d'Azeglio, Signors Predari and Ricotti were constantly at his house; and secondly, his life was most valuable because he was always ready to face the unpopularity of his own class and to express his Liberal opinions regardless of its hatred. By this means, eventually, he did much towards breaking down the ostracism of the literary men and even the press censorship.

It was in 1844 that he produced his great work, *Delle speranze d' Italia* (The hopes of Italy).

With this celebrated book of Balbo we shall deal at some length in chapter XIII. All that it is necessary to say here is that he agreed in a general way with Gioberti's idea of uniting Italy by means of a confederation; but whereas Gioberti suggested a confederation of the existing states under the presidency of the Pope, Balbo advised a more definite league or union, and his whole scheme was far more favourable to Charles Albert and to Piedmont.

3. MASSIMO D'AZEGLIO. It is important to note that Balbo's *Speranze* was directly inspired by Gioberti's *Primato*, to which it was largely an answer. And d'Azeglio's *Degli ultimi casi di Romagna* (1846) was also, indirectly, an outcome of the *Primato*—in the following way: Gioberti had preached the historical and religious greatness of the Papacy; but Balbo pointed out that in modern days it was impossible for the Pope to lead a national campaign against Austria owing to his pacific character as father of all Christians alike, and for the Pope he substituted Charles Albert. After Balbo, there came his cousin d'Azeglio, who in a detailed attack on the Pontifical administration, argued that in spite of its historical greatness, the modern government of the Holy See was entirely incompetent.

A separate account will be given of d'Azeglio's life and work. The other writers of this school need only be briefly mentioned, because their importance is far less than that of the first three. One of their best productions seems to have been a work by Luigi Torelli,[12] *Pensieri di un anonimo Lombardo* (Thoughts of an anonymous Lombard, Paris, 1846), in which he says that independence cannot be achieved by conspiracies: there must be a regular war of princes and peoples against Austria. His settlement of the Papal question is curious: he divides Italy into three kingdoms and leaves Rome to the Pope as a small republic.

More curious still is the *Saggio politico e militare della Nazionalità italiana* (The political and military experiment of Italian nationality), published in March, 1846, by another Piedmontese writer, Colonel (afterwards General) Giacomo Durando, who had fled the country after being involved in Mazzini's attempt on Savoy in 1833 and 1834, together with Fanti,[13] Garibaldi and others. After many years of soldiering and several campaigns in the service of Spain and Portugal, he had returned with the rank of colonel; but he was a republican of such extreme views, says Predari, that he made even Brofferio seem lukewarm (Predari, p. 240). In his *Nazionalità italiana*, Giacomo Durando now proposed to divide Italy into three divisions, the Eridania, a great northern kingdom; the Appeninica, in the centre and south; and thirdly, the Insular. The Pope figured in the latter; he was to have Rome, Civita Vecchia, Elba and Sardinia. That was Giacomo Durando's easy way of settling the Papal question! Naturally it aroused disapproval on the part of Pius IX. Of the other territories, Sicily was to go to the House of Lorraine (of Tuscany); Savoy and Nice, Istria, Gorizia, and Trieste were all allotted to other princes. And the author published his scheme for a campaign against Austria. In this curious

---

[12] Not to be confused with Giuseppe Torelli.
[13] Fanti (as also Cialdini and Fabrizi) had fled from Modena in 1831, but Fanti had joined Mazzini's invaders of Savoy in 1834.

shuffling of the thrones, there are one or two small points of interest: he proposes, for instance, to cut off Savoy and Nice from Piedmont merely in order to give them as compensation to the rulers of Lucca and Tuscany, and adds that "they are not Italian provinces either in their situation or in their tendencies". Naturally this suggestion, together with his republicanism, was displeasing to Charles Albert; but it is an interesting proposal because it is one of those instances which show that the idea of exchanging Savoy and Nice for Tuscany, and for other territory in Central Italy, had been discussed many years before Cavour's time.

About all these writers, there are several points in common: they all speak calmly of diminishing the Papal State; they all want a large kingdom in the north; and not one of them ventures to suggest an Italy fused into one single state. Evidently that was out of the question as yet.

Of the other names mentioned in the list, the most notable between 1820 and 1846 is that of the Marchese Gino Capponi, because he represents the Literary Movement in Tuscany. During all those years he was its patron and one of its chief inspirers; and, until the appearance of Gioberti's *Primato* (1843), the Tuscan literary revival was the most important intellectual phase in the Risorgimento. Moreover, Gino Capponi was known throughout Italy both for his kindliness and for his misfortune, which was singularly pathetic. He lost the use of his eyes at the age of only forty-four, and was obliged to rely for everything on his wife. She died, and her place was taken by their daughter; but the daughter also predeceased him. Notwithstanding his blindness he was Liberal Prime Minister of Tuscany in 1848, and during the rise of the Liberal movement (1842–7) his house in Florence was always open to Moderates of every type. We read of evening assemblages there, rather impressively presided over by their blind host; it was a home where some of the most enlightened men in Italy could meet and freely exchange ideas.

Among his later friends was Marco Minghetti, a clever

young lawyer from Bologna who rose to fame very quickly, as Minister first to Pius IX and afterwards to Victor Emmanuel; but the ablest among the later adherents to the Moderate movement was undoubtedly Dr Farini.

Dr Luigi Carlo Farini's career is one of the most remarkable in the Risorgimento. He began his political life as a rebel in 1831, and he remained an extremist and an active conspirator all through the troubled years of 1843 and 1844 during the preparation for the rising known as the "Moto di Rimini". It was during that period that he became convinced of the futility of the Mazzinian methods, and placed himself in touch with Massimo d'Azeglio; and then, together with Montanelli, wrote the *Manifesto* of Rimini. From that time onwards he was recognised as being one of the ablest of the Liberals: in 1848 he became Minister of Pius IX: in 1850 he founded *Il Piemonte*, a moderate newspaper: and, later on, after the union of Italy, was a member of several Piedmontese and all-Italian cabinets. But the most remarkable episode in the whole of his life occurred in 1860, when the small states were on the verge of fusing themselves into one nation; during that period of uncertainty, no less than three of them elected Farini their dictator. He is perhaps the only man who has ever been dictator of three states simultaneously; and certainly he is one whose ability is only now being realised.[14]

[14] Commendatore Casanova, Director of the State Archives in Rome, was kind enough to tell me that recent research has tended to raise the already high opinions as to Farini's ability.

Chapter XI

GIOBERTI'S[1] GREAT BOOK THE *PRIMATO*

"The Risorgimento, like all phases of Progress, was primarily a development of the human mind; and Gioberti's book is the principal step in that development."

We have already summarised a few of the principal points in Gioberti's scheme of re-organisation. But the *Primato* was not merely a statement of suggestions for reform, it was much more than that: it was a call to the nation, and at the same time a call to the Holy See; a classic, which illumines the whole of the period. As a political work it achieved the unrivalled success of casting its spell not only over the Pope but also over the king. It was due to it that Charles Albert

---

[1] Gioberti's life. Born at Turin, April 5th, 1801, of middle class parents. Poor. Very clever and studious from his earliest years. Educated by the Fathers of the Oratory. Interested in philosophy from his sixteenth year. Doctor of Theology, 1823. Ordained priest, 1825, and appointed member of the staff of the Theological College at Turin. The first years of his priesthood were devoted to the study of philosophy, and he began, even then, to ponder how religion could best be reconciled with modern civilisation. But he was one of those men in whom patriotism seems to spring up like a flame. In 1830 he began to gather round him a circle of friends to study the Italian question and how best to serve their country. Felt that Italians must think for themselves; that Italy was under the physical yoke of Austria and under the mental yoke of France: she must throw them off. In 1830 he was greatly moved by the Paris Revolution, and in 1831 he certainly applauded the advent of the Giovine Italia, and, though a priest, he seems to have written for it. He was hot-headed, honest, but imprudent, says Silvio Pellico, and his views very soon attracted the attention of the police. In 1831 his patron, the Archbishop of Turin, died, and was succeeded by the very conservative Franzoni. Gioberti, who was then one of the king's chaplains, was accused of unorthodox teaching, and, though defending himself vigorously, decided in 1833 to resign his chaplaincy. On May 31st of the same year he was arrested on suspicion by the police, imprisoned for four months and then

ventured forth into the open as a Liberal—and it was certainly the work, which of all others, most fired the imagination of Pius IX during his great attempt to Liberalise the Pontifical institutions. Some of Pius' measures are actually fore-shadowed in the *Primato*, and—which is more important—his conception of the situation, his mental atmosphere during those first two years, certainly appears to be that of Gioberti. One feels it necessary, therefore, to give a short description of this powerful but rather strange book because undoubtedly it initiated a new phase in the Risorgimento.

Perhaps the best way to convey a true impression of a great book is to give extracts from it; and in this instance Gioberti himself has left us a fine preface in which he begins by explaining the true reason why he has not hesitated to make so high a claim for his fellow-countrymen as that of "the civil and moral primacy" of the world. It is a noble reason. He says that owing to long centuries of division and consequent servitude they have lost all confidence and pride in themselves. Therefore, to his own people, now beaten to the earth, he

banished without trial. He settled in Paris, where there were many Italian exiles including Mazzini, Pellegrino Rossi, Mamiani, and others. But in 1834 he obtained a post as private teacher at the Gaggia College in Brussels. In 1838 he published the *Teorica del Soprannaturale*; in 1839 to 1840 he published the *Introduzione allo studio della filosofia*, and in 1841 his treatises on *Il Bello* and *Il Buono*; also the *Errori filosofici di Antonio Rosmini*, which proclaimed to the world the wide differences between himself and Rosmini; he and Rosmini were the two leading Italian philosophers of the day. In 1843 he published his great work *Del primato morale e civile degli Italiani*. In 1845 he published the *Prolegomini*, an attack on the Jesuits which provoked replies; to these he returned a furious rejoinder, *Il Gesuita moderno*. In April 1848 he returned to Italy, and his passage to Rome was a triumphal progress. Everywhere thousands came out to meet him. As he seemed to be the ideal man for founding an Italian Confederation, in the same year he was appointed Prime Minister of Piedmont, and held that office for about three months. After the failures of 1848 and 1849 he retired to Paris, where he wrote another work, the *Rinnovamento*, abandoning his Papal ideas and preaching the unification of Italy through Piedmont. In 1851 he died. (*V.* Massari, Anzilotti, and others.)

addresses his work, in order to show them that, so far from being a weaker brother among the civilised races, they possess both the conditions and the capacity to take first place; and he tells us that if, in saying this, he has overstated the case, he hopes that his doing so will at all events have raised them out of the slough of despond. There is something deeply pathetic in the evident singleness of purpose which inspires his opening sentences:

A man cannot avail himself of his natural force nor completely exercise his powers unless first he is fully confident of possessing them. Similarly a nation can take its true place in the world only in so far as it believes itself worthy to occupy that place.... In virtue of this consideration, when a people has reached the lowest point of abasement and lack of civil courage, when its spirit is beaten to the ground and its strength is prostrate, then there is good reason—and it is a duty of compassion—to take pity on it and to try to reinvigorate it, even by the use of terms which in any other case might be considered reckless.[2]

At the same time Gioberti declares that though writing in praise of his own nation he will never give offence to any other. To hate another people is to offend against the universal law of love which embraces all humanity: for in all the earth there is no nation that has been disinherited by God!

The Heavenly Father endowed each branch of the human family with some special gift so that it should not be ashamed when it takes its place in the council of the brother peoples.[3]

Then he proceeds to write many scores of pages full of long philosophical argument and classical allusions, but through it all he is proving his thesis, namely that Italy owing to her geographical position is intended to play a leading part among the nations; that she was originally the fountain head of Empire, and since then of Christianity, and that her sons have proved their capacity to stand first among the greatest workers and more especially among the greatest thinkers of the human race.

[2] *Primato*, p. 25.
[3] *Ibid.* p. 28.

I. AS TO INDEPENDENCE

Autonomy, he says, or independence—the condition of being a law unto oneself—is of two sorts: firstly, absolute autonomy, which is divine, *a power given from God*; secondly, partial autonomy which is a ray of divinity communicated to human beings. From these words one sees how the servitude of Italy had burnt into his soul: he regarded a free nation as one possessed of something divine! God is the absolutely autonomous being, the Creator, the Preserver and the Redeemer of all things, and, as in Him, so elsewhere the root origin of autonomy lies in possessing the creative faculty; then that of preserving and perfecting the things created; and thirdly in possessing that of redeeming them when necessary.[4]

1. Thus Italy is the nation "autonomous par excellence", because, firstly, it was she who created the civilisation of the young races; secondly, because she still keeps intact its basis and seeds of vitality; and thirdly, because she can purge and renew that civilisation if necessary.[5] She was predestined to this task by her position, for ever since history began, the Mediterranean has been the centre, the "piazza" of the civilised peoples—and even now we cannot tell whether or not the Creator intends the New World to play a great part. Thus, for nearly a thousand years, Rome in being the centre of power in Italy has also been the capital of the world. And in due time from under the wings of the Roman eagle there went forth the white dove of Christ.[6]

2. THE POPE SHOULD BE THE HEAD OF THE ITALIAN NATION AND ITS CAPITAL SHOULD BE ROME. At this point we come to Religion, which to the Abbé Gioberti is all important, "the fountain head, basis, and apex of all social perfection", and the principal and most permanent foundation of the Italian primacy in the world. Italy has been selected to be the home of the Holy See; the Italians are the guardians of the ark, the Levites of Christianity; "Italy and the Holy

---

[4] *Ibid.* p. 36.   [5] *Ibid.* p. 38.
[6] *Ibid.* p. 42.

See are indeed separate and different things...but a union
of eighteen centuries has bound them together so closely
that...a man could not be a perfect Italian without being
a Catholic ".[7]

He then embarks on a sketch of the Middle Ages and tells
us that the Popes, for centuries, had led the national efforts
against the foreign emperors, and had formed the great Guelf
tradition, the only true consecutive national tradition of
Italy.[8] Moreover, when all the world was plunged in darkness
and barbarism, the civilisation of Italy came forth from the
Pope, and that of the other nations came from Italy. "Italy
is the capital of the world because Rome is the religious capital
of the world, and Rome ought to be the seat of the civil and
federal court of the peninsula."[9]

Thus Gioberti has arrived at the first statement of his thesis
that Italy has a natural right to be independent; and that the
Pope should be the leader of the Italian nation. Moreover
that Italy's permanent primacy among the peoples of the
earth is due to her possession of the Holy See. The palace
of the government should be in Rome.[10]

3. GIOBERTI'S DREAM. We now come to what is often
referred to as Gioberti's dream. To him the Roman Church
is the true Christianity; and Christianity is essential to
civilisation and progress. His ideal is a re-united Christendom;

---

[7] *Primato*, p. 44.   [8] *Ibid.* p. 47 *et seq.*
[9] *Ibid.* p. 52.
[10] Professor Montanelli's feeling on this subject is interesting,
because he was a leading nationalist, and he "had gone the round
of all the philosophies" before returning to the Catholic doctrine.
In a letter dated March 5th, 1847, he says: "Modern civilisation
has taken such a form that it is not possible for the Pope to return
to the position which he occupied during the Middle Ages; but
I think that without his power we should lack that centre of unity
at which we should aim, not merely as Italians but as Catholics.
Gioberti seems to me to have said fine things on this subject; things
which we are only now beginning to understand since the comment
upon them which has been undertaken by Mastai". (He refers of
course to Pius IX's reforms.) *Rass. stor.*, Anno x, 1923, p. 145.

a great brotherhood of the Christian nations moving towards the spiritual conquest of the whole world under the aegis of the Pope, with Italy as its vanguard. But he sees that this ideal is far distant.

For the present he continues to dwell on the importance of preserving intact the Rome of the Popes.

Rome...is the eternal city, often devastated by them (the Germans and French) but re-arising each time like a phoenix from the ashes. Thus to Etrusco-Pelasgic Rome of the days before Romulus...there succeeded Latin and Republican Rome; then imperial Rome and finally Catholic and Pontifical Rome....Each of these enlarged its Empire beyond that of its predecessor until at length the Urbs was joined to the Orbis, the City to the World, and became in fact, as in name, cosmopolitan.... [11]

Suffice it for us to know that so long as the vital principle is not extinct we may remain confident, and that the hopes and the life of Italy and all that alleviates the present evils and all that promises blessings to come, dwells in the City that guards the sacred fire, symbolised in ancient days by that of Vesta upon which the immortal fates of the Empire were supposed to depend. Let us guard with great care that spiritual fire, for if it be extinguished, then only need we despair; but if it be preserved with supreme attention, and lovingly sustained, then at the first sign from Providence it will spring up again into living flame and spread fresh heat and light upon all around it. [12]

Theoretical and even mystical as this may sound, its purpose is practical. Gioberti aims at showing that the existence of the Papal State is a permanent safeguard for all Italy; that so long as it remains under the sovereignty of the Popes—nowadays always Italians—so long will there exist a home of refuge for Italian nationality; a home inherited from the historic days of Rome, and re-established in 1815 by the great Powers of the modern world.

In the course of his historical argument he resurrects the names of the patriot Popes Alexander III, Innocent II and Julius II, who stood for Italy against the foreigner—and this no doubt with a purpose. On the one hand to remind

[11] *Primato*, p. 66.   [12] *Ibid.* p. 67.

Italians that the Popes have led them in the past, and on the other hand to remind the next occupant of the Holy See that, in the long list of his predecessors, those whose names evoke enthusiasm are the Guelf Pontiffs, who strove for national freedom.

At the same time he is very careful to lay it down that the Pope cannot possibly become a promoter of violent revolutions.[13]

The civil action of the Pope must not be repugnant to his spiritual and pacific character as Head of the Church; and it would become thus repugnant if the common father of all Christians aroused the peoples against the Princes.

II. AS TO THE UNIFICATION

1. UNION-BY-FUSION. A political union of Italy, he says, is necessary before her regeneration can be achieved.[14] But it need not be union-by-fusion. Fusion is impossible. Its advocates rely either (i) on revolution, or (ii) on calling in the foreigner; and neither of these methods has the slightest chance of success, while both would do irreparable harm.

(i) Revolution would fail. Its advocates rely entirely on their imagination. The Italian peoples are too deeply divided, and there is now no tyranny sufficient[15] to arouse them to

---

[13] *Primato*, p. 84.   [14] *Ibid.* p. 78 *et seq.*

[15] This statement in an epoch-making book is rather a remarkable tribute to the Italian princes against whom so much has been written. What Gioberti says is as follows: "A tyranny such as excites the indignation of a whole people and causes it to rush into extreme measures does not exist, partly owing to the kindly nature of the Italian princes, and partly owing to custom, which softens even the most absolute authority and saves it from abuses either too great or too frequent". Of course Gioberti was a Piedmontese, and in Piedmont the people were satisfied; and he was a priest, so that he would probably prefer to see the kindly side of the Papal rule; but—apart from Gioberti's views—in Tuscany the administration was admittedly lenient. In Parma, the Duchess appears to have been liked; and the Duke of Modena, though hated, was not friendless. In Naples the government is condemned by almost everybody, but even there the king was very popular with the

united effort: neither the governments, the property-owners nor the people want revolution.

(ii) Calling in the foreigner to fuse Italy—either the French or Germans. This, he says, is absurd; contrary to the immutable nature of things and to the experience of twenty-five centuries.

2. UNION BY FEDERATION. Union by fusion is therefore impossible. But union by confederation is possible. Any Italian confederation, however, must be under the presidency of the Pope. This is inevitable, because, firstly, the Pope can never be a subject—for the guardian of Catholic dogma and the interpreter to all Christendom of God's teaching must be free from all civil influence; and secondly—says the Abbé Gioberti—he is the fitting president.

In them (the Popes) I assert, is the true principle of Italian unity. This principle (the Papal principle) is supremely our own and is national.... It is concrete, alive, a reality, not an abstraction nor a chimera; because it is an institution, an oracle, a living person.... It is as perpetual as our own (Italic) family and the terrestrial kingdom of the truth.[16]

Gioberti's scheme is a vision of all the Italian states united into one glorious league or confederation of which the Pope must necessarily be the president; it is to have one joint national army, one navy, and one set of colonies, and to rank as a great nation. And—an immense advantage for this federal plan over all others—no revolution or bloodshed is necessary to obtain the desired unity; the Italian states need only decide to form a league. There is no reason why the great powers should interfere.

To criticise Gioberti's federal scheme. Theoretically there certainly was no reason why the states of Italy should find it

army—a most important point in case of revolution. In his letters Gioberti admits that he wrote leniently about the princes, but this statement, that there is no tyranny in Italy sufficient to arouse united rebellion, is confirmed by both Balbo and d'Azeglio.

[16] *Primato*, p. 83.

harder to form a union than the United States of America
or the cantons of Switzerland. And, though difficult, it was
not actually impossible:[17] in fact it was the only possible
scheme in 1843. But as matters turned out it never had a fair
chance of success. In 1848 the Revolution convulsed everything in the peninsula. For over a year Pius made untiring
endeavours to form the league, but he found that none of the
governments wanted it except that of Tuscany.

3. GIOBERTI'S APPEAL TO THE POPE. Gioberti cast his
net very wide so as to catch people of every class and type
for the national cause, and one of his chief objects was to
convert the Italian princes to his ideas—especially the rulers
of Rome and Piedmont.[18] With this aim in view he writes
many pages. He points out, for instance, that although the
Pope must necessarily disapprove of revolution he need not
disapprove of Liberalism.

Finally he breaks out into an enthusiastic address, evidently
hoping to win the Pope's sympathy for the national cause.

She (Rome) is patient because she is eternal, like God who
founded her. She is aware that whoever wishes to command his
century must stand above it, and compel its wondering admiration
by his rare and magnanimous actions; as she herself was wont to
do in ancient days with her heroic leagues and poetic crusades...

---

[17] Some of Gioberti's minor suggestions were very practical and
were afterwards embodied in a trade agreement between Pius and
Charles Albert, and in a customs agreement between the Papal
State, Piedmont and Tuscany in 1847. Gioberti suggested that the
Italian league should annul or at all events diminish the differences
of weights, measures, currency, custom duties, dialects, administrative civil and commercial orders, "which so miserably and sordidly
divide the various provinces and retard or impede the traffic of
ideas between the various members of the nation. It would make
the lingua nobile the common tongue of the country...". He goes
on to say that by gradually abolishing many sorts of division, and
unifying the peninsula, the confederation would make them safe
against the foreigners. When Cobden visited Italy, in 1847, he made
several public speeches. His view was that Italy should begin by
establishing a customs union.

[18] *Primato*, p. 103.

and as she will again when Providence takes pity upon the
sorrows of Italy and changes the hearts of our princes and grants
to their Head a fresh chance of saving our country...and who can
doubt that, when the moment comes for venturing, the Pontiff
will be eager to seize it?[19]

He gradually works up to a climax and ends with an actual
appeal to Gregory XVI:

What happiness, what glory, what sweet and honoured repose
when the ancient brotherhood of all Italians shall be renewed
through the work of the common Father! Who is the citizen who
will not be grateful to him after re-securing through him our
native land?...Holy Father, if Heaven has not ordained that that
happy day should bless your old age, beyond doubt you must
rejoice when you reflect that it will fall to the lot of one of your
successors.

In this last sentence Gioberti obviously addressed himself
to the next Pope—whoever he might be. And when, in 1846,
Cardinal Mastai-Feretti became Pope Pius IX he had read
this appeal, and he made every endeavour to carry out the
mission which it traced for him, and to be at once the unflinching Pope and the patriot king.

4. GIOBERTI'S APPEAL TO PIEDMONT. Gioberti next
devotes ten pages to winning Piedmont and the House of
Savoy;[20] and here, as in the case of the Pope, he works up to a
climax by a personal appeal to King Charles Albert.

He writes that Piedmont is peopled by a young, vigorous,
military race with more Celtic, Germanic and even Iberian
blood than the rest of Italy; but nevertheless it is a true part
of the Italian nation, the latest emanation of Italo-pelasgic
culture; trained for centuries by the House of Savoy to live
a life of piety and courage.[21]

To the House of Savoy he also appeals[22]—and his appeal
is a masterpiece of suggestion for Charles Albert, as to Liberal
reforms, Italian unity, and war against Austria. The House of
Savoy he says is doubly great; firstly because it has never yet

[19] *Ibid.* p. 106.
[21] *Ibid.* p. 112.
[20] *Ibid.* p. 108.
[22] *Ibid.* p. 113 *et seq.*

produced a tyrant, and secondly because it has trained its people to fortitude and to arms.

But every royal family must advance with the times. It has been the glory of the House of Savoy that it has trained, united and fortified its small nation.[23] But that was the work of the elder branch, which made the mistake of not altering its methods with the changing centuries.

At this point Gioberti, the exile, can speak to his king almost as a fellow-sufferer. The older branch, he says, when it recovered its throne in 1815, did not alter its former methods: hence the discontent of the Piedmontese and the commotion which afflicted Piedmont.[24]

In reality the work of the old branch of the House of Savoy had been that of training the nation to hardihood. But now a new era lay before them, and God had called forth a younger branch on the ancient tree, namely, that of Charles Albert.

Italy does not believe that this coincidence is due to chance. In the coming of the new branch she acclaimed a joyful omen for the common hopes, and a new era for the whole peninsula, congratulating herself on Piedmont's having become Italian and on her having been invested, so to speak, with the national nature by her new prince. All combines to make us believe that the House of Carignano is destined to complete the work of those from whom it descends, by binding the Alpine peoples to those of the Apennines and forming them all into one single family.[25]

And he ends with the direct appeal to Charles Albert.

Generous Prince, the sentiments that I lay before you are not merely my own; they are universal, because they are calm and moderate.... You love and venerate Italy as the native land and mother, both of the Piedmontese who are so dear to you, and of that royal stock of which you are a noble offspring.... You have provided for the security of your people by creating a numerous and well-equipped army, and thus by your own strength for war have laid open the way to the long-desired union of Italy.... We

[23] *Primato*, p. 115.
[24] For taking part in these commotions Charles Albert had been disgraced in 1821, and Gioberti himself had been exiled in 1833.
[25] *Primato*, p. 116.

know that you are armed and posted on the frontiers of the peninsula in order to repulse the attacks of strangers with one hand, and with the other to draw to yourself the Italian rulers.... Therefore, brave Prince, Italy is confident that from out of your House will come forth her redeemer.[26]

III. GIOBERTI ON LIBERAL REFORMS: HIS CONSTITUTION

Having dealt with the question of independence and unity we come, lastly, to that of Liberal reform within the Italian states.[27] On this subject Gioberti outlines a scheme which is important because much of it was afterwards carried out in practice by Pius IX. Before there can be unity between the small states, he says, there must be agreement between the rulers and the peoples; because a government which tries to rule an unwilling people will always be weak. Gioberti has evidently seen this tried.[28]

He who rules in these unhappy conditions knows himself to be disliked, and being moved by fears and suspicions, he has recourse to spies, police constables and machinations of all sorts; relies only on armies, and defends himself from his own subjects as from his most formidable enemies. Progress dies.

The present is the moment for civil reforms;[29] Italy is recovering after 1815, she can take up again reforms such as those of the eighteenth century. Reform is the only way to avoid revolution.

At this point Gioberti gives us an interesting suggestion for the ruling of the state on Liberal lines; he outlines the *Consulta*, or Consultative assembly, to assist the sovereign with its advice. This is especially important to us because a Consulta was the form of assembly adopted by Pius IX: it was one of the institutions whereby he was carrying out ideas which he had studied in Gioberti's work, and elsewhere—

[26] *Ibid.* p. 118.   [27] *Ibid.* p. 119.
[28] Balbo was more or less of the same opinion; but he was strongly opposed to any attempt to force the princes to grant reforms, because that would create bitterness and disunion.
[29] *Primato*, p. 127.

for reform was in the air. But as a step towards Liberalism, Gioberti's Consulta was in reality only a small advance.

His manner of describing it was the following: A sovereign needs advice from his people: their opinion can be expressed either by the spoken word (assemblies) or by the written word (the press). As to the spoken word, the assemblies are of two kinds: either (1) Legislative and Deliberative, or else (2) Consultative.

Of these two types the Legislative assembly imports a division of the sovereign power, so Gioberti refrains from considering it for fear of arousing dissension. But the Consultative assembly has his approval; in fact he calls his Constitution a Consultative Monarchy.

In this *Consultative Monarchy* the ruler remains absolute;[30] the "Consultori" or members of the assembly are entitled to express their opinion to him only on such matters as he chooses to lay before them. They are to be chosen by election (in the second part of his book he speaks of them as principally elected, p. 406), but he does not specify how;[31] and, to give them greater courage, they are to be elected for life. But in

[30] *Primato*, p. 132.

[31] Gioberti has no belief in the wisdom of hereditary legislators or aristocracy, but on the other hand he has no belief in a republican form of government. His ideal Christian monarchy would be of divine origin and very paternal. A benevolent religious sovereign, consulting when he so desires an assembly of the best men: these men to be chosen by election, but he does not say how. Everything for the people, nothing by the people, is a motto he quotes with approval. One notes that when Pius IX set up a Consultative Assembly he arranged that each provincial assembly (elected by the communal councils) should send him in lists of three suitable men for his advisers. Out of each three names he selected one and thus formed his "Consulta". On this subject, *v*. Gioberti's private letters to friends, published by Massari in *Le opere inedite di Vincenzo Gioberti*, vol. IX. He seems to have expressed rather more conservative views in his book than he actually felt, because he wanted his book to be read by the princes and by the clergy (*v*. his letter of August 15th, 1843, to Mamiani), but still he believed in preserving a strong central authority, especially while introducing Liberal views.

this connection we may add that he did not consider Italy yet ready for representative monarchy. (His letter to Mamiani, August 15th, 1843.)

This then was Gioberti's idea of a Constitution;[32] a sovereign who could ask advice from the assembly of members most of whom were elected for life—no doubt on a much restricted franchise; but the ruler was not in any way compelled to follow their advice; though, in Gioberti's view, he would be restrained, insensibly, by their opinion. It may sound a small measure nowadays, but one must remember that in 1843 all Italy was being ruled by absolute monarchs.

This was the type of constitution which was adopted by Pius IX when he set up his reformed government in 1847. But he allowed the members the right of making suggestions, which was an important advance; and there were several other differences.

As to the written word—the Press—Gioberti wishes to see a free press but within reasonable limits.[33] There should be a council of censors.

He feels deeply the need of reform all over Italy.

Certainly Italy has so much to do in raising herself from the depths to which the barbarians have brought her, that she must not complain of too great power remaining with those in authority, so long as it is used to promote civilisation.[34]

For, to establish legal equality between all citizens, public education and charitable institutions for the poor, better law courts, fair taxes and improved municipal authorities—all

---

[32] Balbo gives a different definition of the constitutions of Italy. He calls them (1) Absolute—the prince takes advice from anyone, just as he fancies; (2) Consultative—the prince takes advice from certain counsellors whom he has chosen; (3) Deliberative—the prince takes advice from certain counsellors whom he has chosen, together with others elected by the people (Balbo, *Delle speranze d' Italia*, p. 246). They debate, but apparently only on matters which the prince has referred to them. Balbo's terminology is not quite the same as that of some other writers.

[33] *Primato*, p. 136.   [34] *Ibid.* p. 145.

these reforms[35] and various others which he quotes, constitute such an immeasurable task that, in his opinion, it could hardly be carried out except by an absolute ruler advised by the best brains in the country.

He enumerates many other necessary measures, agriculture, banks, commerce, etc.: but especially he wishes to implant the basis of a Consultative Monarchy in the various states of the peninsula, and to organise the union between them all by means of a patriotic and national league. "So that Italy should not yield the palm to France, Germany or England, nor to any other nation...."

At that point he breaks out into an address to the princes of Italy:

The supreme power is an incomparable treasure....Italian princes, you possess this great good and have the profoundly enviable privilege of being omnipotent for saving Italy—know how to profit by this rare good fortune. Win for yourselves an immortal name here below, and assure for yourselves in the future life that reward which is granted by Heaven to benefactors of their native land and of mankind....Remember that Italy is our common mother, and that from her you receive the air which nourishes you, the sun in which you rejoice and the paternal sceptre which you are privileged to bear.[36]

How truly does this "remember" speak to that degraded class of human being in whom their native air and sky has never been able to infuse a breath of natural patriotism! But it is the nobles of Italy rather than the princes who arouse his anger. A useless nobility, he says, discredits the prince;[37] and to some who seem to have been fond of tracing their descent to foreign conquerors, he observes that the longer their family pedigree the better for them, because it removes them farther from the original robber or thief. These are almost the only bitter passages in the book; directed against these men who belittle their country while accepting from it the high position which it offers and which few of them could obtain elsewhere.

---

[35] Note that these are merely reforms, not political concessions.
[36] *Primato*, p. 146.   [37] *Ibid.* p. 225 *et seq.*

The true reason of course why some people have called Gioberti a dreamer is because so much of his book is devoted to proving that the Pope should be not merely president of the Italian Federation, but also the central arbiter of the Christian nations—in his vision he sees the Pontiff not only presiding over the princes of the peninsula, but at the same time deciding, as Christ's Vicar, all cases that might arise between various powers of Christendom; and he claims that this right is inherited from the Middle Ages; that the arbiter and peacemaker between the nations is still there—for all who seek him—the only existing arbiter in the world.

After all were these dreams quite so impracticable as they seemed? We who are living immediately after the Great War have many ideas in common with those people who lived after the Napoleonic Wars, because our needs are similar, and we all remember that in the year 1917 this method of avoiding mutual slaughter was again suggested. After witnessing three years of unimaginable suffering Pope Benedict offered himself to Europe as a mediator.[38]

What Gioberti felt was that we require a world arbiter of our national quarrels, otherwise we cannot hope to prevent war. At the present time we have founded a League of Nations for this purpose and this is a splendid advance, but

[38] The Vatican Note to the heads of the belligerent peoples, August 1st, 1917: "...Shall, then, the civilised world be naught but a field of death? And shall Europe, so glorious and flourishing rush, as though driven by universal madness, towards the abyss, and lend her hand to her own suicide? In a situation so fraught with anguish, in the presence of so grave a peril, We, who have no special political aim, who heed neither the suggestions nor the interests of either of the belligerents, but are impelled solely by the feeling of Our supreme duty as the common Father of the peoples, by the prayers of Our children who implore from Us intervention and Our own word of peace, and by the very voice of humanity and of reason, We raise again a cry of peace, and renew a pressing appeal to those in whose hands lie the destiny of the nations".

Manifestly, until we have more genuine world-patriotism, Progress will always produce internecine wars, just as in the days of the Heptarchy.

it does not attain to Gioberti's ideal. It is an assemblage of national self-interests, and therefore lives in danger of being poisoned by the cliques, parties, secret agreements, reprisals and all the other characteristics of assemblies of self-interested members; whereas the ideal—and it was seen by Gioberti—would be to submit causes to some arbiter whose whole life and being and tradition should be devoted to representing the principle of eternal justice; not a collection of national voices, but one single international or supernational voice. Certainly in 1843 no established international authority remained in existence except—for Catholics—that of the Pope.

The second part of the *Primato* consists of an immeasurably diffuse analysis of all human knowledge; he quotes great names, such as that of Galileo, in order to prove that Italy has led the way in every branch of thought. And her leadership, he tells us, has been mainly due to her possession of the Holy See, the centre and originator and adviser of all Christian civilisation.

In all, the *Primato* consists of 700 pages containing about 280,000 words, with very few chapters, not many paragraphs and no index. It deals in detail with modern civilisation and incidentally with the ancient Pelasgic, Greek, Indian, Chinese, Buddhist, Confucian, Persian and other cultures, including several references to the Toltecs, nearly all introduced to prove points relating to the present day. It is, in fact, a remarkable instance of an overladen work.[39]

But the views, concerning his own time, of this future Prime Minister are interesting. He examines the position of all the European nations and decides that for the energy of its life and of its national personality the English people is undoubtedly the first in the world.[40] He then dilates for

[39] Unless I am mistaken, it was Massimo d'Azeglio who wrote to his wife that if she read this book she would know all about Adam.
[40] *Primato*, p. 566.

several pages on the strength of England at that time and finally adds that her two "internal ulcers" are the problem of pauperism and the discontent of Ireland—which country is to England as Poland is to Russia.[41] One is kept in constant wonder at the immense reading of Gioberti the philosopher—modern, classical and pre-historic studies alike; at the intense kindliness of Gioberti the *popolano*, especially when dealing with problems of the poor; at his rather indiscriminate historical statements, at his frequent touches of practical common sense, and most of all by the fact that often he intermingles all these subjects and qualities within the space of three or four pages.[42] At the same time, in spite of all exaggerations, he certainly succeeds in demonstrating most forcibly that Italy has always been in the van of civilisation; and his search has resulted in producing a splendid array of great names, in fact one of which any nation in the world might be envious. The gist of his work must have come as a breath of inspiration for his discouraged fellow-countrymen; and to this day it remains a national monument to Italic civilisation—nothing less.

To realise the immediate sensation created by Gioberti one must remember how the press was gagged and distorted at that time. The following description of the Censorship in Piedmont is given by Predari (p. 67):

In the press of those days it was strictly forbidden, not only to speak of politics but even to use the word; and whenever I wanted to speak of *political interests* I was obliged to change the words into *civil interests*; in the place of Italy, native land, or nation, to use the word *country*: the word *constitution* was forbidden even when speaking of the governments of France and England and was replaced by *laws* or *institutions*; the terms Liberty, Liberal or *Liberalism* were not to be used in any sense, and *revolution* was always changed into *upheaval, anarchy* or *government by violence*.

Consequently, from the immediate point of view Gioberti's *Primato* might almost be said to mark an epoch. He had set

---

[41] *Ibid.* p. 572.
[42] *V.* for instance, pp. 403–7.

himself to write a book which firstly should arouse the
lethargic masses and create a public opinion for use at the
next great opportunity; but more especially he had hoped to
reach the usually remote clergy and princes, and to begin to
Italianise them. In this respect undoubtedly he achieved a
great success; it is claimed for him that he not only influenced
Charles Albert but also captured the future Pope. And his
success is proved by the fact that, sooner or later, the sale of
his book was forbidden, in every state except Piedmont, while
even there its buyers were ordered to give their names and
addresses. By that time, however, it was already in the hands
not merely of Liberals, such as his friend Balbo, but also of
the court officials all over Italy. Charles Albert was reading
it and soon afterwards offered Gioberti a pension.[43] At the
same time it had found its way into the houses of the cardinals,
the priesthood and even the ecclesiastical seminaries. The
Bishop of Asti had recommended it in a pastoral letter to his
clergy; Mgr Pecci (afterwards Leo XIII) had praised it without reserve. At first it had aroused opposition, but then
discussion and thought, so its objects had been achieved;
Liberal ideas had been introduced into the court and into the
cloister. Still the chief appeal of Gioberti was undoubtedly
to the Holy See.

For students, his scheme of confederation remains the only
practical suggestion of that day, because it was the only one
which provided for the two great difficulties of the time,
namely, the position of the Pope in a united Italy and the
conflicting ambition of the princes and local patriotism of their
small states.

Gioberti carefully omits all suggestion of driving out the

[43] Gioberti refused to make use of this pension. He accepted it,
out of respect for Charles Albert, but handed it over to a charity.
His refusal was partly due to indignation because some of the
Piedmontese ministers had opposed his being offered a chair at the
university of Pisa, and partly because his enemies were insinuating
that Charles Albert was paying him for what he wrote. Massari,
IX, 378.

Austrians. Nevertheless towards the end of the book his patriotism wells forth, in spite of him, in a passage which aroused admiration at the time and is now celebrated.[44] At that stage, apparently, he has been asking himself whether, after all, his hopes and conceptions are only a dream. Thereupon he breaks out into a long expression of intense pent-up patriotism coupled with a wide vision of his native land, such as often comes from the soul of a political exile:

If dreams can alleviate, even for a few moments, the painful sense of our common miseries, and lay open a weary mind to happy and generous hope—then I do not think it is wrong to dream....

I have imagined Italy not as she is but as she should be and as she might become....

And he pours forth a description of the great majestic nation that is to be; united, powerful, prosperous, with armies, fleets and colonies; and enlightened—a splendid light in the world—the Italy of the future. In those days when the very words Italian nation were eschewed in all truly loyal and law-abiding circles, Gioberti's description came like a vision of the generations yet unborn.

[44] *Primato*, p. 669.

Chapter XII

THE ADVANCE OF PIEDMONT: MASSIMO D'AZEGLIO

Gioberti's book had been addressed primarily to the Papacy; but its appeal was so stimulating that it also initiated a Piedmontese advance of which the chief promoters were Balbo and d'Azeglio.

The life and work of Massimo d'Azeglio, the third of the trio whose writings undoubtedly heralded the new phase in the Risorgimento, have been reserved for a detailed description, firstly, because he is one of the most remarkable figures of his time—distinguished as a painter, as a writer, and as a soldier —and led Piedmont as Prime Minister during its three most critical years; secondly, because his career illustrates from start to finish the advance of Piedmont towards the leadership of Italy; and thirdly, because he represented the Piedmontese party in Rome in 1847, and held a high command in the Papal army in 1848. In fact, he is one of the important characters in this story, and he is a man whose motives and actions cannot be estimated without some knowledge of his early days.

Massimo d'Azeglio was the youngest of four brothers, sons of the Marquis d'Azeglio, head of the Taparelli family. Their father was an exceptionally fine specimen of the Piedmontese nobility; honourable, religious, devoted to the independence of his small country, and imbued with the old-fashioned conception of loyalty to his sovereign—a sentiment which he was ready to prove by the test of self-sacrifice.

Massimo was born in Turin in 1798, but his childhood was spent in exile. In those pre-Napoleonic days whenever the small state of Piedmont was threatened by an invader, the king would call on each of his nobles to train men and raise money; in fact, to perform the same services which in most cases their feudal ancestors had rendered for centuries to the House of Savoy. To many a man among them a declaration of war meant selling his family plate and providing for the safety of his wife and children before leaving home to fight. In 1794 the Marquis d'Azeglio volunteered, and presented most of his silver and jewellery to the king;[1] and in 1795 he served in battle against the French, saw his battalion cut to pieces, was made a prisoner, and was reported dead.

After nearly a twelve-month of suffering, he returned to his home, and in 1798 his last son, Massimo, was born: but when Piedmont was annexed to France he decided to take his wife and family into voluntary exile in Florence rather than live permanently under the foreign régime. And throughout their lives, he and Massimo hated Napoleon with that simple primitive hatred which the conqueror inspired for many years to come, although it is often glossed over nowadays by historians: the same hatred which fought against France at Ligny and at Waterloo, and, in 1870, at Sedan. Even in the year 1864, when Massimo d'Azeglio wrote his memoirs, he still loathed the memory of the dead Napoleon more bitterly than the presence of the living Austrians.

It was therefore in a small house in Florence that Massimo's early childhood was spent; but in or about the year 1809, the family was ordered by the "tyrant" to return to Piedmont, so, very unwillingly, they went to live in their Palazzo in Turin. Here Massimo's misfortunes began. Like many others of the titled youth, he was handed over for education to a Jesuit tutor who seems to have had only two ideas in the world, Religion and Latin, both of which were inflicted for five years on his pupil, until the unfortunate Massimo hated the sound of either. It was to this training that he himself attributed the origin of his lifelong bitterness against priests and against all things clerical and even against religion itself.

In 1814 Napoleon fell, and most of Europe went mad with

---

[1] His direct losses (according to his son) amounted to 400,000 francs; apart from losses of crops during two or three years.

joy; they little suspected that for many of them the régime to be set up in 1815 would be worse than that of the French. No sooner had King Victor Emmanuel I returned to Turin, than the old Marquis d'Azeglio was sent to Rome as ambassador *pro tem.* for Piedmont, and he took Massimo with him as his attaché. This was a great opportunity for a precocious boy of nearly sixteen. During this stay in Rome, he saw the most exalted side of life at the Court of Pius VII, and made acquaintances among the cardinals and among the really old Roman families; and he saw all three sides of it—the civil, the clerical, and the diplomatic. But even at that early age, the people who interested him most were the artistic and literary men: he was introduced to the sculptors Canova and Thorwaldsen, to the poet Ferretti who had written many of Rossini's libretti, and to various lesser celebrities. It was during this period that he became enamoured of pictures and took his first lessons in painting which afterwards became his profession.

In the winter of 1814–15 the d'Azeglios returned to Turin, where already Massimo had been gazetted to a smart cavalry regiment.

At this point in his career, one perceives that he had too much youthful lack of discipline, too much enthusiasm and too high an opinion of his own judgment to be anything but a failure for the time being—and these he coupled with an immense scorn for anything ungenuine. In the army, these qualities very soon got him into difficulties.

The Piedmontese army in 1815 was passing—so it seems—through a period of transition.[2] The legitimist reaction was in power, and, in order to obtain reliable commanding officers, it was distributing the higher appointments, by family interest, to loyal but (according to d'Azeglio) completely incompetent men, while all those officers and N.C.O.'s who had served during the Napoleonic régime were deprived of a step in rank. Massimo was the son of a noble with good

---

[2] Gualterio, vol. I, pt I, p. 512.

family interest, but he was filled with indignation at the conditions around him.[3]

No doubt red tape, influence and incompetence have before now broken the heart of young officers in every army in the world. But in Massimo d'Azeglio's case they had the curious effect of turning him into a Radical. He tells us that he felt the methods of the Restoration to be so unjust—an attempt to put back the clock to the year 1798—that he developed a detestation of the nobles even to the point of hating his own noble birth as if it were a reproach. On one occasion, he actually passed himself off as the son of the factor on his father's estate, rather than give his true name.

In all probability he was generally considered a young whipper-snapper: however, he had the sense not to give up

[3] When d'Azeglio wrote his memoirs some forty-seven years later, he describes the senior officers selected for birth and loyalty as being entirely incompetent; whereas the men and N.C.O.'s were magnificent bronzed Napoleonic veterans who, as he says, had braved the snows of Russia and the burning sun of Andalusia; and so also were some of the junior officers. The adjutant, for instance, in 1812 had crossed the Beresina by wading it—apparently to avoid crowding the bridge—during the retreat from Moscow: he was deprived of a step in rank, and a new colonel and major were appointed over his head, although they were as yet incapable of giving a word of command. In this connection, d'Azeglio describes with perfect seriousness how the colonel had written out all his words of command on a piece of paper, so as not to forget them; but he mislaid it. The result was that when the regiment was drawn up on parade, with all ranks supremely intent on moving off like one man, the command which came forth was: "Fetch my scrap of paper" (v. Ricordi, I, 216). But d'Azeglio is biassed. And, in any case, one must remember that although these legitimist officers had not had time to re-learn their drill, it was fortunate for every one that they were in command when Napoleon returned from Elba. At the same time it seems that there was a tendency to revert to pre-Napoleonic ideas; one is inclined to think that even in 1848 the Piedmontese army, like most others, still suffered from these prejudices, and that it was never at its best until after Cavour had taken it in hand. But these are points upon which perhaps an outsider and a civilian ought not to venture. For criticism of the army, v. Gori, pp. 24–5.

working at his profession, and his knowledge of soldiering was afterwards very useful to him. But he was discontented and reckless and, once off parade, he let himself go. Before long he was turning night into day and associating mainly with riff-raff of either sex. The whole story is that of a boy of seventeen, in reality too young to be his own master. For about two years he remained in the cavalry, and then exchanged into a regiment of foot-guards where, it so chanced, Santarosa was one of his senior officers. But only a few months later he decided to leave the army and become an artist, the one profession which always had inspired him.

In 1818, therefore, he found himself a civilian once again, estranged from Turin society and from his family, without any income or resources beyond his allowance of 135 lire a month, or about £65 a year, an avowed Liberal and a professional artist, both of which creeds were considered at Turin to be objectionable and entirely derogatory for a young man in his position.[4]

Like his brothers he was learning to understand the fine motto bequeathed to them all by their old grandfather: *Ai fa pa nen*.[5]

---

[4] "Because I wished to do something different from what all the young counts of my day were doing, I was voted a madman, *nem. con.*" D'Azeglio, *Ricordi*, I, 21.

[5] "It doesn't matter a jot." The old Count of Lagnasco had had this motto written large in his room to greet him after an unfortunate day at court. The words are in Piedmontese dialect. It was a sentiment well suited to the independent character of the Taparelli family. Balbo, who was their first cousin, and also a Liberal, used to say to Massimo: "You and I have some of that blood in us". The eldest brother, the Marquis Roberto d'Azeglio, was a Carbonaro in 1821, but afterwards served Charles Albert loyally, as a Liberal and a great philanthropist; the second brother, Prospero, was profoundly religious and became a Jesuit; the third, Enrico, died young. Roberto's wife Costanza d'Azeglio, by birth an Alfieri, is described as the loving and sensible collaborator and inspirer of their work, which at that time involved facing social ostracism. But this probably had few terrors for a couple, who in 1835 showed a noble self-devotion in facing the cholera.

By this time Massimo was eighteen years of age, and fully developed: tall, fair, well-bred looking; good at fencing and swimming and "a devil on a horse"; and determined in spite of Turin society and of his family to be an artist.

There are very few boys of his type, one imagines, who would ever have painted a picture worth looking at; but Massimo was the exception. Contrary to the general opinion, he was very much in earnest about life, and his next ten years offer a wonderful instance of a young man deliberately taking himself in hand and working persistently, not merely to learn the dull technical rudiments of his profession, but also to discipline himself both in mind and body;[6] and abandoning a luxurious home to live on £65 a year, simply in order to "make good".[7]

He settled in Rome, and began his studies in real earnest. During the winters he worked in the town, but during the summers he went out into the country to paint from nature.

[6] "I say it sincerely; though there are many things of that date which I am ashamed of and should like to forget, there is one to which I rather cling. Now...tell the truth, dear reader! Do you not think that for a young man who has been a 'scapato' for some years, the change instantaneously to the life, I might say, of a Capuchin novice, some strength of will is required, and that there are not many such instances? It is an absolute fact that after having been constantly tied to some petticoat, I then passed four years and eight months in strict and absolute abstinence from every relation of this nature." D'Azeglio, *Ricordi*, I, 243.

[7] His movements during these years are not perfectly clear either in his *Ricordi*, or in Vaccalluzzo's life of him—the latest published; but apparently they were as follows: He seems to have gone to Rome with his mother in 1818 or 1819, and to have worked in the studio of Verstappen, a Belgian from Antwerp, whose paintings had some vogue in Rome. In the spring of 1820 he and his family returned to Turin (*Ricordi*, I, 305), visiting, on the way, Brescello, Mantua, Verona, Padua and Venice. On returning to Turin, he found the political atmosphere troubled, because the situation was working up towards the mutiny of 1821. In any case, he was out of touch with the social life there, and far preferred to be in Rome. He seems to have returned to Rome before the end of the year 1820, and remained there for the next seven or eight years.

The whole of these summers, from May to October, were spent in the Roman Campagna where he lived incognito as a poor artist among the poor, studying not merely art but also the innumerable types of people whom he met. At first the lofty village of Rocca di Papa became his headquarters, and from that glorious height he could gaze[8] across the plain of Lazio (Latium) and take in all its wonderful lights. Few people ever have had such a training; he would travel from place to place, conquering the *castelli* one by one, from the artistic point of view, paying for his lodging in the house of a peasant; living, dressing and feeding like one of the family—and no one knows Italy fully until he has had friends among her peasants—and thus learning life among the great world brotherhood of the toilers for their daily bread. His adventures during these days rather remind one of those of Du Maurier's heroes, for he went about making friends with men and women of every class and description, from the villano to the Roman Marchesa, charming them with his talk and his songs and his guitar. But the people who appealed most to him were the more picturesque types, as, for instance, the drivers of the great mule-carts whose wine business was in Trastevere. One wonders whether he ever met the cheery wine-carter Ciceru-acchio, that hero of the populace, who was destined to become his associate during the crucial years of 1847 and 1848.

During the winters he lived in Rome and again became the Marquis Massimo d'Azeglio among his old friends; dined with Cardinal di Gregorio about once a week—a remembrance which gave him a slight twinge of remorse in after life when he thought of his subsequent abuse of the Papal government in *Degli ultimi casi di Romagna*. But at the same time he

---

[8] "As we are at Rocca di Papa on my balcony which commands the whole of Lazio, from whose farthest horizon line there rises, solitary, the cupola of St Peter's, while the highest buildings of Rome remain half hidden amidst the vapour and mingled with the plain...." D'Azeglio, *Ricordi*, II, 25. That house now has a tablet on it with Massimo's name and a quotation from his writings. For this period of his life, *v.* Vaccalluzzo, *Massimo d'Azeglio*, p. 33.

studied the undersides of the town; he had acquaintances among the Carbonari. He himself was a Liberal, and a pan-Italian, but he tells us that at that time no one in Rome thought of a united Italy, except some of the lowest of the people;[9] and he knew Rome exceptionally well.

Within three years he sold his first picture, a view near Castel Sant' Elia, to the Marquis Lascari of Ventimiglia, a friend of his; and not so very long afterwards, in the winter of 1825, he achieved his first real success with a painting called *La Morte di Montmorency*, representing the death of a hero of the Crusades. This work created some sensation in Turin, and was presented to King Charles Felix by the old Marquis d'Azeglio who by then had become quite reconciled to his son. From that time onwards, life became easier. Unfortunately, Massimo d'Azeglio's artistic career cannot be described here; one may say, however, that his natural inspiration led him to paint romantic historical episodes, but that he had a keen appreciation of landscape, and especially loved trees: the "patriotic landscape" was his type. During the next ten or fifteen years he produced various well-known pictures, notably the defence of Nice against the Corsair Barbarossa, which he was commissioned to paint by King Charles Albert himself. From 1830 onwards he was one of the best known artists in Italy.

An unusual training! But not entirely bad for a man who was to be a conspirator, revolutionist, soldier and Prime Minister: he had been to the bedrock for his experience and knew how to talk to all types of men. But it is with d'Azeglio as a writer—it is with his books—that we are concerned. In reality his literary career came to him through his art and

[9] "In all Rome, who was there then, who thought of Italy, of her independence, or her regeneration? With a few exceptions only the extremist scum of the lowest of the people, which used to meet mysteriously in the vendite of the Carbonari, in public houses, etc." He is speaking of the early period after 1821. But even among the poor people one knows that the great majority were very loyal to the Pope. D'Azeglio, *Ricordi*, II, 199.

through his patriotism, for he was, above all things, a patriot, and he hated the Austrian domination. He tells us how, while in Venice, he went to visit the "Arzana de' Viniziani", the historic arsenal, where the Venetians used to build their ships in the great days of the Republic: "Ove bolle d'inverno la tenace pece", where Dante had seen the tenacious pitch boiling in winter. But Massimo found the Austrians at work there, and he says, "it made his own blood boil far more".

From time to time he had made some attempts at writing, but it was in 1830 that his literary successes began. He was busy completing a painting descriptive of a celebrated historical episode, the *Disfida di Barletta* (Challenge of Barletta) in the year 1503. It was a "subject which for me possessed the great merit—in fact the *sine qua non* for all my work of any significance—that of helping forward the pensiero italiano, our Italian ideals". It was certainly an inspiring theme. It was the story of contemptuous references spoken by a Frenchman anent Italian valour; of this proffered insult being taken up; of thirteen knights being carefully selected on either side as champions; of a long and stirring struggle between the horsemen in the lists, ending at last in a complete victory for the Italians.[10]

D'Azeglio himself lived much among chivalrous and poetic[11] imaginings and was in spirit a knight errant.

Working away with the fever zeal upon me, for the beautiful and the poetic, and above all, with the belief that I was doing

[10] For a description of the *Disfida di Barletta*, *v.* Sismondi (in French), *Républiques Italiennes*, vol. VIII, p. 230, and also Giucciardini (Italian), vol. V, chap. V, p. 362. It was a great triumph for the Italians, and especially suitable for d'Azeglio's propaganda, because their champions were drawn from many different Italian states and might almost be regarded as representing all Italy, or, at all events, the southern half of the Peninsula and Sicily. Ettore Fieramosca of Capua was the name of the knight who heads the list of Italians.

[11] For instance, his idea about music: "What is music?" he asks in his *Ricordi*. "No one knows what it is, yet all nations understand it. Perhaps it is a forgotten language."

well...in a month I had got on so far with my painting that already it was quite in a condition to be viewed....One day—I remember it as if it were this moment—I was just finishing the group of horses close-locked around one another in the centre, and the idea came to me that, given the importance of the episode and the desirability of recalling it so as to put some national fire into the Italians, a written description of it would have been far better and more efficacious than a mere painting of it. "Let us write it then!" I said..."Let us write it in prose—in words that can be understood in the byways and marketplaces, not merely in Helicon."

It was to be a book that would arouse the national pride throughout Italy.

He threw himself enthusiastically into the new work of writing about the Challenge of Barletta without even pausing to think what form the book would take. "I shall never be able to put into words the intimate pleasure, the inward joy which I felt then, in depicting and describing those scenes and characters; in living entirely within that life of chivalry, practically oblivious of the present". Before long, he had made such progress that he was able to read some chapters to his cousin Cesare Balbo; and eventually, in 1833, the book was published in the form of a novel called *Ettore Fieramosca*. Honesty compels one to say that it is not considered a classic, though it contains some fine passages and situations. But it suggested driving out the French foreigners—and for "French", most people read "Austrian". Consequently it proved a great success. Henceforth Massimo was known as a writer more widely than he had been as a painter.

Meanwhile his father was dead and his brother was established in the family place, the Castello d'Azeglio; so Massimo decided to leave Turin and settle in Milan, and there he remained for the next twelve years. This is a very striking fact: he actually elected to say good-bye to Turin and to settle down under the Austrian administration in Milan, because he felt freer there. It speaks well for the Austrians; and Massimo, although as a patriot he hated them, always said that they were better than the French, because they took great trouble to make their rule agreeable to those whom they insisted on governing. But this preference for Milan as compared with Turin is accounted for partly by the fact that he was still out of touch with his own class in Piedmont—as was also the case with his brother Roberto and with the young Cavour and other Liberals during these years.[12]

He remained in Milan from 1831 to 1843 painting, and sometimes writing. During those twelve years he married Manzoni's daughter and had one girl, Rina, the future Marchesa Ricci. Then his wife died and in 1835 he married again, a widow named Luisa Blondel, one of the same circle. He had already become one of the leaders of the artistic and literary revival there, and lived among the friends with whom in reality he had most in common. In 1841 he published *Nicolo de' Lapi*, another historical romance, which had some success: it dealt with the siege of Florence. In 1843 he was with Balbo when the *Speranze* was composed. But his own

---

[12] Even in his memoirs, written at the age of sixty-four, he still remembers those early days during which he and other young men suffered from the fearsome weight of an eighteenth-century restoration. He complains that no one in Turin society of the twenties and thirties ever ventured to think for himself: "Just as in certain countries there is a standard measure or weight for the use of the public, so that anyone can verify his own measures and weights and be sure that he is quite accurate, so for the nobility of Turin, God wished to limit His expense to making only one single brain: and He placed it at court, in the camera di parata, so that anyone could go there and provide himself with the idea which he required". To do them justice, this state of things is characteristic of almost every small society, especially after a class-war. It has been necessary to mention this social influence to account for the otherwise surprising fact that d'Azeglio made his home in Milan rather than in Turin. But the fact remains that the Restoration party succeeded in shutting out of their circle at Turin the two men with whom lay the future of Piedmont, Massimo d'Azeglio and Camillo Cavour. Young Cavour "was hated by the whole of the reactionary aristocracy who came to the house of his father. To some of them Cavour was a *Protestant*, to others a revolutionary, and to all of them a foolish youth whose head had been turned by the Liberals". Predari, p. 38.

political career—the collecting and dissemination of propaganda for the cause of Italian independence—did not begin until 1845.

It was not until 1846—as will be described—that he produced his best known book, *Degli ultimi casi di Romagna*, an outspoken, adverse criticism of the Papal administration in Romagna. This book will be criticised in detail, for it is one of the landmarks of this period.

Chapter XIII

THE ADVANCE OF PIEDMONT: BALBO'S WORK

BALBO'S PROGRAMME

The three great aims of the Italian nationalists were—as already stated—independence, unification and the introduction of Liberal institutions. And the two chief difficulties in their path were the existence of the Pope, and of the state patriotisms.[1] Gioberti had solved this problem by suggesting a confederation of which the Pope should be president.

Balbo's work, *Delle speranze d' Italia* (1844), appeared in the following year. It takes the Piedmontese view of the case, but it is the direct outcome of the *Primato*.

Its inception came about as follows. Soon after the publication of Gioberti's great volume, Massimo d'Azeglio was staying with Balbo at the Villa del Rubatto near Turin. D'Azeglio as usual was hard at work painting, while his cousin, whose studious soul was greatly stirred by the *Primato*, sat with him reading out various eloquent passages and noting down points that should be made if another work were written on the subject. "You write the book", said d'Azeglio; and it was this suggestion which started the project. In 1844 Balbo's *Speranzε* duly appeared, dedicated to Gioberti; and eventually, in 1846, d'Azeglio's first political work made its appearance, *Degli ultimi casi di Romagna*, dedicated to Balbo.

---

[1] "Turin, Milan, Florence, Rome, Naples, Parma and Modena are seven capital cities of the present day (without counting Lucca which is to be joined to Tuscany). In six of these there are reigning princes.... It is a dream to expect from one single capital city that it should be willing to reduce itself to a provincial level; and a greater dream still to imagine that all six will agree to submit to one; and the greatest dream of all to think that the six will agree to select one of their number." Balbo, *Speranze*, p. 20.

The books of these two Piedmontese gentlemen undoubtedly represent a disposition to capture the federal movement for Piedmont.

According to the original scheme of Gioberti, the small states were to join the confederation just as they stood; no frontiers were to be altered between them so as not to destroy the balance of power; as to the fate of Lombardy and Venetia —both under Austrian occupation—he made no statement, but he assumed that his plan could be carried out without bloodshed.

Balbo's scheme, however, claimed the leadership, the dangers and the subsequent gains of territory for Piedmont. Evidently he contemplated ousting Austria by arms or by diplomacy, and he did not want the Pope to be President of the Italian league, because he felt that, as head of the Church, no Pope could really lead a militant campaign against his Austrian spiritual subjects.[2] In fact he thought it best that the exact terms of the confederation should be left open.

[2] Balbo, *Speranze*, pp. 43, 64–6; also p. 256. Speaking of former Popes he says: "Who could blame, or even avoid praising these men who set their own duties above those of others; and also their own greater duty above the lesser; who, having in their hand the interests of all Christendom and likewise the interests of a principality or portion of Italy (the whole of Italy they never had), devoted their attention to the former rather than to the latter" (Balbo, p. 65). And of Alexander III, the Pope of the Lombard League, he says: "He abandoned the victorious communes and I do not know who could say that he was wrong; or that, for the sake of the interests of Italy, he ought to have expelled the Emperor and half Christendom from the Communion of the Church. And if anyone were to argue that he ought, as Pope, to have made an end of the schism, and at the same time, as Prince, to have continued the war, such a person would be drawing a distinction which was probably impossible to maintain at any time and was certainly impossible then". Only three years later all Italy was calling on Pius IX to declare a holy war of excommunication against Austria and calling him a traitor because, as Pope, he felt this to be impossible. Consequently, one attaches great value to Balbo's reasoned opinion on this point, definitely published before the advent of the war fever; also concerning the difficulty of separating the Spiritual from the Temporal power.

(This, one may observe, offered no guarantee of safety to the smaller states which were all afraid of being swallowed up by Piedmont.) He believed that the great hope for Italy would be in her taking advantage of some European crisis—some "great opportunity".

As yet the only future opportunity that he can see sufficiently near to justify any preparations is the probable disruption of the Turkish Empire. This he regards as fairly imminent, and suggests that, on the downfall of the Turks, some of their Christian provinces should be given to Austria on condition of Metternich's resigning Lombardy and Venetia to the Italians. Austria would probably be ready to accept these terms from the Great Powers if she found herself faced in Italy by a strong confederation; and then the balance of power in Europe would be maintained.

But which Italian state is to be the happy recipient of these liberated Italian provinces? Undoubtedly, says Balbo, they will come to Piedmont. Owing to her position Piedmont is obliged to face the dangers of the enterprise and therefore she is entitled to receive the gains; and she alone would be able to Italianise Lombardo-Venetia. Moreover it is necessary for her to have them in order to form a strong kingdom across the north of Italy; without such a kingdom the whole peninsula will always remain open to invasion. In this connection he makes an observation which is rather significant: that the peninsula is divided naturally by the Apennines into two distinct parts, northern Italy and southern Italy. Now this division (by the Apennines), one notices, would assign the Papal "Legations", that is to say the provinces of Bologna, Ferrara, Ravenna and Forlì, to the northern half of Italy; in fact to the enlarged kingdom of Piedmont. Hitherto, since 1815, the dividing line had been the River Po, which left them to the Pope. Balbo does not actually suggest annexing the Papal Legations to Piedmont, but he refers to a well-known plan for doing so. The project of forming a strong northern kingdom which should include these Papal territories had long been suggested by Piedmontese sympathisers;[3] and later on, in 1846, when the Papal question seemed likely to be re-opened at Gregory XVI's death, Massimo d'Azeglio published his great attack on the Pontifical government in Romagna, and tried to prove that that government was unbearable (*v.* chapter xv).

What Balbo says is as follows:

To speak of the enterprise for winning Italian independence is almost the same thing as to speak of the foundation of a big Ligurian-Lombard[4] Kingdom. Parma and Modena might have some share in this gain of territories; but Tuscany could be given nothing, or hardly anything; Rome could get nothing, and Naples could get nothing.

On these terms their rulers were not likely to join in the enterprise; nor were most of their people. They were too comfortable. As matters stood Naples was far away, remote from the scene of action; the Papal State was safe, guaranteed by the Great Powers; and Tuscany was a peaceful haven of refuge for almost any type of fugitive. Some people, says Balbo, have suggested taking the Adriatic provinces of the

[3] Compare, for instance, the *Catechismo italiano* of Giuseppe Pecchio written in 1830. In it he proposes the formation of a strong northern kingdom in the following terms:

"Piedmont, the guardian of the Alpine gates, has hitherto enjoyed this honourable title without being able to fulfil its duties; she has the keys, but she cannot close the way. Would it not be much better for her...to become the protector of Italian independence?

What would be the frontiers and forces of the new kingdom?

The Alps, and the Apennines of Tuscany and Tronto would be its boundaries. It would have a population of twelve million inhabitants....Genoa, Ancona and Venice would put life into its commerce.

But how would the Pope bear the loss of the Legations and the Marches?

The Patrimony of St Peter might suffice for the successor of St Peter—*Regnum meum non est de hoc mundo*".

This writer, therefore, limits the Pope to the territory immediately around Rome, *v. Rass. stor.*, 1917, p. 525.

[4] "Ligurian-Lombard" means the same as "Piedmontese-Lombard".

Pope and dividing them between Tuscany and Naples; but
he, Balbo, is opposed to this scheme. He realises the value
of the Papacy to Italy. He says that in being the home and
defender of the Holy See, Italy has a primacy which is better
assured and more permanent than the primacies of the other
nations; and that, apart from this, to attack the Pope would
sow dissension throughout the peninsula, and would arouse
all Catholic Christendom against the national cause.

Finally, after thus dealing with the independence and
unification questions, Balbo comes to the great third aim of
Italy—that of winning Liberal institutions within each state.
On this point he says that independence must be considered
before anything else. Some people think that if they win
grants of free institutions they will be able to use them for
achieving independence; he agrees with them, and thinks too
that the concession of free constitutions would leave the
Austrian bureaucratic rule distanced and discredited in
Lombardo-Venetia. But he is opposed to any attempt at
forcing the princes to grant constitutions, because that would
create bitterness and disunion. His advice is: "Leave it to
the princes to decide when the people are ready for grants of
liberty". In other words he does not want them to try and
force the hand of Charles Albert.

It will be seen that Balbo's conception was very different
from that of Gioberti. Gioberti had described a confederation
which maintained all the existing frontiers, and functioned
under the presidency of the Pope. Balbo held that the exact
terms of the confederation could not be fixed until after the
Austrians had been driven out: and that, when set up, it
should be protected by a greatly predominant state of
Piedmont which should stretch right across northern Italy.
And strangely enough, as fate willed it, Balbo was himself
Prime Minister of Piedmont in 1848, when Charles Albert
made his great effort to carry out this programme.

It has been necessary to lay stress on these differences
between Gioberti and Balbo because, virtually, they founded

two schools of thought concerning the proposed Italian confederation; and it was this divergence that prevented any of
the efforts at confederation from ever coming to completion.
During the first two years of his reign, Pius IX constantly
endeavoured to federate Italy more or less on the lines of
Gioberti's scheme; but the Piedmontese ministers did not
want definite terms of confederation until after the expulsion
of the Austrians; and at the conference of Turin in 1848 they
boldly claimed the possession of the liberated provinces before
coming to any federal agreement at all. It must have been,
and apparently was, a great grief to Pius that at the conference
Gioberti declared himself in favour of the Piedmontese point
of view.

Looking back on the scene now one feels that most of
Balbo's contentions were right. The fact was that the
ambitions of Piedmont happened to coincide very genuinely
with the practical interests of Italy. He was right in saying
that Italy required a strong nation—and a very strong nation
indeed as we all realise now—across her northern frontiers.
A mere confederation under the Pope, as outlined by Gioberti,
was not a good permanent arrangement, although it was the
nearest approach to unity that could have been achieved before
1849. It was a great suggestion; one which founded a new
phase in the Risorgimento.

As to the lesser princes and governments being afraid of
a really strong Piedmont, this fact was conclusively proved
in 1848. They feared that a northern kingdom of Piedmont-
Lombardy-Venetia would soon swallow up its lesser neigh-
bours; and—to do them justice—this is exactly what happened
in 1860. No sooner had the Piedmontese acquired Lombardy
(after the campaign of Solferino) than they raised an army of
200,000 men and overran the rest of the peninsula. In
fourteen months the process was complete, but by that time
most people had realised that it was the best form of settlement for the new nation.

The foregoing is a broad sketch of Balbo's tenets, and

especially of the differences between him and Gioberti. Incidentally, one notes that he entirely condemns the idea of a national insurrection, on the ground that small risings are useless and that there is no tyranny in Italy sufficient to arouse a general rising. "To have good revolution you must have good tyranny." But he gives some consideration to the idea of initiating an agitation similar to that of O'Connell:[5] the actual method of agitation he does not consider possible for Italy, but in the matter of choosing a single leader and all uniting under his orders, Balbo strongly urges that Italy should follow the example of Ireland.[6] No doubt he was thinking of Charles Albert as Dictator.

Balbo was a genuine historian, and he is not carried away by Gioberti's idea of an eternal Italian primacy among the nations. In his view the following nations have led the world during the Christian era:

[5] Speaking of Italy and Poland, he says (p. 157): "It does not matter that it now seems near to destruction; farther off than ever from all hopes of resurrection. *The Christian nations cannot die*; Ireland has not perished after seven centuries of an oppression which might have seemed like destruction". It was Gioberti who had written this phrase about Italy: "The Christian nations cannot die", but Balbo quotes it and repeats it several times with a depth of feeling and conviction that is rather pathetic, v. *Speranze*, pp. 61, 157, etc.

[6] He says (p. 232): "Great mutations within a state can only be carried out with difficulty and danger by the multitude, so it is necessary to entrust them to the few...as was well known to many of the ancients; even to those who were democratic republicans". He recalls how in classic days a dictator was appointed, and argues that the modern idea of a constituent assembly or convention is wrong: "Therefore I cannot but turn to that specially fine instance which I have already mentioned; to that of the Irish who in their enterprise, whether it be for liberty or for independence, have set up for themselves almost a dictator or a prince, and follow his directions; to him they look and around him they stand unanimous and therefore strong, with a wisdom which is both truly classical and truly Christian". He continues "that the strength of their enterprise has been its legality, and that a similar legality can be obtained in Italy by acting under the princes"; he evidently means under one prince, no doubt Charles Albert.

A.D. 1–476. Period of breaking up of the ancient Roman civilisation.

A.D. 476–1073. Germanic preponderance, until Gregory VII broke the power of the Emperor.

A.D. 1073–1494. Italian primacy in civilisation.

A.D. 1494 to present day (1844). Various Christian nations.

      1550–1650 (*circa*). Spain.

      1650 onwards. France.

Nineteenth century. The British Isles.

The British now lead the world. They stand first as conquerors, extending Christianity; in the spreading of population; in commerce; in industry and scientific and material progress, which,

in spite of much stupid contempt, are still, and will be the occupation, the subject of work, and the path for many noble intellects both present and future. If all this is not to be called a primacy I do not know what can or ever will be called by that name.

The three "vices" with which the British will have to cope are

bad public charity; the tyranny of the territorial magnates; and the injustices accumulated on Ireland,[7]

all of which, says Balbo, are outcomes of the Reformation, and could be settled by Great Britain's returning to Roman Catholicism.

---

[7] *Speranza*, pp. 334 and 350.

Chapter XIV

THE ADVANCE OF PIEDMONT: CHARLES ALBERT, 1835 TO 1845

I. CHARLES ALBERT'S ACTIVITIES[1]

To Charles Albert the Reform Movement was destined to come as a great encouragement of his secret hopes.

It will be remembered that in 1835 he had emerged from the First Period of his reign, during which he definitely established his independence of the Revolution (*v.* chapter VI).

The Second Period. The next period is 1835–43, during which years his Foreign Minister is Count Solaro della Margherita,[2] and his Minister for War is Count Pes di Villamarina. At home, this is an era of excellent Conservative reform;[3] in 1838 a new civil code is introduced; in 1840 a new

---

[1] So much has been written about Charles Albert that it is hard to select the most suitable works. The following will cover, at all events, the statements in this chapter. The general histories of the Risorgimento: Tivaroni, Masi, etc., *v.* chap. VIII, note I. Special: Vidal, Lemmi, Luzio, Vaccalluzzo, Rodolico. Contemporary writers: Solaro della Margherita, Cibrario, Gualterio, Farini, Predari, d'Azeglio, Montanelli, Rinieri, Hübner, Brofferio, and others. Diplomatic: Metternich, Bianchi (documents), de Sambuy, and the various Archives. No attempt has been made to find new facts about Charles Albert's reign, as that is work for a specialist, and this can only be a summary; but all facts given have been verified from the writings of contemporaries who played a leading part in them, such as Solaro della Margherita, d'Azeglio, etc.

[2] His name is spelt della Margherita by M. Vidal, the latest biographer of Charles Albert. He himself often used the French language and spelt it de la Marguerite; but on the fly-leaf of his Memorandum it is spelt della Margarita. Charles Albert, when addressing him in French, sometimes spelt it la Marguerite (*v.* Memorandum, p. 181), omitting the "de". But this is according to Piedmontese custom. General della Rocca, for instance, was called La Rocca in his young days; a similar instance is the name La Marmora.

[3] He was not a political reformer in the sense of introducing

penal code, and in 1842 a new commercial code; all mainly based on the Code Napoléon. Meanwhile, abroad, Count Solaro della Margherita aims at developing commerce; some nineteen new consulates are founded and fifteen commercial treaties are signed. But the main objects of which Charles Albert never loses sight are his finances and his army. On them depend all his secret hopes and plans.

The revenue rises from 60 million lire in 1831 to 85 millions in 1845.

The army mobilisation in 1840 gives 48,000 men (Count Solaro refers to the number as 40,000); and it claims that for war Piedmont can raise 163,000 men, all told. In 1848 we shall find her with nearly 70,000 men in the field against Austria; and in 1849 with 80,000. But unfortunately the military training under Villamarina seems not to have been quite as good as it became, after the war, under Cavour.

Even the navy has now some importance; in 1840 it consists of twenty ships and 2000 men.

In foreign affairs the situation remains rather curious during this period. Charles Albert pursues a twofold policy: on the one hand he is Conservative, anti-revolutionary and correct in his relations with Metternich; but, at the same time, secretly he hates Austria, and as the years go by he tends to become more independent in his measures of reform.

And, actually, throughout this long period he has two ministers, men of entirely divergent views, to carry out simultaneously the two different lines of his policy. The one is his Foreign Minister, Count Solaro della Margherita, a true

Liberal ideas or popular institutions; but he pursued a steady policy of Conservative reform, and he was not afraid to abolish some of the worst privileges that had been re-introduced by the Restoration of 1815, although this policy gave bitter offence to many of his most loyal supporters. The royal forests, the uncultivated communal lands, the silk trade, the administration of justice and the codices: the fine arts, science, literature, were all subjects for his reforming hand. But his chief interest by far went out to the army and the finances of the state. *V.* Predari, pp. 280–5.

Conservative; and the other is his Minister for War, Count Pes di Villamarina, whose opinions are Liberal, and who sympathises with the king's hatred of Austria. It is the most extraordinary arrangement. For about ten years they work on opposing lines, and the king holds the balance between them.

Charles Albert's constant care is not to commit himself before the great moment arrives. And it must be admitted that he achieves his object. He has been called in derision the "Re Tentenna" (the vacillating king), but those who deride him cannot deny that for eighteen years he kept his people in hand and finally struck with all his might when the very best opportunity occurred. One doubts whether anyone else of his day would have done as well.[4]

Count Solaro della Margherita is an interesting figure in this story; small, thin, with a narrow forehead, an ex-diplomat only forty-two years of age, endowed with a considerable power of self-assertion. Fortunately he has left us a "Memorandum" or detailed account of his whole term of office. His own description shows him to have been almost as Conservative as Metternich himself: he dreaded the Revolution, hated Liberal constitutions and believed in Divine Right. But at the same time he had a fine determination to maintain the individuality, independence and prestige of Piedmont both in Italy and throughout Europe. He held that all sovereign states had equal rights, great and small alike,[5] and that in Europe there were only six nations more powerful than his own, namely the five Great Powers and Spain; "to none others should Sardinia go second".

[4] In 1840 he wrote to Count Solaro: "Tout ce que l'on dit et on fait en ce moment se réduira très probablement en fumée, mais le grand jour finira par arriver, et il ne faudra pas que nous eussions d'avance gâtée notre position".

[5] He quotes Klüber, *Droits des Gens*, pt II, titre I, chap. III: "This equality (between sovereign states) cannot be affected by the accidental qualities or attributions of a state; such as its antiquity, its population, the extent of its territory, its military power, the form of its constitution, the title of its sovereign, its culture of all sorts, the consideration which it enjoys, etc."

From the first, della Margherita was perfectly well aware of Charles Albert's secret hopes and ambitions, but he regarded them as the merest dream:[6] and in so regarding them he felt that he was out of sympathy with his king—as, indeed, he was also, for various reasons, with all the ministers.[7] Nevertheless he remained the leading adviser of the crown for eleven years (1835-46). This was because he could play with perfect genuineness the twofold part required at the moment. When dealing with Metternich he was a most whole-hearted and willing ally against revolutions and constitutions, and he honestly regarded the "War of Liberation" as absurd. But at the same time he entirely refused to be treated as one of Austria's Italian marionettes; in diplomacy he made himself difficult to deal with,[8] always insisted on acting independently, and gradually built up a separate position for Piedmont.

So Conservative was he that between 1835 and 1839 he allowed Piedmont to become almost a base of action for the legitimist claimants Don Carlos in Spain and Don Miguel in

[6] "It needed no great acuteness on my part to discover...that from the very depths of his soul he was opposed to Austria and full of illusions as to the possibility of freeing Italy from her dependence; ...as for the revolutionists he hated them and despised them, but was afraid and convinced that sooner or later he would be their victim." Solaro, p. 21. In his very first report della Margherita advised the continuance of the old traditional Piedmontese policy "without inebriating ourselves with fantastic illusions which would end in weeping". *Ibid.* p. 25.

[7] "I was destined to be alone; never to have anyone who would second me; never a colleague to whom I could open my soul." Solaro, p. 220. An extraordinary position for a Foreign Minister! He was quite aware that when the great day arrived it would bring his dismissal because he did not believe in attacking Austria.

[8] Speaking of the Austrian ambassador, Count de Bombelles, della Margherita says: "He had a mania for interfering in our affairs and giving, unasked, advice to Ministers of the King... [after trying polite methods in vain] I was obliged, by means of actions which seemed discourteous, to convince him of the necessity of changing his attitude". Solaro, p. 41. He says that he told de Bombelles that "we wished to show ourselves the friends of Austria, not her vassals".

Portugal—and this in defiance of the Liberal powers, France and England. So openly did he send supplies that both Spain and Portugal closed their ports against Piedmontese vessels, and the British Admiralty gave orders to intercept them to prevent their landing arms (1838).

But on the other hand, in 1836 when Metternich called upon Piedmont to co-operate with France and Austria in a blockade of Switzerland, della Margherita refused:

However close may be the ties between our royal cabinet and that of his Apostolic Majesty when supporting the cause of monarchy, the people of Vienna can hardly suppose that we shall adopt without consideration any ideas which the Austrian Minister may lay before us.

In the same year,[9] 1836, Metternich wanted Piedmont to act with him in a joint complaint in London about the asylum granted by Malta to revolutionists. Della Margherita refused. Although he regarded the conspirators in Malta as a danger, he would not allow Palmerston to think that Charles Albert took his instructions from Vienna.

In 1838 Metternich made another attempt to embroil Piedmont with Switzerland and again failed. In this year Charles Albert refused to attend the coronation ceremony of the Austrian Emperor at Monza, and merely went to see him, incognito, at Pavia.[10]

In 1839 Metternich published a threat that any state in which a rising took place would be occupied by Austrian troops, and he wanted Charles Albert to print it in the *Gazzetta*. Charles Albert refused.

From the above instances it will be seen that, although Charles Albert had been driven by the Revolution to make a treaty with Austria, he meant to preserve a free hand, and avoid being included in Metternich's system. After 1843 he tended towards friendship with France.

[9] *V.* Luzio, p. 46, note 2.
[10] Metternich says that at this private meeting Charles Albert was extremely humble and friendly. Probably he thought it necessary to make private amends for not having gone to Monza.

Nevertheless, it seems that he was at least equally careful not to let Metternich consider him anti-Austrian. In April 1842 he arranged for his son Victor Emmanuel to be married to the Archduchess Adelaide of Austria, daughter of his brother-in-law the Archduke Rainer (Italian *Rainiero*, French *Renier*), Viceroy of Lombardo-Venetia; and in 1843 he entered into negotiations for an engagement between his second son, Prince Ferdinando di Carignano, with the Archduchess Maria, another daughter of the Archduke Rainer. This princess died. But had this marriage taken place he would indeed have had an Austrian ménage; his own wife was an Austrian, a daughter of the Grand Duke Ferdinand of Tuscany; his sister was married to the Archduke Rainer; and his two sons would have been married to two sisters, Austrian archduchesses, their first cousins. And these marriage negotiations were begun in the very midst of the dispute with Austria over the salt. Well might della Margherita moralise on the idea that "cold reasons of state maintain their antipathies even while marriage-beds are flowered".

Finally while dealing with his foreign policy we may note that in 1839 Charles Albert improved his already good relations with the Holy See by prevailing upon Gregory XVI to re-establish the Papal Nunciatura at Turin. There had always been Papal representatives at Turin, but since 1750 there had not been a Nunzio. In 1839, however, della Margherita visited Rome, for it was a year during which five saints were canonised. Old Gregory XVI had already known him for a long time and was attached to him and to Charles Albert; and Cardinal Lambruschini appreciated their Conservative views. So to Charles Albert's great satisfaction the affair was settled. The first Nunzio was Monsignor Massi, Bishop of Gubbio, "a real gift from the Holy See". He died in 1841 and was succeeded by Monsignor Gizzi who had already been in Turin as Chargé d'Affaires. In 1844 Gizzi returned to Rome and was created a cardinal; in 1846 he became Secretary of State of Pius IX.

The Third Period. In the year 1843 Gioberti's *Primato* started the neo-Guelf movement, and from then onward Charles Albert undoubtedly took a bolder line *vis-à-vis* of Austria. He feels around him the growth of popular enthusiasm for the enterprise which is his secret hope. He means to come forward and to be regarded as its leader. It is a task for "a man who is wise and imaginative, of high courage and great emprise", as Froissart once said when describing a similar venture by a Count of Savoy in the fourteenth century.[11] At the same time his common sense tells him that immediate action is impossible: at all costs he must avoid being swept into actual conflict with the immense power of Austria until the true opportunity arrives.

Still from 1843 to 1846 he comes to be regarded undoubtedly as the leading, and in fact the only patriotic, Italian prince. But then, in June 1846, there appears Pope Pius IX, a genuine Liberal. For a year and nine months Pius becomes the popular hero all over Italy, and it is he who makes the movement national; the Pope's name can move the peasants and the parish priests and every other class of men; so it is mainly owing to the influence of Pius' movement that the great opportunity comes into being in 1848.

From 1842 onwards, says Vidal, there is a triple attack in progress against Austria; we see it in the work of the neo-Guelf writers all over Italy; in the question of the salt between Charles Albert and Metternich; and in the question of the Piedmontese railways. Of these three headings the first has already been described.

The question of the salt was the chief subject of contention between Charles Albert and Austria. It dated from the eighteenth century. Before 1751 Piedmont had been ac-

[11] Froissart was speaking of the Duke of Anjou's expedition against Naples in 1382, upon which there rode with him "le gentil comte Amé de Savoie, bien accompagné de barons et de chevaliers, qui fut aussi de son cousin le pape grandement bien venu". Such enterprises were in the blood of the Savoys since the days of Amadeo, and earlier. *V.* Froissart, *Les Chroniques,* livre II, chap. cxxxv.

customed to draw supplies of salt from Venetia (from Comacchio on the River Po). But this route involved carrying it along the river through Lombardy, and paying duty to the Austrians in possession there. Consequently in 1751 a convention was drawn up whereby the Piedmontese were no longer to pay duty; they were entitled to carry, duty free, enough salt for their own needs, but were bound not to re-sell it or trade with it; previously they had sold some of their supply to the Swiss of the Canton Ticino. Thus the Austrian government, which already possessed a salt monopoly in Lombardy, succeeded in capturing the Piedmontese trade with the Swiss Canton Ticino.

By the Treaty of Vienna in 1815 the old Convention of 1751 was re-enacted—which was unwise, because it no longer applied to the existing conditions. Piedmont no longer wanted to draw salt from Comacchio on the Adriatic side of Italy; she could now obtain her supplies from Genoa, newly ceded to her. However the Convention of 1751 was never denounced and consequently remained valid.

In 1841 the Swiss of Canton Ticino, unable to get enough salt from Lombardy owing to the Austrian monopoly, applied to Piedmont to send them supplies from Genoa. At this point begins the quarrel between Piedmont and Austria.

Charles Albert and his treasurer Gallina were anxious to trade with the Swiss, but their own Foreign Minister, Solaro della Margherita, was obliged to tell them that they were prevented from doing so by the Convention of 1751. So this offer was refused.

In 1842, however, a way was discovered of evading the Convention. Trading in salt was forbidden; but transit of salt was not forbidden. It was arranged therefore that the Swiss should buy foreign salt from the French at Hyères or from traders in the free port of Genoa, and merely ask leave to carry it across Piedmontese territory. In this manner Charles Albert agreed to furnish the Canton Ticino with three to four thousand quintals per annum for twelve years.

The Austrians again raised complaint, but this time, Count Solaro tells us, he considered that Gallina was within the terms of the Convention of 1751. Charles Albert refused to give way. The utmost that he would concede was a reduction of the contract with the Swiss from twelve years to four.

In 1843 he signed a commercial treaty with France.

In 1844 the Canton Ticino was supplied with four thousand quintals of salt from Genoa. Nominally, this salt had come from Hyères; it was supposed, at all events, to be merely in transit. By this procedure the Convention of 1751 was rendered nugatory.

But in 1845 Count Buol, who had been Austrian ambassador at Turin for a year, warned della Margherita that Austria would retaliate; and it was in vain that della Margherita tried to prevent the outbreak of the quarrel. For some months to come he could only live in expectation of the coming blow—which fell in 1846, as will presently be described.

Before 1843 Charles Albert's policy had been independent of Austria but in sympathy with her Conservatism. After 1843 he moves gradually into a position opposed to her: firstly over the salt, but soon over a matter a thousand times more serious. It was the advent of the most splendid new idea of the nineteenth century—that of the railway—which aroused fresh rivalry between him and Metternich, this time over a question of vital importance to the future of Italy: was it to be Piedmont or was it to be Austria which should garner in the trade of Central Europe and connect it with the East? On February 13th, 1845, Charles Albert promulgated a railway plan whereby Genoa should be the chief southern port and terminus; whereas Metternich favoured Trieste. These were the rival ports for inlet into Central Europe, of the Mediterranean commerce, including goods from India; and Charles Albert's railways would carry them to the North Sea;[12]

[12] Count Petitti wrote a book on the railway scheme and it is in reality one of the best works of the period; owing to Charles Albert's

moreover, these lines running north and south down the peninsula would tend to promote unity.

Strange! These rival schemes could be discussed in the Austrian or even in the English or French papers, but in Piedmont their very naming was forbidden. Charles Albert worked in silence, for he did not yet feel equal to a rupture with Austria (Predari, p. 80).

Partly owing to his own inward wishes and partly owing to the force of circumstances Charles Albert was being borne forward, before 1846, into the first place among the princes of Italy. But he could make no appeal to the people: he was compelled to work with great circumspection; the "King's secret" was known only to his ministers and was well kept by them. Like many other moderate men in revolutionary times, he was entirely misunderstood by the majority of the nation. The Conservatives distrusted him, the revolutionists hated him, and even the neo-Guelfs felt very uncertain as to his ideas. He seemed to be destined to work almost alone— the solitary prince whom Mazzini had named "the Hamlet of Savoy".

Yet he was right: and soon he was to be approached by men who realised that fact.

II. MASSIMO D'AZEGLIO AND CHARLES ALBERT

Massimo d'Azeglio has been called the most "complete", that is to say the most all-round, man in the Moderate Party.[13] His advantage lay in his many-sided experience: he knew how to talk to everyone from a king or a cardinal to a Carbonaro, and had seen the national question from every point of view. As a Piedmontese noble he was loyal to Charles Albert, and to serve the House of Savoy was his true mission in life; but

unwillingness to risk a rupture with Austria, this book had to be printed at Capolago outside the state, but it was allowed to circulate in Piedmont.

[13] Montanelli, p. 113.

he had been brought up in Florence, had soldiered in Turin, had worked for his living in Rome, had travelled and made friends in Naples and Sicily—to say nothing of his visits to Venice and elsewhere—and finally had married and settled in Milan, so that he felt equally at home in every part of Italy. And he must have been a fascinating companion for—so his biographer tells us—he spoke just as he wrote. At the same time he had not knocked about among all classes without picking up some of the wisdom of the serpent; but he used it mainly in the interests of his cause, which in practice was the cause of Piedmont.

In politics Massimo was genuinely Moderate. His main creed was to substitute agitation for revolution, and, like the other Moderates, he cited Ireland under O'Connell as a successful example of this policy. He had a rooted dislike of the Giovine Italia and of all Mazzini's methods;[14] he refused to join any secret societies and consequently could say what he liked without any fear of his name being unearthed by the police from a roll of conspirators. He was essentially a practical politician, looking for results, and had disapproved of the risings of 1821 and 1833 because he regarded them as useless and harmful. For secret conspiracy he wished to substitute "public conspiracy", namely agitation. But, like Charles Albert, he was a good hater of the Austrians, and

---

[14] "I did not share the opinions of the Giovine Italia; I recognised that all the fuss made by its trusty followers was useless; moreover, I hated their habit of continuous lying (not to mention the dagger) and kept myself outside the whole concern". D'Azeglio, *Ricordi*, II, 344. "The Giovine Italia was a bad example and a bad school for Italy, owing to the absurdity of its political principles, the foolishness of its proposals, the perversity of its methods, and finally owing to the melancholy example set by its directing body, which, from a safe distance, sent to the shambles its open-hearted young fools who did not perceive that they were being knocked on the head, not for the sake of Italy, but in order to rejuvenate the now sterile zeal of its partisans." *Ibid.* p. 343. One advantage of d'Azeglio's memoirs is that he never leaves one in doubt as to whom he dislikes.

when, some years later, the moment came for regular war against them, Massimo d'Azeglio at the age of 49 was one of the first to volunteer for active service.[15]

Two points, however, must be remembered when estimating the value of his opinion: firstly, from the days of his boyhood to the end of his life, he hated the priests and the clerical rule; secondly, he was an Albertist; he believed that no one but Charles Albert could lead Italy, because no one else had an army. This belief was practical, but it led to his Italian patriotism becoming virtually narrowed down into Piedmontese patriotism. He was ready to push the interest of his king, Charles Albert, at the expense of any other sovereign.

On June 29th, 1843, d'Azeglio's sister-in-law, Costanza, wrote from Milan to her son that Massimo's vogue, both socially and as an artist, was on the down grade, and that therefore he was discontented and wanted to change his home.

If true, this speaks ill for the foresight of his contemporaries. Massimo was then at the very height of his powers: three years later, in 1846, he was to write a political book of European interest; in 1848 he was to hold an important command in the firing line; in the same year he refused the Ministry for Foreign Affairs in Tuscany, and a few months later, he refused the Presidency of the Council in Piedmont— to which country however he returned in 1849, to be its Premier during its three most perilous years. In after life he was the successful and popular ambassador in London where he made many friends. But while at Milan he was usually very busy either painting[16] or writing, and he preferred the society of Grossi and Manzoni and their circle, to any other.[17]

---

[15] He was able to go as a colonel on the staff of the Papal army, and did excellent service.

[16] In one of the earlier years he painted, between large and small, no less than twenty-four pictures; and, what is more, he seems to have sold many of his works satisfactorily.

[17] A reason which may account for his leaving Milan was the fact that he and his second wife could not live together. This was due

The fact, however, remains, that whatever the cause, d'Azeglio was now on the verge of a new advance in his life; the political phase. At the end of the year 1844, on his return to Milan after a visit to Balbo near Turin, he suddenly received a letter asking him to go to Rome in order to help an old friend out of a serious difficulty. This at all events is the story which d'Azeglio tells us in his memoirs, but his biographer, Signor Vaccalluzzo, thinks that, in reality, his going to Rome was part of a plan previously arranged with Balbo when they were talking over the *Speranze*, and that Massimo felt himself ripe for political conspiracy. Whatever his motives the following points are certain: that he settled his friend's difficulty in a day or two; that he stayed away from home for the next eight or nine months, and that then he was offered an extremely important, secret, political mission.

It was one evening in Rome[18] at the house of a Signora Clelia Piermarini, an ex-lady-in-waiting to Queen Christina of Spain, and now a Roman hostess of theoretical revolutionary leanings, that he was taken aside by an acquaintance— whose name he still, in 1864, conceals under an initial, but whom now we know to have been Dr Filippo Amadori—and, under pretence of a medical consultation, they entered on a long political discussion. Dr Amadori said to him that Gregory XVI was near his end; that on his death Romagna would break out into Mazzinian rebellion; that such rebellion involved useless suffering and must be prevented at all costs; that all sensible people were tired of the Carbonari and the Giovine Italia. And that what was required was that some trustworthy person should go round and persuade the people that risings merely injured the cause of freedom, and should, in fact, preach the doctrine of the Moderates to them; that for this purpose there must be found a new man and one of

to incompatibility of temper. But, as has been said, they lived "in tender separation"; they remained on the best of terms, and nearly all Massimo's most interesting letters were addressed to her.

[18] D'Azeglio, *Ricordi*, II, 426.

genuinely Moderate opinions, personally popular, well known in Italy: and, in short, that the influential members of the societies had decided to ask him, the Marquis Massimo d'Azeglio, to be their representative.[19]

D'Azeglio was astounded, for he had never yet belonged to a secret society, and this request amounted almost to making him the generalissimo, temporarily, of them all. But after some consideration he decided that it was his duty to accept it in order to try and prevent bloodshed; and by the first day of September, 1845, he was already on the road. Ostensibly he was travelling in search of documents for his projected romance about the Lombard League, of which he actually wrote eight manuscript chapters.[20]

This journey of d'Azeglio's through the Papal State in 1845 is one of the most important episodes of the period, because it led, firstly, to his celebrated interview with Charles Albert at the end of that year, and, secondly, to his writing *Degli ultimi casi di Romagna*, in which, rightly or wrongly, he pilloried the Papal government before Europe. It was during this round of enquiry that he obtained the material which five months later he used in *Degli ultimi casi* against Gregory XVI's administration. And in fairness to the Papacy one should

---

[19] "Was this a chance meeting? Was it true that d'Azeglio 'flew' from Milan to Rome—as he tells us—merely to help a friend out of a difficulty? To me this seems too small a motive for so serious and unpremeditated a step, which decided the whole remaining current of his life. Massimo d'Azeglio had his own projects in his head, and believed himself to be now ripe for a political mission, and it is not unreasonable to suppose that the invitation concealed a different reason. But it is strange that to this man—who always wished to be thought the most anti-secret-society person in our whole Risorgimento—the mission seems to have presented every appearance of being a conspiracy; and so, indeed, it appeared to the governments of that day, and not to them alone." Vaccalluzzo, p. 85. Vaccalluzzo also quotes Predari, Cantù, Torelli, and others, who believed that at this time d'Azeglio had taken part in a conspiracy. Vaccalluzzo, p. 342.

[20] D'Azeglio, *Lettere a sua moglie*, August 25th, 1845. (Letters to his wife.)

remember that his facts were all derived from revolutionists; that he himself always had been an opponent of all that was priestly; and finally, that he went out into the Papal State with the avowed purpose of persuading the Liberal subjects of the Pope to look to Charles Albert as their leader.

Owing to the help of his revolutionary friends he was able to travel from one end of the state to the other by *trafila*,[21] that is to say by the secret Mazzinian organisation which was spread all over the country. In every place of any importance there was a trusted man known as the *anello* or ring in the plate (*trafila*); and d'Azeglio on arriving there would enquire for him, would hold the necessary discussion with him, and then would obtain from him the name of the next *anello*. In his *Ricordi* he tells us that during all the years of their existence not one of these *anelli* was ever betrayed.[22]

By this means d'Azeglio went all round the Papal State; his route was Terni—Spoleto—Fuligno—Perugia—Colfiorito —Loreto—Ancona; and then through the temporarily peaceful province of Romagna; by Senegaglia—Pesaro—Rimini— Cesena—Forlì;[23] and after that he did some work in the state of Tuscany. His doctrines were those of the Moderates; he advised the people to give up insurrections and to substitute agitation for them; by agitation to train the Italian peoples politically—for the Italian peoples themselves needed re- forming and unifying before Italy could be unified. He urged boldly that Charles Albert must be regarded as the leader,

---

[21] Literally, "plate for wire-drawing". Vaccalluzzo says that this was a Mazzinian network; that d'Azeglio did not go to Bologna because Mazzini's organisation did not extend to that town.

[22] It is rather hard to understand how he could use Charles Albert's name as boldly as he did, unless he had first had some communication with him; this would probably have been through a third party. But d'Azeglio definitely denies that Charles Albert knew anything about his expedition until after it was over. *V.* d'Azeglio, *Ricordi*, II, 441; and his letters to his wife of September 9th and 15th.

[23] There is a good account of his doings in the *Nuova Antologia* for January 1927, Article by Marcus de Rubris. *V.* also *Archivio triennale*, I, 47.

because no one else had an army, and the Austrians could not be turned out of Italy without an army.

This Albertist propaganda is very important; and, at the risk of needless repetitions, stress must be laid on the fact that although d'Azeglio's tour may not have been foreknown to Charles Albert, in practice it had certainly become a piece of Piedmontese proselytism in the Papal State, and to a lesser extent in Tuscany. And it marks a change in the situation: the following change. In Italy there existed two states either of which might perhaps lead a national movement—Piedmont and the Papacy. Of these two the Papacy had been brought to the fore by Gioberti's *Primato*; but ever since the appearance of the *Primato* we find Balbo and d'Azeglio busy substituting Charles Albert for the Pope in the popular mind. The avowed purpose of d'Azeglio was to win over the Liberals and the revolutionists of the Papal State and teach them to look to Charles Albert as their leader when the great day should dawn,[24] although this attitude, of course, would be difficult to reconcile with their allegiance to the Pope. At the same time d'Azeglio was working to moderate and to constitutionalise, under the Piedmontese banner, both the Carbonari and the Mazzinian revolutionists. In fact the Reform movement which had been inaugurated by Gioberti under the shadow of the Holy See, was now, owing to Balbo and d'Azeglio, becoming a peaceful agitation under the aegis of Piedmont.

On the whole d'Azeglio's propaganda was very successful. Most people were sick of the Giovine Italia and ready to fall in with his views and become Moderates: it was only in Romagna that he became aware that there was a secret insurrection of some sort in progress. It broke out soon afterwards and is known as the Moto di Rimini.

But what struck him most of all was the profound and widespread distrust of Charles Albert. This became one of his

---

[24] We know this from Massimo himself, and also from Aurelio Saffi, the well-known Mazzinian, who lived in Forlì. *Archivio triennale*, I, 47–53, and other sources.

chief difficulties. His king was still regarded as "the traitor of 1821 and the executioner of 1833 ". In order to overcome these bitter recollections d'Azeglio was obliged to point out that it was Charles Albert's own interest to attack the Austrians. "Invite a thief to rob others and there is no reason to suppose that he will disappoint you."

It was actually in such terms[25] that he was reduced to defending his sovereign! Poor Charles Albert! During those years his apparently reactionary policy had taken in his own sympathisers more effectually than it ever took in Metternich. Yet he was pursuing the true course: most undoubtedly he was in the right.

The other great difficulty lay in persuading the people that before moving against Austria they must wait until the great moment should arrive. "When will that be?" they asked, and d'Azeglio could only reply, "God alone knows".

Nevertheless he was well satisfied with the results of his tour; well enough satisfied at all events to ask for an audience with Charles Albert, in order to ascertain that the king approved of the line that had been taken more or less in his name: d'Azeglio asserts that there had been no kind of pre-arrangement between them; that he himself was nervous as to his reception, and hailed as a good omen the fact that the audience was granted immediately.

This interview, though it exercises no decisive influence over the Risorgimento, is at all events a gleam of light upon its path. It reveals a fresh step in its progress and fills the wayfarers with renewed courage. "At that time", says Massimo,[26] "the king was a mystery, and however explicit may have been his later conduct, to the historian he will perhaps always remain partly a mystery. The secret of his life was well kept, and no one knew what might be its true purpose."

This audience was granted, according to Charles Albert's

---

[25] *Ricordi*, II, 430.   [26] *Ricordi*, II, 456.

custom, for six o'clock in the morning, which in winter meant before daybreak:[27] and when Massimo passed into the palace he found it all lit up and busy, whereas the town outside was still asleep. With beating heart he waited for a minute or two in the ante-chamber and then was shown into the king's room. As he entered, Charles Albert, who was standing in the bow-window, returned his bow courteously, pointed to a seat in the window-space and himself sat down just opposite.

"Even his appearance", says d'Azeglio, "conveyed an indefinable suggestion of the inexplicable. He was very tall and slender with a long pale face of habitually severe cast, but when speaking he had a very gentle expression, the tone of his voice was attractive and his words were affectionate and friendly. He exercised a real fascination on the person to whom he spoke, and I recollect that when he began his first phrases of polite enquiry after not having seen me for some time, with a kindness and a courtesy entirely his own, I was obliged to make a continual effort and to keep repeating to myself—Massimo, be on your guard!—in order to avoid being conquered by his manner and his words.[28]

"Povero Signore! He had a share of greatness and of goodness within him—why would he insist on believing in underhand methods?"

Massimo then poured forth the whole story of his own doings: "Your Majesty, I have been from town to town through a great part of Italy", and told Charles Albert that the people were tired of revolutions, but that they were convinced that without force nothing could be done, and that force existed only in Piedmont; moreover, that they must wait for the right moment. But the question was: would they be able to wait? When would the moment come? And he ended up by saying: "Now Your Majesty will tell me whether you approve or disapprove of what I have said and done?"

---

[27] Probably in the middle of October. *Nuova Antologia* for January, 1927, Article by Marcus de Rubris.

[28] Charles Albert was "shy of talking to a gathering of people, but fascinating in an interview". Genova di Revel, *Dal 1847 al 1855*, p. 6.

He had expected a guarded, indefinite reply, but instead of that the king showed no hesitation;

did not avoid my gaze but on the contrary fixed his eyes on mine, quiet but resolute, and answered: "Tell these gentlemen to remain peaceful; not to move; because at present there is nothing to be done; but let them rest assured that when the opportunity comes, my life, the life of my sons, my treasure and my army will all be spent in the cause of Italy".

This was nothing less than a confession of faith from Charles Albert himself, and in saying "Tell these gentlemen", he had authorised the dissemination of the good news throughout the party. D'Azeglio left him, he tells us, with his heart in a tumult, "over which there seemed to hover a great hope with outspread wings".

III. MASSIMO D'AZEGLIO'S MOVEMENT

Thus Massimo d'Azeglio had won for himself a great hope, and the right of spreading that hope among the Liberals throughout Italy. But the question remained to be answered: Would it ever be fulfilled? Was there any real probability that Charles Albert would ever lead his little nation of four and a half millions against the Austrian Empire?

Manifestly it was most unlikely, indeed almost impossible. D'Azeglio, and perhaps Charles Albert himself, realised that fact even before the end of the interview. When they parted— so d'Azeglio tells us—the king took leave of him with an embrace so cold and formal that it chilled him to the bone. Perhaps, as king, he feared that he had gone too far. But Massimo's whole soul was invaded by an icy wave of distrust; the same ineffaceable distrust that had attended every action of Charles Albert ever since the day in 1821 when he had unwittingly led Santarosa to his ruin. Up to the very end of his life Massimo never ceased regretting that distrust. Nineteen years after his audience he still felt a poignant remorse for having misunderstood his sovereign that morning.

Who could have told that...when, through me, he was offering his arms, his treasure and his life to the Italian people, I was doing him injustice in not being inwardly and immediately convinced by his offer? Who could have foretold that the great opportunity which seemed so far beyond all prevision in 1845, which, in fact, we both despaired of ever beholding, had been fixed by God for only three years later? And that in the war which seemed at that time so impossible, he was to lose his crown, and then his native land and his life; and that I myself, as Prime Minister to his son, should actually have the sad duty of signing the deed of interment for his burial in the royal tombs of Superga.

On leaving the royal palace, Massimo's first care was to send a complete account of the interview to his friends. It was written in cypher and ended as follows: *These are his words; but God alone knows his heart.*

It seemed, therefore, that Charles Albert's declaration of faith was little more than a passing vision. For one moment the tall, pale recluse had drawn aside the curtain which cloaked his real life; but as yet his real life was only a dream. He had bound himself to act "when the opportunity comes", but the question remained to be answered: could the moment ever possibly come? The hard facts seemed to say no. Piedmont with four and a half million people could not attack a huge Empire. The Piedmontese field force would be only about 70,000 strong, whereas Massimo d'Azeglio himself said that Italy would require some 200,000 trained troops to drive the Austrians out of their oblong stronghold of rivers and fortresses, the impregnable Quadrilateral: and, as the event proved, it cost between 30,000 and 40,000 casualties to do so in 1859.

Italia farà da se was a noble motto, the noblest imaginable, but at that time it meant *Piemonte farà da se*. As matters stood before 1846 Charles Albert would have to fight single-handed, disapproved by all the other princes and by the Pope;[29]

[29] Solaro della Margherita, whose judgment might perhaps rank first of all, was definitely of opinion that Charles Albert would not have taken any violent step but for the advent of Pius IX. "His common sense would have prevented his putting his hand to a

and the peoples, if they rose at all, would be rising mainly
against their own rulers, not against Austria.

The first necessary step was to arouse and unify the Italian
peoples, by means of agitation.

IV. THE BEGINNINGS OF AGITATION

It must have been very soon after the audience with the
king that Balbo and d'Azeglio settled down together at the
Villa del Rubatto near Turin to organise their new political
campaign. On October 27th, 1845, d'Azeglio wrote to his
wife, from whom he had now been absent for over a year:

You must have had about enough of my romance, but now
I have another work on hand which you did not expect, so you
will see that I have lost no time.... I am reserving the surprise for
you until I come to Milan.

He and his cousin had the great advantage of being entirely
in sympathy with one another; and, from Turin, Massimo
placed himself in touch with the more moderate Mazzinians,[30]
kept an eye on the state of affairs at Court, and on the other
hand set himself to curb the spirit of intolerance and the lack
of discipline of the impatient spirits in Romagna, where, to
the number of his former friends, had now been added

hazardous enterprise, if the death of Gregory XVI had not changed
the condition of Italy." Solaro, p. 541. "Naturally it made an
immense difference to him when the Papal influence justified his
enterprise among all classes of Italians and among the nations of
Europe. The exultation of all the Liberal party for Pius IX, though
mistaken, also reached the king, and for him it was entirely a
religious exultation...." *Ibid.* p. 541. He no longer doubted that
it was lawful for him, just as it was for the Supreme Pontiff. Count
Mortier, the French ambassador at Turin, was asked to write his
considered opinion as to Charles Albert's aims on northern Italy,
and he answered in a long despatch, of which the pith is in the
following sentences: "He (Charles Albert) will listen with pleasure
to dreams about the future of Italy which promise him a fine and
great rôle in history. But—I repeat it—at the moment of action it
will all fade away". This document is printed in *Rass. stor.* 1924,
p. 634.

[30] Vaccalluzzo, p. 94.

Minghetti and Farini. To all these people he made mention of his intimate talk with the king and distributed significant symbols such as Charles Albert's mystical medal representing a lion with his paw on an imperial eagle and the historic motto, *J'atans mon astre,* I await my star, an ancient motto of the House of Savoy dating from Amadeo VI.

His doctrine remained the same as heretofore; to unite the Italian people by means of agitation. Meanwhile one definite advantage had accrued to d'Azeglio from his famous audience; when he wrote to his wife, he was able to tell her that "un altro", another unnamed person, had approved of what he was doing. The king had authorised the starting of a review called the *Rivista Italiana.* And far more important was the book on which Massimo was now working with great secrecy and assiduity. This was *Degli ultimi casi di Romagna,* the best known of all his successes. It was to be nothing less than an outspoken criticism of the whole system of government and administration in the Papal State: in fact it was intended if possible to pillory the Papal system before Europe.[31]

At that point we must leave him.

[31] About this book Charles Albert was kept informed; indeed, afterwards Massimo could not remember whether the original suggestion to write it had come from himself or from the king.

Chapter XV

THE PAPAL STATE, 1840 TO 1845

(THE MANIFESTO OF RIMINI)

I. THE MOTO DI SAVIGNO 1843[1]

We must now return to the Papal State, to complete our sketch of the pontificate of Gregory XVI, by reviewing his last six years, those from 1840 to 1846. It is a period during which the two great contending influences are again looming large: the Revolution which, in Italy, had been temporarily discredited by Mazzini's failures in 1833 and 1834, is now re-arising under his leadership; at the same time Metternich, still all-powerful, starts upon a long series of unremitting efforts to save his vast "system", which in reality has just reached the beginning of its last days. Between these two extreme, uncompromising antagonists there is visible the new moderate, literary, reforming, federalist movement whose prophet was originally the Abbé Gioberti but which is now being converted into a pro-Piedmontese agitation by Balbo and d'Azeglio.

Within the Papal State, during the last six years of Gregory XVI, there occurred two risings, both in the Legations: the first in 1843, near Bologna, the Moto di Savigno, a comprehensive scheme which in practice degenerated into a few fights against local bands of insurgents; the second in 1845 near Ravenna, the Moto di Rimini, a far more serious movement because it discarded revolution and substituted for it a written manifesto as an appeal to Europe;

---

[1] For authorities there are: The general histories. Special article in the *Rassegna storica* of 1916 (Article by Menghini). Contemporaries such as Farini, Gualterio, Montanelli, Fattiboni and Masi (quoting Aglebert).

an appeal written by Farini and Montanelli and soon to be
confirmed and corroborated by their Piedmontese friend
Massimo d'Azeglio in his celebrated political pamphlet *Degli
ultimi casi di Romagna*.

It results therefore that during these six years the sovereign
authority of the Pontifical government was being attacked
simultaneously in three different ways: firstly, undermined
by the Revolution; secondly, overawed by the Great Powers,
especially Austria; and, thirdly, edged out of Romagna by
Piedmont.

It is only fair to preface the description by saying that in
1841 the Pope went on a most successful tour throughout
his dominions. He did not venture to visit Romagna,
but everywhere else he was received with the most enthusiastic demonstrations; with deputations, ovations, and with
every sign of joy. One knows that these receptions may
mean much or may mean little, and in this case it is hard to
say how much. At that time there were very few conspirators
in Umbria, but very many in the Marches—according to
Farini, himself a conspirator.

Firstly, to describe as shortly as possible the Moto di
Savigno in 1843. It marks the revival of the Revolution
throughout Italy. Some of the Mazzinians took part in it,
but it was not the work of Mazzini himself who still remained
rather discredited, especially in Bologna. By now there were
many revolutionary societies in existence, and in order to insure
united action the "Comitato misto", or mixed committee,
had been formed in Paris; at the same time, of course, the
Giovine Italia had its organisers not only in Paris but in
London and its usual *trafila* all over Italy; and it was in touch
with Malta. In 1843 this mixed committee evolved a plan
for a rising on a large scale.[2] At that moment the most

---

[2] Srbik, I, 124, quoting Raulich, accepts the statement of the
Italian writers, that in 1842 a Mazzinian betrayed to Metternich the
plans of a general rising to take place in 1844. There was to be
revolution in Italy and Sicily; movements in Spain and Switzerland,

inflammable districts were Calabria in the Kingdom of
Naples, and Romagna and Bologna in the north of the Papal
State, so a scheme was elaborated whereby both these centres
should rise simultaneously and receive assistance from
Tuscany. It was hoped that the movement would spread
throughout all three states, perhaps even as far as Leghorn
and Rome.

The result was almost ridiculous. Neither the northern
section around Bologna nor the southern section in Calabria
were willing to strike the first blow; each, in fact, was waiting
for the other to begin. After several cross-messages the
movement was still hanging fire, when suddenly the pontifical
police took the initiative, and surrounded a house inhabited
by Dr Pasquale Muratori and his young brother Saverio, the
leaders of the fighting men. The Muratori had plenty of
courage: they resisted, broke their way out, and were joined
by some of their adherents. But unfortunately these adherents
were not of a very desirable type. For this fact Farini blames
the Mazzinians.

"As there are few men nowadays ready for a desperate venture,"
he says, "these satellites of Mazzini threw themselves amid people
accustomed to party factions, and joined connection with cut-
throats, smugglers and even worse sets, of whom there are a good
many in Bologna."

Farini is certainly well informed, for, at that time, he was
himself an extremist and took an active part in this plot,
spending whole nights on horseback; but he was not impartial,
for he emerged from it a Moderate. However, it is stated that
some of these men rather disgraced the movement; that, after
taking the small place of Savigno, during their retirement they

as also in South Slavia and Poland, so as to keep Austria busy.
Metternich was forewarned; thus the movement was limited to that
of the Bandiera brothers, and of the small risings in the Papal State.
I have followed the accounts given by Farini, who was one of the
ablest of the revolutionists, and by Masi, who drew his information
from a narrative written for him by Augusto Aglebert, the Bolognese
revolutionary envoy to Tuscany. *V*. Masi, 1, 582.

killed the Papal officer who had surrendered to them. They then
fled to the mountains under command of the elder Muratori,
and tried to start guerilla war, a plan which, though disapproved
of by Mazzini, was the cherished dream of the exiled Italians
serving as Carlist officers in Spain. But the rebels soon found
that what had been so gloriously possible in the southern
Pyrenees, where every guerillero could rely on being concealed and fed in every village, was entirely impossible in the
Apennines owing to the lack of sympathy among the peasants;
and after some weeks of extreme hardship they escaped over
the frontier into Tuscany. Once there, they were kindly
received by Professor Montanelli and his friends, with whose
assistance they travelled right across the state and finally
embarked for Corsica.

By that time the movement had died out. Its chief result
was to prove to the government that it had failed to establish
the rule of law and submission, and on the other hand to
prove to many of the people that revolution was a mistaken
method of making their wishes known.

Among the prisoners and fugitives after this rising there
are several names that re-appear in history, and one or two of
them are rather noted for recklessness. Firstly there is the
well-known revolutionist Carlo Poerio, who became leader
of a rising in the following year; next we hear of a pale,
sensitive, dark-haired young man, Felice Orsini, then aged
only 25, experiencing simultaneously his first arrest and his
second or third love-affair, but already the same cool, con-
ceited, fearless patriot who ended his career in 1858 by
throwing a bomb at Napoleon III and the Empress Eugénie,
and hitting 158 innocent bystanders. But the most interesting
man in the Moto di Savigno is the Nizzard Ribotti, the exile
of 1831, lately returned to Italy, with a great reputation for
reckless courage, earned during his career as an officer in
Spain. On this occasion Ribotti, at all events, justified his
reputation. Some weeks after all was lost, when he was
returning to Bologna, he heard that three cardinals, Amat,

Falconieri and Mastai-Ferretti (Pius IX) were living together in a villa near Imola. Instantly a plan[3] struck him; he would capture them, hold them as hostages and march on Rome. For his ambitious enterprise he succeeded in collecting some 200 to 300 men, and received various promises of being joined by more. On the night of September 8th he started; he arrived outside the town of Imola only to find that all was silence along its walls, and that its gates were safely barred; at the next town, Castel-Bolognese, he fared no better; and when finally he reached the Cardinals' villa he merely discovered, in the words of one of his party, that "the cage was open and the three goldfinches were flown". It was fortunate that Mastai was not taken in this way; his capture might have changed the history of the Risorgimento. One may add that Ribotti's scheme was certainly somewhat ill-judged, seeing that Mastai and Amat were two of the very few Liberal cardinals, while Falconieri was a learned and kindly ecclesiastic.

After this disappointment Ribotti, nothing daunted, disbanded his companions and started single-handed on a fresh Mazzinian *trafila*, this time with the intention of raising Ancona and the Marches; but this attempt also proved a failure, although he actually penetrated as far as Rome.

II. REPRESSIVE MEASURES

The rising was followed by repression. It must be admitted that such exploits as those of Ribotti went far to justify repression; for although Nice was his birthplace and Spain his home, he was now ranging about the Papal State, on the *trafila*, trying to kidnap cardinals. A military commission was set up at Bologna with apparently almost unlimited powers. During the next year, 1844, it tried 116 people, of whom 103 were convicted and sentenced; of these unfortunates 21 were condemned to death, but only 7 actually shot; more than half of the remainder were condemned to the galleys for life

---

[3] *Rass. stor.* 1916 (Article by Menghini).

or for a term of years. Apparently only 13 were acquitted.[4]
These sentences were very severe for political offenders, more
especially as prison life was a terrible ordeal in those days.
As the severity of prison life is one of the principal accusations
against Gregory XVI it is necessary to give some account of it.
The following description is that of Tivaroni, who is a republican, but usually impartial:

The political prisoners of the Pontiff were treated in the same
way as political prisoners all over the rest of Italy. "At San Leo",
says Orsini, "the cells were horrible; narrow, with walls often over
a metre in thickness and the windows about three decimetres
(about a foot) wide; one sack of straw and one blanket per prisoner.
At Rome, in the new prisons, the cells were full of insects, the air
fetid; the food consisted of twelve ounces of bread and four of bad
minestra (vegetable soup) in hot water, for every twenty-four hours.
At Civita Castellana in 1845 there were 120 prisoners, 40 of them
condemned for participating in the affair at Viterbo in 1837, the
others for their share in the risings at Bologna and Rimini. Bodily
tortures (tormenti) d'Azeglio noted,[5] the scarcity of almost any
comfort, the unhealthiness of the prison, the methods of obtaining
confessions and revelations were matters of daily custom; the
prisoners were dragged from one prison to another in chains and
handcuffs and thrown into squalid and dark verminali (verminous
cells?), and subjected to the pains of hunger and thirst. In the
summer of 1845 those accused of political crime were moved from

---

[4] Tivaroni, *Domin. Austr.* II, 243, says that 116 were tried. Later
he gives (pp. 244–5) a list of 103 sentenced during the year 1844;
namely, 21 death sentences (? carried out, the remainder commuted to galleys for life); 16 to galleys for life; 7 to galleys for
twenty years; 33 to galleys for fifteen years; 26 to sentences of ten
years or less. One does not know whether the sentences for years
were reduced on the same scale as the death sentences; it is noticeable
that Vannucci, a violently anti-Papal writer, gives a much shorter
list of names, only 62 in all. *V.* Vannucci, *I martiri della libertà
Italiana*, p. 336.

[5] This sentence is quoted from d'Azeglio, *Degli ultimi casi*, p. 46.
Whether d'Azeglio meant merely the torments of discomfort, such
as cold or hunger, whether he meant the physical knocking about
which was and, even in modern nations, still is resorted to on such
occasions to obtain evidence, or whether there was anything worse
it is hard to say for certain.

prison to prison during the hottest hours of the day, and crossed
the city under a blazing sun covered with dust and treated like
common thieves.

When the court of Sacra Consulta pronounced a sentence
against the political prisoner, the sentence was seldom less than
twenty years at the galleys. In political trials the judges, all
ecclesiastics, considered themselves confronted by an enemy, and
treated him as such, and sometimes even reached the pass
of abusing him.[6] The ration of the political convict in the
fort of Paliano consisted only of two rolls weighing two ounces,
and a big spoonful of semolina pasta or rice cooked in water
and seasoned with melted lard; broth twice a year and minestra
always made of damaged material. Every prisoner put into the
common stock whatever he received from his family. Croci and
Lipari, both of them afterwards generals in the Italian army, spent
some years at Paliano, as also Major Berni, a Roman, and the
mathematician and philosopher Ercole Rosselli, brother of the
general; he bore the chains with spartan pride for a long time.
A man called Ciacca died there after thirty years of prison, refusing
any sort of assistance from a priest, and also a young man called
Cristallini of kindly and refined nature. (*Martiri pontifici*, by
Uno dei detenuti politici. *Pontifical martyrs*, by One of the political
internees.)

It took some courage to be a rebel! And descriptions such
as the foregoing are the best means of bringing that fact
before us.

It must be remembered, however, that Tivaroni prefaces
his description by saying that the prison system in the Papal
State was similar to that all over Italy.

Moreover, one point, at all events, is absolutely certain—
that few, if any of the other powers are in a position to cast
a stone against the Pope. The first half of the nineteenth
century was everywhere a period of terrible prisons. In

---

[6] It must be remembered that in this second paragraph Tivaroni
is apparently quoting from a book entitled *Pontifical Martyrs*, by
"One of the political internees". This book expresses the view of
the political prisoner, which is naturally a kind of retaliation. As a
matter of fact the sentences passed were often reduced, sometimes
even by two-thirds. The prisoner Ciacca above-named was possibly
a man sentenced for life during the Napoleonic régime.

Russia, for instance, we have a state of affairs of which the celebrated case of the nuns of Minsk is only one example out of thousands and thousands. In the British Empire the Norfolk Island convict settlement has left a record of organised cruelty which is comparable only with that of Russia. In Austria the stories of the Spielberg are familiar to us all. No doubt in most other countries a similar enquiry would reveal similar horrors.

Throughout the year 1844 the progress of the military commission kept bitterness alive in the Legations. Gradually but steadily it was getting through the 116 trials already mentioned, and publishing the sentences. One can imagine the feelings of the prisoners' relatives and friends.

Several retaliatory assassinations took place; but, on the whole, conspiracy was less general in the Legations, and almost at an end in the rest of the Papal State: in the state of Naples, however, the long-postponed risings had at length broken out; and in June 1844 there came the heartbreaking episode of the Bandiera brothers which stimulated both sides to renewed action. Fresh plots and preparations were begun in Romagna, while, in Tuscany, Professor Montanelli founded a new secret society, *I fratelli italiani*, a national association to combat the three egoisms: the personal, the municipal and the provincial.[7] On the other hand the Papal government was equally active. In fact, Romagna was now virtually under the rule of the various perambulating military commissions, a species of tribunal where those who had recently been shot at could have an unusually good chance of retaliation. But their methods were gradually bringing matters to a crisis.

During the first half of the year 1845 one of these commissions approached the Province and Legation of Forlì, but, to his honour, Cardinal Gizzi, the Papal Legate, refused to receive it there, so it proceeded to Ravenna. At Ravenna the Legate was Cardinal Amat, one of the three whom Ribotti

[7] Montanelli, p. 64.

had tried to kidnap. His action was remarkable; although he was Legate—that is to say, the Pope's own civil administrator —he issued passports to the five leading Liberals[8] so as to get them out of the state before the military commission arrived. He was recalled by the government, apparently on this account, but by that time the five Liberal leaders had made their escape. Contemporaneously we read about Cardinal Mastai-Ferretti (also one of Ribotti's three) that he had to suffer impertinences from the Papalini on account of his Liberal tendencies. Such indications as these three show that the crisis was coming: things were happening as they so often happen in struggles of this nature. The machine was beginning to break in Lambruschini's hand: even in high places there were good men and true who would no longer serve him. In fact both sides—the Papal and the Mazzinian—were giving proof of disliking the methods of their leaders, and this was a matter of European importance. It meant that a cog-wheel was running weak in the great system of Metternich.

III. THE MANIFESTO OF RIMINI 1845

Conditions were but little better when, in September, 1845, d'Azeglio appeared on the scene—as already described—with his peaceful Albertist propaganda: "cavaliere aggraziato", says Farini, "a knightly gentleman", and one "who was liked by many people". During his short stay he seems to have had a pacifying influence on those whom he met. But the military commissions aroused such hatred that, no sooner was d'Azeglio gone, than a fresh outbreak took place among the more extreme revolutionists.

[8] The five Liberals were Count Francesco Lovatelli, Count Tullio Rasponi, Dr Farini and Signors Foschini and Strocchi. At Ravenna two soldiers were killed, and the military commission, determined to make an example, executed two people and sent thirty-six to the galleys. *V.* Gualterio, vol. I, pt I, p. 214; d'Azeglio, *Degli ultimi casi*, p. 45; Tivaroni, *Domin. Austr.* II, 248.

It is known in history as the Moto di Rimini.[9] A rising was planned in Rimini and Faenza with arms from Marseille and leaders from Châteauroux. On this occasion, however, the less extreme members remained at home—perhaps owing to d'Azeglio's teaching—and Mazzini himself was either not enthusiastic (Orsini) or else was not greatly credited (Farini). The result was that, as often occurred, the unfortunate men on the spot were sacrificed. In Rimini several hundreds rose under a leader named Renzi, killed three Papalini, wounded seventeen, and plundered the bank, though apparently for political purposes only, and then sought refuge in Tuscany. But the real importance of the episode lay in the fact that some of the quondam extremists had refused to rise, because now they had definitely made up their minds to a moderate policy and had decided to draw up a remonstrance and send it to the Powers of Europe. They therefore issued what has since become known as the Manifesto of Rimini.

The Manifesto of Rimini marks another great step in the progress of reform as an alternative to revolution. It is a resuscitation of the Memorandum of the five Great Powers in 1831, when first they definitely recommended the Papal government to reform its administration. And as justification it quotes Seymour's protest almost in full. In fact this Manifesto of Rimini is virtually an appeal to the Great Powers to make the Papal government carry out the terms of the Memorandum or their equivalent. It is one of the four landmarks in the history of reform in the Papal State, from whence the movement spread to the rest of Italy, namely, the Memorandum of 1831; Gioberti's *Primato*,[10] published in 1843; this Manifesto of Rimini in 1845; and finally the Reforms of Pius IX during the years 1846–48.

[9] Andreini, who took part in this rising, gives rather a different account. I have followed that of Tivaroni (p. 250), who quotes Orsini, and that of Farini; the differences are of no great importance. *V. Rass. stor.* 1916 (Article by Commendatore Menghini).

[10] *v.* chapters VIII and XI.

The Manifesto was probably the work of Farini and Montanelli. It begins by a very bitter review of the Papal administration since 1815, but it ends up with a list of twelve claims which are comparatively moderate. A short summary of them is given at the end of this volume.

These twelve claims of the Manifesto of Rimini are important, firstly because they form the culminating point of the agitation, and secondly because they were used more or less as a programme by Pius IX when he started on his reforms.

The chief demands are:

An amnesty for political prisoners.

An improved system of government machinery. It is claimed that

1. Municipal or Town Councils should be freely elected by the citizens: and above them there should be

2. Provincial Councils: the Councillors to be selected by the sovereign out of the lists of three names (*terne*) sent up to him by each Municipal Council.

Above these there was to be

3. The Supreme Council of State: similarly its members were to be elected by the sovereign from lists of three names sent up to him by each Provincial Council: it was to sit in Rome.

The Supreme Council was to have important powers in financial matters. Its members were to superintend the national debt: they were to deliberate and vote on the estimates and budget: but on ordinary matters to have only a consultative vote, not to interfere unless they were consulted by the sovereign.[11]

A civic guard was to be raised and the foreign troops disbanded.

---

[11] The following summary shows the chief differences in the three principal schemes of reform proposed before 1848.

1831. *The Memorandum of the five Powers* (*v.* chapter VIII).
    Communal and Municipal Councils, to be elected by the people.
    A new Junta for the state finance, consisting partly of members

All civil, military and judicial posts to be open to laymen (secularisation of the great offices).

The political demands may be considered fairly moderate—if indeed the revolutionists ever intended to accept them as final. The authors evidently wanted to keep' in the good graces of the five Powers to whom they were addressing themselves. But the dangerous point in this scheme of Farini and Montanelli was that they also asked for a civic guard. This meant that they would have command of an armed force and consequently be able to dominate the whole situation.

These armed civic guards were always a danger to their own government and rarely so to foreigners. Having no

elected by the communal and municipal councils and partly of nominated members.

A Council of State, nominated by the Pope, but perhaps to include the Junta.

Besides these it suggested provincial councils to help the provincial administrators, which should consist, preferably, of members chosen from the municipal councils.

1845. *The Manifesto of Rimini.*

The Municipal (which presumably includes the communal) *Councils*, to be elected by the people and approved by the sovereign.

The Provincial Councils, to be selected by the sovereign from terne (lists of three) presented to him by the municipal Councils.

The Supreme Council of State, to be selected from terne presented to him by the provincial Councils. This Council to have deliberative powers in matters of finance, but only Consultative in other matters.

1847, October 4th. *When Pius IX set up his Consulta in the Papal State.* (Not included in this volume.)

A consultative assembly of twenty-four members plus a president and vice-president. They were selected by the sovereign from terne sent to him by the Provincial Councils, which were themselves selected by the sovereign from terne sent to him by the Communal Councils.

But Pius did not introduce the elective principle into his Communal Councils. They remained co-opted, as directed by Bernetti's edict of July 1831. But he made various additions to their powers. For instance, his Consulta had the right of being heard as to the question of reforming or re-organising the Communal Councils.

military tradition and very little discipline they were swept by
every passing gust of political passion.

The important point about this Manifesto of Rimini is that
it represents the definitely thought out scheme of the Moderates
in 1845, the year before Pius IX came to the throne. During
the next two years, 1846–7, Pius dealt with nearly all the
claims here raised, but by then the people were very far from
being satisfied, and demanded more and more after each concession. This was partly due to the change of circumstances;
but it is a striking instance of how a revolution usually tends
to pass into the hands of extremists. Undoubtedly this forms
some justification for the views of Gregory XVI, but not for
his methods of government.[12]

[12] For a more complete summary of the Manifesto of Rimini, v.
p. 277.

Chapter XVI

MASSIMO D'AZEGLIO'S BOOK
DEGLI ULTIMI CASI DI ROMAGNA

During the Moto di Rimini (1845) the Legations had been in revolt, but the remainder of the Papal State had remained peaceful. Nevertheless the government was in a disagreeable position. The revolutionists had issued the Manifesto of Rimini appealing to the Great Powers; and very soon their protests were to be supported and reiterated by the Piedmontese propagandists, Massimo d'Azeglio and his Liberal friends, acting with the approval of Charles Albert: d'Azeglio was hard at work upon his proposed pamphlet, *Degli ultimi casi di Romagna*, which was to criticise the recent events in Romagna, and to proclaim publicly the shortcomings and the crimes of the Pontifical government.

This might be called a bold step on his part. He meant to pillory the Papal government before the whole world, and to put his name to the accusations so as to attract attention. It would probably involve him in a great deal of unpleasantness, social as well as political, but he was ready to lay his case before public opinion both at home and abroad. Perhaps the chief value of Massimo d'Azeglio at this moment consisted in his realising better than other men the force of public opinion both national and international.

Before completing his book he decided to show it to some of the Liberals in northern and central Italy, and already on December 16th, 1845, he was able to write to his wife that Balbo and "another"—no doubt the king—had seen and approved of the manuscript as far as it had gone. On December 25th he held a meeting at Balbo's house and read a portion to Lisio, Villamarina, Provana and Sauli, all Piedmontese friends or relations of his, whose names were well known in Turin;[1] later on at Cesena he held another reading to which Amadori and Gasparre Finali were invited; then, in Professor Montanelli's house at Pisa,[2] another reading to which Giusti came: and, on January 21st, 1846, he discussed it for the fourth time in Florence at the house of Count Gino Capponi. In this way he had obtained a large body of Liberal opinion on his scheme before publishing it, and had answered a good many objections. Most of the objections were raised by Montanelli and Giusti, but they resulted in only a few corrections—notably one from the passages in which he censures the insurgents in the Moto di Rimini; he now omitted the word "colpevole" meaning "guilty", because that epithet would have hurt the feelings of Farini, Canuti, Mamiani and others who had taken part in the rising.

The next difficulty was to get the book printed. This could not be done at Turin as it would have involved Charles Albert in the scheme, so d'Azeglio made for Tuscany, the "Refugium peccatorum" as he named it—most suitably during this period—and managed to get the printing done secretly in Florence.[3]

In March 1846 *Degli ultimi casi di Romagna* made its appearance. It was not much more than a fine pamphlet, being wisely restricted to 100 pages of small size so as to be easily hidden, and was dedicated to Balbo, just as Balbo's *Speranze* had been dedicated to Gioberti. Both the manner and the matter of the book were excellent. Krauss has rightly called it "the first real political writing that Italy then saw, and one that had definite political aims". But certainly it is not, as

---

[1] Guglielmo Moffa di Lisio, Emanuele Pes di Villamarina, Luigi Provana del Sabbione and Luigi Sauli d'Igliano.

[2] *V*. Montanelli, pp. 116–17.

[3] De Rubris says that the publishing was done by a courageous French publisher, Le Monnier, an exile since 1830, and that d'Azeglio was very possibly in touch with Vieusseux, the founder of the celebrated library in Florence. Vieusseux was half a Swiss and very well known among the Liberals. *V. Nuova Antologia for 1927* (Article by Marcus de Rubris).

some people seem to have supposed, an impartial opinion about the Papal government written by an unprejudiced outsider: it is in reality an excellent Liberal party pamphlet: the best of its day.

It may be divided roughly into two parts: firstly, that which concerns the Moto di Rimini, and, secondly, his criticisms of the Pontifical government.

He begins by condemning the Moto di Rimini and all other partial risings; and so important did he consider this theme that he actually spent some twenty pages on it.

"The events in Romagna", he says, "are merely part of the whole question of Italian independence: a question which might be compared to a great powder-mine underlying all Italy: a mine which no one has the right to fire except by agreement of the majority."

Moreover he adds (p. 7), in reality there is no tyranny in Italy:

To call the existing governments of Italy tyrannical is a piece of Alfierian childishness, just as it is a piece of childishness worthy of a Caesarian imperial poet to fix the name of robber on everyone who wants independence.

This statement of d'Azeglio's is another remarkable testimony in favour of the rulers of the Italian states, who, except Leopold of Tuscany, are so often described as petty tyrants.

So, he continues, there will never be a rising *en masse* in Italy because the poor, who are always at grips with the obstacles of life, have too much common sense: they know that a universal rising is impossible and that small revolts have no chance of success.

He goes so far as to say that no national rising has ever been successful without help from outside: Spain and Greece have lately won their freedom; but Spain won it by the help of the Duke of Wellington's army, and Greece won it by means of the English and French fleets at Navarino. Meanwhile the small Italian insurrections merely excite ridicule, and do we not want to find means whereby our misfortunes may arouse pity just as it is aroused by the cases of Poland and of Ireland our sisters (their positions, if not precisely similar to ours, are at all events analogous in many points): I mean the indignation which generous minds feel against those who oppress others: and the ancient, honourable compassion that is a comfort and a hope, not an insult to the oppressed....[4]

D'Azeglio's purpose was to preach the doctrine that agitation was a far superior weapon to insurrection:

Ireland and Poland! Why do they obtain this sympathy? Because they suffer more than we do, and more worthily and more tangibly. The opinion, the sympathy and the wishes of the whole of civilisation is with them, and nowadays these feelings are powerful allies. But what about ourselves? We are merely laughed at.

Moreover these partial risings are not merely failures; they are actually harmful. For one reason, "they may draw upon us the fearful calamity of an Austrian invasion". It looks rather as if Massimo foresaw a rising on the death of Gregory XVI and thought that, by means of peaceful agitation before Europe, the Legations might perhaps be joined to Piedmont, provided that they were not already undergoing an Austrian occupation.

Perhaps the best way of extracting the pith of this book is to ask the same test questions which were applied to the works of Gioberti and Balbo: what answer does it give concerning the three main problems of the period, those relating to the Independence of Italy, the Unification of Italy, and the introduction of Liberal institutions? And what solution does it suggest for the two main difficulties: the position of the Pope, and the inter-state jealousies?

As to independence, he says definitely that that is the first and the greatest necessity: far more important and a far more stirring war-cry than the demand for Liberal institutions.[5] The way to win it is by agitation.

[4] P. 18.
[5] "There may indeed be diversity of opinion in Italy as to the best way of re-ordering the individual states and as to the forms of

As to the unification of Italy he gives no practical advice. The idea of a confederation is not even mentioned. This is a very noticeable omission.

One feels that his book represented Piedmontese and Tuscan Liberalism, and had the approval of Charles Albert, so that his silence as to the proposed confederation was probably due to its being unpopular in Piedmontese circles. And this became a very serious question in 1847 and 1848 when Pius IX tried to unite all Italy by means of a confederation—especially in 1848 during the campaign against Austria. For various reasons the Piedmontese never wanted to be bound by any federal treaty. As to the introduction of Liberal institutions, Massimo d'Azeglio says that they, like independence, must be won by agitation.

And he adds boldly that the Pope must become a constitutional king: "the Pope reigns but does not govern" must be his guiding principle; this reform, he considers, was partly or wholly promised in 1831 (the Memorandum).

But he feels that this would be so great a change that at first it seems impossible,

but with a prudent devolving of powers, if it be guided as I have said, by a love of justice, with a firm will and a supreme loyalty

government, but from Trapani to Susa you may ask any Italian if it is a good plan for Italy to free herself from the dominion and influence of the foreigner, and no one, thank God, will answer anything but yes, or refuse to put his hand to the work.... In the century in which the slavery of the individual is an object of universal abomination...who could affirm that what is considered unjust between individuals can be just between nation and nation...." d'Azeglio, *Degli ultimi casi*, p. 11. As a matter of fact d'Azeglio probably overstated the case. When the crucial moment arrived in 1848, throughout the kingdom of Naples there was very little real self-sacrificing enthusiasm to drive the foreigners out of Lombardy and Venetia. Even some of the most reputable Liberals cared more for "arranging a Liberal assembly" in their own state than for war or even for confederation against Austria. This was the opinion of Baron Griffini, who was sent to Naples by the Tuscan government to negotiate an Italian confederation: he found it quite hopeless.

of intention, the government of Rome might, if it wishes, obtain what at first sight seems very difficult, not to say impossible.[6]

He then goes on to say, that the Pontifical edifice is crumbling, and that those beneath it must choose between prudent counsels or the danger of the roof falling in on them. From the above quotations it will be seen that even so anti-ecclesiastical a Liberal as d'Azeglio regarded the conversion of the Pope into a constitutional monarch as a very difficult operation indeed. He saw its difficulties far more clearly than Protestants such as Bunsen and Seymour. In fact he says on the next page that if the Pope considered it too dangerous a change he should at all events grant some of the lesser reforms.

Finally, one may ask: if d'Azeglio did not approve of a confederation or a republic, what did he himself suggest? What are the people to do? He says: agitate firstly for the general national aim, namely independence; but agitate also within the individual states. And though he does not say so in this book, one knows that his propaganda was always Albertist. He wanted all Italy to be agitating openly for independence, and to look to Charles Albert as their leader.

The second portion of this little book is devoted to criticisms of the Pontifical government, especially in connection with its repressive policy in Romagna.

The only verdict possible on these pages is that they represent the anti-government point of view. Indeed it would have been impossible for d'Azeglio to represent anything else: and, although he had lived in the Papal State, he had no experience of Romagna except for such items as he had picked up from revolutionists and Liberals during a journey of a week or two in 1845 along the Mazzinian *trafila*. All the principal points in his book figure also in the work of Farini, who was one of the original organisers of the rising. But these were both great men—as is proved by their writings and by

[6] P. 66.

their subsequent careers—and some of their accusations carry weight. Thus d'Azeglio as long as he is criticising the Papal government and not merely engaged in defending the rebels of Rimini, makes some very definite points against the administration of Gregory XVI.

His scheme is to prove that reform is absolutely necessary; the gist of his contention is: We must reform or die! and any reform must necessarily take the shape of grants of Liberal institutions. How often has this train of argument been used in the history of other nations! It is always easy to make a strong and perfectly true case against any unrepresentative government.[7] D'Azeglio draws up an array of some fifteen or more accusations of which the following eight are perhaps the most important:

He begins by blaming the system whereby the Pope delegates his authority to so many Legates and Delegates in the provinces. He says that the Romagnols could suffer a tyrant but not an infinity of tyrants.

In law: he says that the laws require codifying and that the whole legal system should be reformed.[8] There seems to be

---

[7] There were people of all types who accused the Piedmontese of ambition and said that d'Azeglio's work, both his tour of Albertist propaganda and his *Degli ultimi casi*, was simply designed to win the Legations for Piedmont. The following is the opinion of a representative of the Roman republican assembly of 1849: "Although Piedmont, by means of Gioberti, Balbo and Azeglio, professed to advise the Roman subjects to work on legal lines, and although they appeared to be Guelfs, yet this deceived no one; the pretence was so crude. . . . Meanwhile the Piedmontese wanted to have all the Legations; to the rest of the country they aspired as to a possible goal given certain political conditions—the election of the Duke of Genoa to be King of Sicily, and the agents sent into Romagna, Rome and Calabria, leave no room for doubt on the subject". *Archivio triennale*, 1, 55.

[8] Massimo probably knew little about law; but Pellegrino Rossi condemned the whole Papal system of law and justice without reserve. He said that between 1843 and 1846 inclusive some 25,000 cases of criminal or correctional nature had occurred and only 5000 had been decided. Paris A.E. Rome, 1847–8.

no doubt that that was true. Gregory XVI had issued a code in 1832, but that can only have been a partial measure.

Finance: he says that the finances were entirely in the hands of state officials both for taxation and for expenditure: that the Treasurer, an ecclesiastic, was not *obliged to publish returns* (!). It was known that there was a deficit each year but that was all. This was true: there was no popular control over finance and actually no budget for ten years! He says that a deficit existed owing to the expenses caused by the rebellions. True; but as a matter of fact the sums borrowed were small and so was the deficit.

Railways: that Gregory XVI had refused to have any. This also appears to have been true. He was not the only ruler who feared the advent of the railway, and especially of its vast company promotions, which recently had caused scandals in Paris. D'Azeglio adds that at the time of writing he was informed that the railways were to be started after all. Unfortunately, however, Gregory XVI died three months later, before any scheme had been initiated.

The Customs: that they were too high, and that they were farmed out. Whether they were too high is a question for Tariff Reformers. It seems to be true that their collection was farmed out, but this miserable system had been adopted only during the rebellion, because at that moment the credit of the state was temporarily so low that loans were almost unobtainable.[9]

The Swiss regiments: that these were paid at a higher rate than the Italian regiments and were hated by every one. The Swiss, of course, were the traditional defenders of the Holy See, as previously of the French Bourbon kings, but it was very regrettable that they should have been employed in preserving law and order, because in practice it meant that the Pope was paying foreigners to hold down his Italian subjects. It must be remembered, however, that in 1848 the Swiss proved themselves to be the best fighting units in the

[9] Tivaroni, *Domin. Austr.* ii, 6.

Papal service. They did splendid work against Austria and lost about a third of their number at the battle of Vicenza.

The Centurioni: of course he attacks this universally-hated police force:

A vile generation—obscure men of irregular and criminal life, given to idleness, rioting and tavern-rows; but it proclaims its devoted loyalty to the Pope, to his government, to the faith and to religion. It is allowed to commit any violence against political enemies, and invents false accusations against them of alleged conspiracies and murders.

The Military Commissions: these were the Papal substitute for the courts-martial when the country was in rebellion, and Massimo d'Azeglio condemns them without mercy. One can only say that by their very nature they were party tribunals.

The above eight [10] headings seem to make an overwhelming case for reform: also for the introduction of popular control, at all events in matters of finance.

But whatever the weight of d'Azeglio's accusations, the true case against the Pontifical government was not what it did, but what it was. It was a bureaucracy which refused representative institutions. All its highest offices were held by ecclesiastics, so that any young man about to enter the government service found himself faced by the following dilemma: either he must enter the Church and renounce marriage, or else he must resign all prospect of ever occupying

[10] D'Azeglio included six or seven more, but they are not at all so convincing. He says, for instance, that the government discouraged the setting up of banks: but one rather doubts whether the banks wanted to come there, just then; that Gregory XVI would not hear of Agricultural Associations: but this is mere propaganda on the part of Massimo, because he was perfectly aware that the Agricultural Association meetings and the scientific congresses were used chiefly for talking pan-Italian politics. He says that there was no commerce although the land was rich with mines: but those mines are still undiscovered; that the ministers' salaries were too high and their officials too many: but this last accusation is one that has often been made against every government in the world, and in this case one can only say that the total expenditure, at all events, was small.

the highest appointments; and it was a matter of common complaint (at all events) that the junior posts were ill paid.

D'Azeglio ends up with the following summary of his advice to Liberals.[11] No revolution; but agitation all over Italy. Agitation in each state in order to win free institutions from the princes. Later on there will come the military movement to drive out the Austrians: for that is the true national purpose. Evidently he meant that the people of each state should capture their government and then use it against the Austrians: but apparently he did not believe in forming a confederation.

In the existing conditions, he says, it is useless to attack the Austrians: there would be no chance of success without a force of 200,000 men and 200 guns.

Once again he preaches the advantages of agitation over revolution, and one wonders how far he afterwards went in assisting this agitation against Pius IX.

When, in a nation, everyone recognises that an aim is just and everyone wants it, then that aim is already achieved; and in Italy all the most important work for our regeneration can be done with our hands in our pockets....I merely say that the greater the number of people who discuss our affairs publicly and wisely and protest in any way against the injustices inflicted on us, the more rapidly and happily shall we advance on the way to our regeneration.[12]

In his final paragraphs he says confidently that the agitators will have the sympathy of the civilised world and that their work will have the blessing of God.

This detailed and tabulated condemnation of the Papal government made a great sensation throughout Italy, the more so as it came openly and avowedly from a Piedmontese noble whose father was the head of a Jesuitical society, the *Amicizia cattolica*, whose elder brother was a Majordomo of the king, and whose second brother was a Jesuit; and who apparently was imperilling his own successful career by publishing these statements. It was known to have been printed secretly and consequently it was bought far and wide.

"They write to me", said d'Azeglio to his wife in his letter of March 22nd, 1846, "that the whole edition of 2000 copies is sold out—it will be reprinted in various places and also a French translation—From Turin they write that owing to the Nunzio it is impossible to print the book, but that I am to *send all the copies that I can.* The King likes it and says that the only thing required is that they should take my advice."

In spite of his popularity in Florence the Tuscan government refused to allow him to remain there, which made him still more popular. Lord Holland and the Dutch Minister in Florence were among the first to sympathise with him. But Milan with its Austrian rulers could no longer be his home, so he returned to Piedmont, where Charles Albert allowed him to take up his abode but told him not to come to Court. Certainly to sign a political pamphlet had its drawbacks in those days, in spite of the fact that it brought renown.

In reality it is very hard to know how far d'Azeglio's accusations are true: but the Papal administration was certainly at a low ebb during the last years of Gregory XVI. The following description is given by Bishop Pelczar, who is a broad-minded writer, but naturally a defender of the Papacy:

The clergy,[13] formerly so eager about reform, had become lukewarm in its zeal and negligent in its studies: moreover the secret societies had netted in a group of the unwary, so that even Mons. Cocle, Archbishop of Patrasso, and confessor to Ferdinand II, was enrolled among the Carbonari—the nobility, in most cases, was given up to idleness and, as it lived in the towns, would squander in riotous living the money which the poor and ignorant people paid in small rents.[14] Consequently the sowers of discord had a fine field among the nobles and proved equally successful among the professors and lawyers who were always

[13] Pelczar, I, 101.

[14] Deschamps, *l.c.* T. III, 161. Even in Rome some bishops, as for instance Foscoli, Calcagnini and Monticelli, caused scandals among the people. (Note by Bishop Pelczar.)

thinking about the unification of Italy: and regarded the Pontifical government with a special bitterness because it would not entrust its principal offices to anyone except ecclesiastics. On their part the lower officials were not impervious to bribes, nor the army to conspiracy—It is not surprising, therefore, that the worst elements from outside the state prevailed, and fused themselves with those within.

In the first days of 1846 the Pope underwent a successful operation for cancer in the face.

Chapter XVII

SUMMARY OF THE SITUATION DURING THE FIRST HALF OF 1846

The beginning of the year 1846 may be regarded as the final moment before the first great crisis in the Risorgimento. It will be best, therefore, to follow the example of the Italian historians and to give a short résumé of the situation during those six months: one dealing more especially with the chief forces already mentioned in the Introduction of this book as passing through the years of trial, 1846 to 1849, namely: The Revolution (Mazzini); The Conservative reaction (Metternich); Piedmont (Charles Albert); The Papal State (Pius IX).[1]

I. THE REVOLUTION

The Revolution of course had agents everywhere in Europe, but for Italy it was mainly dependent on Mazzini. During the previous five years his value as a leader had been vindicated. At first in 1836 he had been compelled to leave Switzerland and had retired to England utterly dispirited and filled with doubt, and so completely discredited as a man of action that he could no longer raise supporters. In fact for nearly four years the Giovine Italia had remained in other hands than his. But during that interval it had languished and virtually died away. Not until Mazzini again became its inspirer and director did it start on its second period of activity. One may say that the signal was given when, in 1839, he wrote to his friend Lamberti: "we are not doing our duty".

On March 1st, 1840, they started on the great work of

---

[1] In the Introduction there are five chief influences whose development is traced in this volume: but we need not recapitulate that of the fifth, the Moderate movement.

resuscitating the Giovine Italia[2] and the Giovine Europa, and rebuilding the belief in Italy. At that moment Mazzini was in London, and Lamberti was in Paris where he was soon joined by Giannone. Most of the men of 1831, even Fabrizi,[3] who had now seen active service in Spain and Portugal, refused to rejoin the society. But to Mazzini they were already a generation of the past. His appeal was addressed to the young and it is one which expresses the very spirit of nationality:

This is the banner of youth—your banner. That one generation of young men should achieve its triumph has never been said. But this has been said: that one generation shall receive it from another until the day of victory.

This second great period of activity in the history of the Giovine Italia lasted from 1840 to the Revolution of 1848, when (on March 5th, 1848) the members broke up the Society and transformed it into the Associazione Nazionale Italiana, because many of them were going back to fight in Italy.[4]

During the years 1840 and 1841 Mazzini reorganised his fellow-countrymen all over the world.[5] The Italian exiles and

[2] "The Giovine Italia is the name in being, the name which has caused most fear to the governments and has been made holy by our martyrs: the name which is recognised abroad by the Poles and the Germans with whom some day we must make fresh ties....We must be men with a religion, not merely a faction: in short we must be like the early Christians...." Mazzini, *Scritti* (E.N.), vol. XIX, letter of August 30th, 1840. Members swore to consecrate their lives to the Society "ora a sempre", now and for ever.

[3] Fabrizi, one of four exiled brothers, had served in Spain and Portugal and on his return had settled in Corfu and then in Malta, and had formed the Legione Italica (the Italic Legion), a corps of fighting men. His plan for freeing Italy was to carry on guerrilla warfare such as he had seen in the mountains of Spain. This plan was strongly condemned by Mazzini, who, among other reasons, objected to a scheme which did not include the towns. *V.* Mazzini, *Scritti* (E.N.), XXIII, 30.

[4] *V.* Mazzini, *Scritti* (E.N.), XIX, vii; also vol. XX.

[5] During these years Lamberti kept a Protocol or summary of the letters which he sent out or received, and thus we now possess "the complete documentation of that vast work of conspiracy under-

emigrants were to be found in every country. In Paris, therefore, and in New York and Monte Video, Mazzini placed his central committees for Europe, for North America and for South America respectively. In Paris, Giannone was president (February 1841), and Lamberti was secretary under the name of Raimondo Montecuculi.[6] In every other town containing Italians they organised a revolutionary committee, with a president, a treasurer and a secretary, working under an assumed name. In this way they gradually formed a network of revolutionary committees all over the world:[7] in towns of France, Switzerland, Spain; in Brussels, Constantinople, Algiers; and throughout the New World; and, of course, in many of the towns of Italy. Mazzini himself, as director of the whole organisation, remained with his "section" in London.

The duties of the local committees were to control the Ordinatori (affiliators of new members); to raise and send in the local subscriptions to the Central Committee; to forward all revolutionary letters and disseminate their newspaper, the *Apostolato Popolare* (started June, 1840). Many of the members who took these risks were poor Italian workmen, for the society was now democratic. In 1831 it had béen rather more in the hands of the intellectuals.

As to the policy of the movement one of the most important

taken by Mazzini and his companions in faith during the whole of the second period of the Giovine Italia". This was an invaluable work of Lamberti. *V.* the *Protocollo della Giovine Italia.*

[6] In New York the president was Dr Felice Foresti, an ex-prisoner of the Spielberg; the secretary was Giovanni Albinola, who worked under the name of Masaniello. At Monte Video, where there were many Genoese, the secretary was G. B. Cuneo, a Genoese exile of 1833; the committee worked under the name of Girolamo Olgiati. Garibaldi was a member and was in touch with Mazzini. Already in March, 1842, the New York Central Committee was subscribing for 500 copies of the *Apostolato*, now in its fifth number, and it had started a school, and was beginning to employ travellers. *V.* Mazzini, *Scritti* (E.N.), XXIII, 90.

[7] Mazzini, *Scritti* (E.N.), vol. XIX, letter of September 29th, 1840.

characteristics is its exclusiveness. In order to set up a united republic Mazzini was compelled to exclude and oppose all other movements, such as Gioberti's federalism, Charles Albert's monarchism, and the Pope's authority, not only temporal but also religious. Moreover he felt it necessary to have one large society instead of a plethora of small ones, so, as a general rule, he would not allow the Giovine Italia to work in alliance with other societies, nor its members to have any action in common with theirs. The Giovine Italia was to represent a great national proselytising religion with branches all over the world.

It is necessary—although one rather regrets it—to record Mazzini's working agreement during these years with the *Christian Alliance* of the United States, because this shows that already, before 1846, he meant to make an end of the power of the Papacy both temporal and spiritual. It is best to let him describe this curious alliance between them in his own words :[8]

This work is a secret alliance of the *Giovine Italia* with the vast Protestant societies of the United States, for the purpose of over-throwing the temporal power of the Pope and recognising and causing to be recognised the Unity, Independence and Liberty of Italy. You know me and my religious beliefs which abominate equally both Catholicism and Protestantism. I have far wider hopes for Europe and for Italy. But there is ground common to us both: something which we both wish to destroy. We want to overthrow what exists and arrange matters so that the conscience of each individual freely expresses his belief.

A little further on he gives the terms of the alliance:

The methods of this Society (the Christian Alliance of the United States) will be two: free schools on the model of ours, in North and South America, in Europe, and in the Levant; and a distribution of books. For these schools the Society will supply the funds; but they will be in our hands. The books on religion, history, and literature will be proposed by us, and we are always to be consulted on the choice even of those which the Protestants

[8] Mazzini, *Scritti* (E.N.), XXIII, 269, 271.

themselves have proposed. Depôts of the said books will be established in various places. This will be the Society's action before the public. But the officials of the Society, who will be chosen from those among the Protestants who have fully grasped the bond between the two Societies, will use the discretion allowed them and will provide substantial means towards assisting our work.

Moreover, the Alliance was to spread Mazzini's cause by means of the press, and to try and influence the great forces in Europe—especially the Protestant Powers—to support non-intervention in Italy.

This agreement was carried out for some years. In December, 1845, the agent of the Alliance was still working in Italy.[9]

Thus outside Italy Mazzini had laboriously built himself up an immense organisation all over the world. Certainly as an organiser of propaganda and propaganda machinery he was unrivalled. But within Italy itself he does not seem to have been regarded as a good director of rebels; indeed it would have been very difficult for him to direct them from England.

During the years 1843–5 inclusive, there were four risings: the Moto di Savigno (1843), the fight at Cosenza (1844), the death of the Bandiera brothers (1844) and the Moto di Rimini (1845). None of these was organised by Mazzini: in none of them did the Giovine Italia take part officially.

Except perhaps the Moto di Rimini they were no better planned than Mazzini's Savoy attempt in 1834. Each one in turn seemed more heart-breaking than the others, and such a series of tragedies could not continue. Their chief result was to disgust the people with revolution and to drive them into the Moderate camp. For the next two years they follow the advice of Gioberti and Massimo d'Azeglio, and substitute agitation for insurrection.

In 1846, therefore, notwithstanding the widespread dis-

---

[9] Mazzini, *Scritti* (E.N.), xxviii, 213; *Protocollo*, iii, 350.

content and consequent unrest throughout Italy, the Revolution had been temporarily superseded by the Moderate and Albertist movements. And Mazzini himself evidently realised that the moment was unpropitious for armed risings.

The protocol of the Giovine Italia during these months[10] is not very exciting to read: most of its communications are devoted to finding work or money for revolutionists abroad. But some of them are interesting—as, for instance, the following entry of March 18th, 1846, referring to a letter from a well-known revolutionist, Dr Pietro Sterbini, then living in exile at Marseille:[11]

They (in Marseille) are certain that we (at headquarters) must be meditating some way of causing a rising in Italy: we should know what a propitious moment this is, and how great is the importance of supporting Poland. They (in Marseille) are busy with something of this sort and are collecting war-seasoned men. The only thing lacking is money for arms and ships. Consequently they are having recourse to us and are sending us Grandi, one of the leaders of the late rising at Rimini (1845).

Mazzini's reply is practical:

There is no money; and if there were any I could not conscientiously give it to them, for in small affairs of this sort the party only discredits itself without the slightest probability of success. Our people do not move except for an important and effective action; and such an action must either start from within Italy or, if from outside Italy, it must have the advantage of favourable circumstances. And these circumstances—although the Polish movement has fallen—will come perhaps sooner than is commonly supposed.

He spoke no doubt with "inside knowledge", and this last opinion perhaps referred to the growth of revolution in France and Austria; but in Italy[12] the Moderate policy was undoubtedly predominant for the time being.

---

[10] *Protocollo*, IV, 8, 35.

[11] *Ibid.* p. 24; *v.* also Saffi, *Ricordi*, I, 142.

[12] In May, 1846, Cavour wrote an article to the *Revue nouvelle* in the course of which he said: "En Italie une révolution démocratique n'a pas de chances de succès. Pour s'en convaincre il suffit d'analyser

In 1846, therefore, "the united Italian republic" was again before the world; but for some time to come the party of action in Italy was to bide its time.

II. THE CONSERVATIVE REACTION

The first half of the year 1846 was a period of energy on the part of Metternich. He himself has summed up the situation as follows:

The whole of Europe he regarded as broadly divisible between the forces of Conservatism and the forces of Destruction. In his eye the western nations, France and Spain, were already given up to the principles of the Revolution; throughout the central countries, namely Germany, Italy, and, no doubt, Switzerland,[13] the struggle was still in progress. Austria was the true rock of Conservatism, but her authority had been temporarily shaken by the Polish rebellion, which, if successful, would, he asserted, have been followed by one in Italy.

His suppression of the Polish rebellion of 1846 evidently was regarded by him as a salutary example of strong government; and in one sense it certainly was so, because it demonstrated how such methods of repression defeat their own ends.[14] It entirely failed even to postpone the Revolution,

les éléments dont se compose le parti favorable aux mouvements politiques. Ce parti ne rencontrera pas de grandes sympathies dans les masses qui, à l'exception de quelques rares populations urbaines, sont en général fort attachées aux vieilles institutions du pays. La force réside presque exclusivement dans la classe moyenne et dans une partie de la classe supérieure. Or, l'une et l'autre ont des intérêts très-conservateurs à défendre....

"Sur des classes aussi fortement intéressées au maintien de l'ordre social les doctrines subversives de la Jeune Italie ont peu de prise".

[13] Metternich, VII, 225–7. A year later he wrote: "In Switzerland we may shortly expect the revolutionary lava to overflow".

[14] "In any case it seems that these executions have produced the very worst effects and have given rise to demonstrations which cannot have afforded much satisfaction to the authorities. The government received information that, when the two condemned men Wisniewski and Kapncinski passed by, the road before them

which duly arrived in 1848 only two years later: at the same time it left an eternal stain on the name of Austria; and on that of Metternich himself.

It is necessary just to give the leading facts of this episode, because Metternich evidently relied on it as being a triumphant consolidation of his position in 1846.

For the time being he was enjoying an exceptional freedom from opposition because the Liberal powers, France and England, were already at variance with one another and rapidly becoming more estranged over the question of the Spanish marriage. Their disagreement gave Metternich a free hand, and he seized the opportunity to occupy the small Polish republic of Cracow.

The republic of Cracow was only an old city of 136,000 souls with some 23 square miles of territory; but it was the last free remnant of the ancient Polish nation, and—be it noted—it was guaranteed to the Poles by the Treaty of 1815. In spite of this guarantee, however, Metternich had long been planning its suppression. He complained—and not without justification[15]—that it was the chief centre of conspiracies all over Europe, and from 1836 to 1841 he had organised its joint occupation by the troops of Austria, Russia and Prussia. That first occupation had only been temporary, but in 1845 he determined to annex it permanently as soon as all danger had ceased of any joint Anglo-French opposition.

At the end of that year the three eastern governments stationed their troops at suitable points near Cracow, where,

was to be strewn with flowers, the windows were to be covered with flags and every woman within sight would be in mourning. It sent them by another road." Letter to Guizot of August 10th, 1847, from the Comte de Marescalchi, French chargé d'affaires, Vienna.

[15] "In February 1846 came the turn of Cracow, the last asylum within their native land of a considerable number of proscribed Poles and, at the same time, a refuge for exiles of other countries." Mazzini, *Scritti* (A.E.), vol. xii. This extract is from the Proemio (Preface) by Aurelio Saffi, the Triumvir of the Roman republic of 1849.

according to their police reports, plots were being hatched for the provinces. On February 19th, 1846, a Polish revolutionary movement against Austria broke out in Galicia, and was suppressed by the brutal expedient of appealing to class hatred and encouraging the peasantry to sack and burn the houses of the gentry and to massacre their occupants.[16] But on February 18th, even before that rising had come to a head, the troops of the three northern powers had already occupied Cracow.

Henceforth Cracow was treated as conquered territory; but the three invading powers had not yet given out that they intended to annex it. Already there was some indignation in France over their illegal action, and in the English House of Commons Palmerston spoke his mind with fine independence: he said that if the Treaty of Vienna did not hold good on the Vistula, there was no reason why it should hold good on the Rhine or the Po. So the three powers of the Holy Alliance called a conference in Berlin and decided to delay their final annexation until the Anglo-French *entente* had completely broken down. The matter was not finally settled until October 10th, 1846.[17]

[16] Many of the rebels were of the gentry and noble classes, and the Austrian government is said to have offered ten florins for every dead insurgent (Debidour, I, 427). The peasants took full advantage of this offer and invaded the houses of the rich proprietors; no less than 1458 people are said to have been thus killed in the circle of Tarnow alone. Montalembert vividly described this episode in the French House of Peers on July 2nd, 1846 (Gori, p. 116). The commander responsible for the brutality is said to have been Benedek, the same officer who distinguished himself in 1848, who in 1859 won immortal glory by his defence of the Hill of S. Martino during the battle of Solferino, and who in 1866 met his great defeat at Sadowa. He certainly fought alongside the peasants, but his story is that he saved prisoners from their hands. His letters would lead one to suppose him a man of the kindliest nature devoted to his wife, his soldiers and his horses. The results of this class war certainly afforded satisfaction to Metternich (v. *Benedek's nachgelassene Papiere*, Friedjung, Leipzig, 1901).

[17] The above, of course, is only a very brief summary.

Thus Metternich had proved his power in eastern Europe, and from that lofty height he surveyed the world.

In Italy the contest was less unequal. Hatred of Austria had been re-embittered by the events in Galicia. Metternich had taken the offensive: on the death of Francis IV, Duke of Modena (January 21st, 1846), he had sent troops to occupy that town and, owing to the weakness of the young Duke, Francis V, they had remained there permanently. Parma was to be his next victim, and then perhaps Tuscany: already there was great anxiety in Florence. On the other hand, however, Metternich was far from being satisfied with the Italian situation. The blow which he had aimed at Piedmont had proved a failure, and everywhere he found himself opposed by the skilful tactics of the Moderate party.

III. CHARLES ALBERT'S MOTTO: "ITALIA FARÀ DA SE"[18]

It is not known, I think, at exactly what date Charles Albert spoke these words which are certainly a fine expression of his patriotic hopes, and denote the difference between his own policy and that of Cavour. Cavour relied on foreign alliances, but Charles Albert had hoped that Italy could fend for herself.

The story told by Predari (p. 99) about the origin of the saying is that one day a strong Conservative, Marshal La Tour, was arguing with the king, trying to dissuade him from risking a breach with Austria. "What will Piedmont do", he said, "if, instead of being on our side as she always has been, Austria should be against us?"

To this suggestion Charles Albert replied with a calmness and a certainty which created a profound impression upon La Tour and on those around him. "If Piedmont loses Austria she will gain Italy; and then Italy will be able to fend for herself."

It was a great hope, though impossible of realisation: and, it was the cause for which Charles Albert lived and died.

[18] Italy will fend for herself.

In March 1846, when *Degli ultimi casi* made its appearance, the differences between the Piedmontese government and Austria were on the verge of a crisis. The Austrians were tired of fruitless negotiations over the question of the salt (*v.* p. 200 *et seq.*), and had already warned Charles Albert that there would be reprisals.

A few months later their blow fell. For years the Piedmontese wines had found a ready market in the province of Lombardy. On April 20th, 1846, the Austrians imposed a duty of 21.45 lire per metric quintal and this meant that the trade was virtually annihilated.

It was a purely punitive measure, a reprisal; and naturally it aroused great resentment in northern Italy. But the Piedmontese wine-growers showed some signs of being discontented with their own government, because they thought that the quarrel could have been avoided,[19] so Solaro della Margherita considered it advisable to issue a statement on the subject.

On May 2nd he published an article in the *Gazzetta* simply stating the Italian case in a few paragraphs of plain but forcible words. The result was electrical. Not only Piedmont and Lombardy,[20] but the Liberals all over the peninsula saw in this article the spectacle of an Italian state defying the power of Austria, and they hailed Charles Albert's action with enthusiasm; while even among the Great Powers of Europe there was some anxiety as to the result. In Turin there surged up a wave of national pride, and that town, ordinarily so calm, prepared itself for a great demonstration.

Massimo d'Azeglio was one of the principal organisers and decided to hold the demonstration on May 7th. On that morning every proof of popular enthusiasm was to be poured forth upon Charles Albert as he rode out on his usual Thursday inspection of the troops in the Campo di Marte:

[19] Vidal, p. 150, quoting a despatch of the Papal Nunzio at Turin; *v.* also Solaro, p. 351.

[20] Predari, p. 101.

Bunches of flowers had already been prepared and garlands which fair hands were to shower upon the head of the king as he came by; odes and sonnets had been written to celebrate his happy stroke of daring....Acclaimed to the skies on account of his bold statement, he was to hear amid the clamour of the cheering people, that well-loved cry of Evviva il re d' Italia! Long live the King of Italy.[21]

That was the plan of Massimo d'Azeglio. It would, says Gualterio,[22] have produced a demonstration such as never had been equalled in Italy, and perhaps have been a beginning of agitation throughout the whole peninsula.

But such plans are dangerous. At eleven o'clock on the morning of May 7th hundreds of flags were flying and an immense crowd had assembled in the piazza and along the streets and balconies. It was waiting for the king; but he did not appear. Instead there came an order that the troops were to return to their quarters. The people were greatly disappointed. They waited for some time, but then, perhaps fortunately, the rain came down in torrents so they dispersed.

Charles Albert had been ready in full uniform. He had been seen—a tall thin figure with a black moustache and grey hair—moving to and fro from the window, pale, anxious and uncertain. It was a supremely harassing moment. To go might lead to revolution and war; but to hold back would be regarded as a "great refusal". He had been on the point of mounting his horse; but various advisers had come to him one after another, some urging him to go and others to stay. He had ended by not mounting the horse; and probably he was right. The people would have received him with shouts of "Viva il re d' Italia", and that would have given Metternich a handle against him. As matters stood the demonstration had shown clearly enough that the people, to a man, supported his anti-Austrian movement.

True, his reputation certainly suffered among the enthusiasts; they were bitterly disappointed. But it was

[21] Solaro, p. 353.
[22] Gualterio, vol. I, pt II, p. 115; v. also Bersezio, II, 4, 33.

necessary to avoid an actual breach with Metternich: he had only Piedmont at his back, and Piedmont was not nearly strong enough to fight Austria single-handed: that fact was proved most tragically in 1848 and 1849.[23]

The wine question was by no means closed. It remained in existence for some time to come as a matter for negotiation between the courts. In this connection Metternich complained bitterly—especially in a letter of May 29th, 1846—of the changed attitude of Piedmont towards himself, and if we are to believe Count Buol, on June 26th Charles Albert gave a more or less reassuring reply:

"My conduct since I came to the throne has always been consistent and undoubtedly entitles no one to believe that there is a change in my principles—Never", he added, "will I grant a constitution, and never will I accept one, or allow one of any sort to be imposed on me."[24]

Thus at each step forward he takes care to regularise his position.

[23] In 1848 he had a temporary chance of success; but this was due to the fact that Austria was in revolution, and so were Venetia and Lombardy; moreover, Charles Albert received eight or ten thousand men from the Papal State and some thousands of volunteers from other states. Even so the Quadrilateral proved impregnable. All these advantages were non-existent in 1846 and 1847: the moment to strike had not yet arrived. One rather feels that Massimo d'Azeglio and his friends ought not to have tried to force the hand of their king.

[24] *V.* Metternich, vii, 237. His unwillingness to grant a constitution was undoubtedly genuine. The following story is told by Predari. By the beginning of December 1847 progress had been hastened by the Ferrara episode. Balbo became convinced that it was time for Charles Albert to grant a constitution. He therefore drew up a draft constitution and got it placed before the king by one of the private secretaries: on the following day the secretary brought to Balbo, as an answer from the king himself, the following question: "What account must a Christian make of a bond which is equivalent to an oath?" Balbo was shaken by the unexpected form of reply and he remained a few moments in thought; then with an expression of profound conviction he said: "His Majesty is right; honour first, even before glory!" Predari, p. 231.

Nevertheless, from this time onwards Charles Albert's activities become far bolder and more extensive than heretofore. Although he cannot yet face an open rupture with Austria, he seizes every chance of strengthening his position in Italy: firstly within Piedmont itself, and secondly in Lombardy, Tuscany and the Papal State and the Duchies.

Within his own kingdom we find societies springing into being nominally for social, but in reality for political ends: such, for instance, as the *Società del Whist*, the Whist club, originally founded by Cavour in 1841; the *Associazione agraria*, the Agrarian Association—under its state-appointed president —which included among its 4000 members of all classes some of the Lombard landowners, and certainly dealt with politics as well as agriculture; indeed its importance lay in the fact that it was the first assemblage in which national politics could be discussed: at the same time the *Nuova Enciclopedia popolare*, the New Popular Encyclopedia (5000 subscribers), was edited by Predari, Balbo and others, avowedly for propaganda: and Charles Albert invited the scientists of Italy to hold their annual congress (September 1846) in Genoa. This was a significant step, because the scientific congresses were so political in character that Gregory XVI had refused them permission to meet in the Papal State.

During these months Charles Albert was working hard and secretly in Lombardy, getting into touch with the anti-Austrians especially in Milan. This undermining of the Austrian rule in Italy became one of the chief Piedmontese activities during the next two years. At the same time in Florence he had Massimo d'Azeglio who kept him in touch with Liberal opinion there; and also with Farini and others in the northern provinces of the Papal State.

So evident was the Piedmontese advance that many people began to ask themselves whether Charles Albert would ever really break bounds or not. It is interesting to read the best opinions on either side.

Mazzini of course thought not—he disliked Charles Albert:

The nature of the man is too weak. The enterprise is not difficult, but to succeed, one would require an energy sufficient to make the first steps decisive.[25]

The two men most likely to know were his two ministers, Solaro della Margherita and Villamarina. Of these two, della Margherita was afterwards definitely of opinion that Charles Albert would never have taken action but for the advent of Pius IX.

His common sense would have prevented his putting his hand to so hazardous an enterprise, if the death of Gregory XVI had not changed the conditions of Italy....[26]

The exultation of all the Liberal party for Pius IX, though mistaken, also reached the King and for him it was entirely a religious exultation....He no longer doubted that it was lawful for him, just as it was for the Supreme Pontiff.

Villamarina would probably have held the opposite opinion. The historian Gualterio, who is said to represent Villamarina's views, wrote after the event:

I do not doubt that if other events had not supervened to distract the minds of Italians, one single cry would soon have issued from every loyal heart in the Peninsula. The Piedmontese vied with their King in patriotism, and all announced to Italy...that that country (Piedmont) would give them deeds rather than words.[27]

These phrases are misleading; outside Piedmont Charles Albert might have won for himself a great deal of sympathy, but he never could have got the essential element, namely trained soldiers. They were all under command of the princelings. This was proved in the year 1848, especially after Pius IX refused to declare war.

An impartial opinion is that of Count Mortier, the French Ambassador at Turin. In the spring of 1846 he was asked by the somewhat anxious French government to send it his considered opinion as to Charles Albert's aims in northern

[25] Mazzini, *Scritti* (E.N.), xxx, 15.
[26] Solaro, p. 541.
[27] Gualterio, vol. I, pt II, p. 486.

Italy. In reply he wrote a long and reasoned despatch of which the pith is in the following sentence:

He (Charles Albert) will listen with pleasure to dreams about the future of Italy which promise him a great rôle in history. But—I repeat it—at the moment of action it will all fade away.[28]

Count Mortier and Mazzini were equally wrong about Charles Albert's character; that, at all events, was proved in 1849. Before the event most people considered Charles Albert wanting in audacity; but after his failures in 1848 and 1849 they accused him of rashness. Looking back on the scene now, we may surely admit that he took a true view of his position; he was far more sensible than his critics.

His aim seems evident: what he wanted was to place himself in the forefront so as to be the recognized leader of Italy when the great opportunity should arrive. He knew that it was madness for Piedmont to strike at Austria unless she were followed by the rest of Italy. As the event proved he succeeded, most undoubtedly, in selecting the right moment for his blow.

But—the question remains—would he ever have found himself in a position actually to march against Austria? But for the lead given to him by Pius IX one can hardly imagine it. Even as matters turned out his chance was never more than fleeting. Single-handed, opposed by the immeasurable influence of the Holy See, he would never have been strong enough to take the plunge.

What the situation required was that a ruler should arise who would have the moral courage to declare himself a Liberal: to fly in the face of Metternich and break the ring of the petty princes: and to appeal to the peoples in the name of Progress. No such man was to be found among them all.

In reality no one could do this so well as a Pope, for, justified by the Memorandum of 1831, he could play off the Liberal powers against Metternich. If the Pope turned Liberal he would justify and inspire the Progressives in every

[28] *Rass. stor.* 1924, p. 634.

state; his own political advance would compel a corresponding advance by other rulers; his movement would supplant Mazzini, would appeal to the peasants and would oppose moral force to the material power of Metternich. It was only when the press became free and when, consequently, the people were aroused, when the ministers were responsible and when the Pope was on the side of freedom, that the Austrian bureaucracy in Milan and Vienna would be shaken, and discredited as a despotic anachronism. The advent of a Liberal Pope would be the beginning of the end; but what was to happen to the Church?

IV. GIOBERTI'S POPE

During the first half of the year 1846 all parties seem to be waiting for the old, old monk at the Vatican to die. At his death there will be a possibility of reopening the issues, and consequently the politicians are all on the *qui vive*: the Revolution is watching for an opportunity: Metternich is consolidating his position in the Italian fortresses: Charles Albert's confidants are at work in Lombardy, Venetia, the northern Legations of the Papal State and elsewhere. At the same time many thousands of the Italian nationalists are looking for a leader.

But what is required in reality is a leader who can send out a call to Liberalism, and one whose voice will stir the whole peninsula, not merely Piedmont or the republicans. And, contrary to all expectation, this call is now to come from the Church.

The man destined to inaugurate the next great step in the progress of the Risorgimento was at that moment a prelate little known outside his own diocese, Cardinal Giovanni Maria Mastai-Ferretti, soon to be famous as Pius IX.

Undoubtedly the best way to form a mental picture of Pius IX, in 1846, is to read the charming memoirs of Count Pasolini,[29] for Pasolini, though by far his junior, may be called

[29] A book compiled by his son, Count Desiderio Pasolini. Of course there are scores of descriptions of Pius IX; every fresh

his most genuine friend. He was a man of his own class and ideas, and he conveys to us the personal attraction of Cardinal Mastai-Ferretti with a vividness lacking in the compilations of historians, and in the memoirs of men whose dealings with him were merely official.

During the critical and troubled years of 1845 and 1846 Cardinal Mastai often used to visit the Pasolini family at their "villa" at Montericco—which is not a "villa" in the English sense, but an ancient stone house with machicoulated walls, built to guard the passage of the river below—and was greatly attached to the young Conte, Giuseppe, and to the still younger Contessa, Antonietta. These visits, and the evenings spent together, must have seemed to him like a haven of peace in the sea of troubles around them. They were in sympathy with him. And certainly these three friends formed a trio of exceptional talent: Pasolini was an active-minded landlord and farmer, and at the same time endowed with good ability in political and intellectual matters, as is evident from his subsequent career.[30] Of his young countess, Antonietta, we know that she was pretty and fond of reading, the daughter of a Milanese professor, and an enthusiastic student of national problems. But it is, of course, the third figure of the group, that of the cardinal, which chiefly concerns us; and the descriptions by his contemporaries give us more or less the following picture: Cardinal Mastai was unmistakably a person of distinction; slightly above the average height, broad shouldered, and, by 1846, naturally, rather tending towards stoutness; but in spite of his fifty-four years he had remained a handsome man, owing to his regular features, to his good dark eyes and more especially to the charm of his kindly,

historian tries to unearth something new about him; but the old one by Pasolini seems to me to be the best, for the reasons stated in the text.

[30] Only two years afterwards he was appointed by Pius IX to be Minister of the Papal State; later, he served in the Cabinet of Piedmont and, finally, he became Foreign Minister of United Italy under King Victor Emmanuel.

half-humorous expression; he was clean-shaven, of course, and consequently looked young for his age. And—perhaps for his help and consolation in life—he had been endowed by Heaven with a wonderfully attractive smile, with a gift of inspiring sympathy and happiness in those with whom he spoke, and with a sense of gentle fun: traits which, together with his cheerfulness under great misfortune, were destined always to win him devoted friends among those around him, for thirty years to come—whether they were servitors, guests, foreign potentates, Papal Zouaves on duty at his Castello, or merely popolani to whom he gave alms.[31]

These were the three friends whom the troubles of the year

[31] Pius lived to be nearly eighty-six and his portraits usually represent him as an old man. But during his younger days he must have had an exceptionally taking personality. There are many descriptions of him so flattering that they sound like exaggerations.

Spada, i, 50: "He was exceptionally handsome in person. Knightly, by birth and by manner, attractive, taking (*simpatico*); dignified but without constraint, and unconstrained with dignity; open-hearted too and so persuasive in conversation as to convince any listener".

Gualterio, vol. i, pt i, p. 604: "In person he was handsome, and his face was gentle and lovable, but not without a certain air of dignity (maestà = literally majesty), due to the regularity of his features. He smiled often in a natural and almost ingenuous way, with a movement of his lips that charmed people. He talked easily and his speech was frank and thoughtful and his manner refined, that of a gentleman". This description of him is quoted by the republican historian Tivaroni in *Domin. Austr.* ii, 264, and he adds that Pius inspired affection among those around him. There are many other similar testimonies by writers of every shade of opinion.

Maguire (Papal writer) saw him in 1857, a man of sixty-five worn with trouble. But he also was captivated by his smile, and by his "musical and sonorous" voice and expression of "rapt piety".

De Sanctis Scritti politici Pio IX a Gaeta, p. 98: "Pius' serene and pure soul which shone forth in the laughter of his face and in the wit of his bon-mots, in which there was never any ill-nature".

Minghetti, *Ricordi*, i, 213, quotes a note which he made after his first interview in November 1846: "Pius IX was stately in person and very affable in manner. In his appearance dignity was combined with kindliness and in his conversation courtesy alternated with wit".

1846 had united by a great bond of sympathy: the hope of finding a way of salvation for their native land.

Already Cardinal Mastai, though not very widely known in the Papal State, had the reputation of being an exceptionally enlightened Churchman. He too happened to be of "gentle blood"—being by birth Count Giovanni Maria Mastai-Ferretti, son of Count Girolamo Mastai-Ferretti and of the Countess Caterina, "a lady well known for her piety". And his family, though not one of the great historic houses of Italy, had figured among the provincial nobility of Sinigaglia for almost three hundred years. However, he himself had certainly eclipsed, by his own talents and personality, any standing due to the accident of birth. He had been a hard-working priest and bishop, a man of prayer, a devoted servant of the Church, yet one who had progressive, Liberal ideas and patriotic tendencies, which seemed almost a contradiction in terms in Metternich's Italy of 1846. What a prolonged tragedy he was preparing for his old age!

One asks oneself the question: Was he the right person to succeed Gregory XVI? He was a man whose guiding principle would be duty; but supposing he were called upon to carry out two contradictory duties—that of the Italian patriot and that of the steadfast Pope—would he not be torn in two between his patriotism and his religion? Moreover, he was a good man; but had he enough hard shrewdness to hold his own among the worldly? Had he enough stored up experience to cope with so great a crisis as that of 1846?

The following description of him by Count Desiderio Pasolini (the son of his friend) gives an idea of the character that he bore as Bishop of Imola just before his election to the Papal throne.[32]

As a jealous custodian of ecclesiastical discipline, the aims which stood nearest his heart were that his priests should lead a straightforward life, should live frugally and should bear an honourable reputation. On one occasion when visiting a certain parish he

[32] Pasolini, I, 61.

returned to the donor a splendid fish without even tasting it, and told the priest to save his small stipend for feeding the poor, and not for the table of the Bishop. In his charities he was liberal, perhaps beyond his means; and he carried them all out secretly without ever caring for thanks or praise.

He believed that the affairs of the world were very far from being well-ordered, either in the Government or in the Church. He used to say that the tax-payer has the right to know and to regulate public expenditure. He tried to re-order the charitable institutions of Imola and he attached some active-minded laymen with experience of modern customs and requirements, to the ecclesiastical administrators who were often too much bound by ancient custom.

In fact he had the temperament of the reformer. The writer then describes his constant determination to make his clergy take their life more earnestly, and ends up:

Every action of the Cardinal arose from a sincere desire to do good. He became full of interest and pleasure over any generous idea or anything right, or any project which he believed to be, or which was represented to him as being, useful and beneficent. But a long physical infirmity and also his labours during his mission had interrupted the regular course of Mastai's studies, and had left him neither the time nor the possibility of gaining experience of public affairs. Consequently the practical results obtained did not always correspond to his good intentions, and his words and actions were not always accompanied by a sufficient knowledge of men and of human nature.

All this I have heard on very many occasions from some of the citizens of Imola, and from individuals who did not agree with one another in politics, but were all agreed in making the above statements as coming from people who had known Bishop Mastai personally.[33]

Cardinal Mastai evidently disliked the policy that he was forced to carry out. On one occasion, when it was suggested that the political troubles could be settled by a meeting of the

[33] The above translation is rather different from that of Lady Dalhousie who, in 1885, published a most interesting English version of Count Pasolini's *Memoirs*. But her work was an abridgement, and in it the above description of Mastai is somewhat shortened.

three reactionary Cardinal-Legates, he opposed the idea and even wrote to Monsignor Polidori: "If God does not help us, it will certainly not be the congress of the three Eminentissimi which will save us ".[34]

It was towards the end of this period that he had an unpleasant experience with the Centurioni, which gives one a vivid idea of the distraught condition of the country and shows how the secret police and the secret societies fought savagely in the Papal towns, knifing each other in side alleys in the dark. On February 24th, 1846, as Cardinal Mastai was praying in the church of S. Cassiano, at Imola, about an hour before the Ave Maria, suddenly a wounded man staggered into the building and made his way to the sacristy where he fell exhausted; in those days the Church's right of sanctuary was still enforceable by law. The cardinal at once went to help him, and in another moment found himself face to face with the pursuers. His position seemed dangerous, but their leader promptly called out: "You can search me and you will find that I am entirely unarmed, whereas those who waylaid and provoked us were armed to the teeth", and to this statement the pursuers have always adhered. They were five young Liberals who said that they had been set upon by five other young men, members of the secretly-armed Papal volunteers; that in defending themselves they had stabbed one of the Papal party with a cobbler's awl. That was their side of the story, but the wounded man afterwards denied that he had been the aggressor. Whatever may be the true version, he certainly had been severely stabbed in the lower part of the stomach and after two days of suffering he died.[35] One can imagine the influence of this scene on the kindly nature of Mastai.

During these years the land was full of plotting, killing and suffering, and in the evenings of these autumn and winter months he often sought the home of the Pasolini. In it he

---

[34] I give Masi's version of this letter; that given in *Il Risorgimento* of 1908 is slightly different.   [35] Pasolini, I, 74.

could exchange views with a man of his own standing and of religious principles which satisfied even the Papal government; thoughtful, endowed with progressive ideas, and ready to face the troubles of being a Liberal. "And beside him a lady, very young, but cultured, pious and gracious, full of joy in her domestic happiness; a true ray of sunlight amid the darkness of Romagna in those days."[36]

Mastai was an interesting talker:

"It was very pleasant", wrote Count Pasolini many years afterwards, "when the Cardinal discoursed to us. He was a man of reflective mind and took great pleasure in the beautiful, whether it were in letters, in art, in a garden or even in horses. And he had been a diplomat, and had gone to America and was thus to be the first, and hitherto the only Pope who has visited the New World. So he had seen a great deal, and hoped to be able to see and do a great deal more in the world."[37]

Here we have one of those situations which make history, and yet are often ignored by historians. These three friends talked for hours, as people do in troubled times, about the distressed state of their country, and searched together for the right way between the points of danger. The Pasolini were Liberals and reformers, whereas Mastai, though of Liberal tendencies, was duty-bound as a cardinal of Gregory XVI. But he was broad-minded and patriotic, and during these talks the young couple were strengthening the bonds of sympathy between his political ideas and their own. He was becoming more and more indignant at the excesses which the Centurioni were perpetrating in the name of loyalty and religion. Pasolini says:

They moved his honourable soul to profound indignation because he did not understand the iniquitous political arts that were used then, and could not share in passions so manifestly contrary to Christianity.

"One evening", so Pasolini continues, "when talking to a certain Count, a citizen of Ravenna who had come to his house, he expressed himself as follows: 'I do not understand the provocative attitude of our government, which mortifies and persecutes

[36] Masi, p. 157.   [37] Pasolini, I, 60.

our young men because they breathe the air of their own century. It would take so little to make them happy and to win their affection! And I cannot imagine why it opposes railroads, gas-lighting, suspension bridges and scientific congresses.

"'Theology is not opposed, so far as I am aware, to the growth of science, art and industry....But there!...I know nothing about politics, so perhaps I am mistaken.'"

During these months the Pasolini were able to introduce him to the literature of the reformers. When *Degli ultimi casi di Romagna* made its appearance he read it with great interest. Then, one evening, the Countess Antonietta lent him a copy of the *Speranze d' Italia*, by Cesare Balbo, and asked him for his judgment on it. It spoke, as we know, of "the hopes of Italy". And after that she gave him the *Acts of the Congress of Italian Scientists*. But the book which aroused him most of all was Gioberti's *Primato*, lent him by Pasolini himself. And one can easily imagine the impression that would have been made upon him by the resonant sentences in which the abbé combines into one great movement the service of the Church and the patriotism of the new Italy.

Italy is the capital of Europe because Rome is the religious metropolis of the world.

The design of an Italian federation under the auspices of the Pontiff, if ever it is destined to bear fruit, must start its first roots in Rome and Piedmont which are the special dwelling-places of Italian piety and Italian force.

There lay the way of combining religion with patriotism. How far these ideas had already been in his mind one cannot tell, but it is certain that when he became Pope, he tried to set up a consultative monarchy on the model described by Gioberti, and that he thought that his difficulties as spiritual leader would be realised by his people just as Gioberti had realised them.

Meanwhile Pasolini did not cease from urging upon his friend that, however bad might be the present days, they two must never give up hope or cease to believe in humanity.

Appealing to him on his religious side, he drew the picture of a church purified and triumphant, and justice and peace in the land; and more than once quoted the text: "Blessed are they who hunger and thirst after justice for they shall have their fill".[38] On one of these occasions Cardinal Mastai became so deeply stirred that he raised his arms to heaven and solemnly called on God to purify His Church and grant peace to Italy.[39]

When that close intimacy had lasted almost a year, on June 1st, 1846, the news went out that Pope Gregory XVI was dead, and a few days later Cardinal Mastai started for Rome to attend the Papal Conclave. It was a great moment in his life, and a turning-point in the history of Italy. He himself had no expectations of being elected Pope and king,

[38] This text is taken from the Vulgate.

[39] The political views of Cardinal Mastai about three months before his election are clearly expressed in the following letter. At Shrovetide, a certain informer living in Imola wrote a detailed letter to the Governor of Rome (as Director of the Police) to complain that the Liberals of that town had too much freedom. The Governor, Monsignor Ciacchi, forwarded it to Mastai, as Bishop of Imola, for information. Mastai replied boldly that the police were not all flowers of virtue, and as to the doings in Romagna he added: "There are so many people writing about the doings in Romagna that some of them may be actuated by personal motives of grievance against the Authorities about whom they write. In Imola, for instance, the Governor writes, the Carbineers write, Captain Pagani writes, Captain Buferli writes, Benacci writes, Count Vespignani writes, some priests write and other people write and bother one or other of the government offices. In a country such as is most of Romagna, where passions run so high, where *sicut nos dimittimus debitoribus nostris* is a virtue so seldom seen, how can one be surprised if among so many writers there are some whose reports are dictated by their passions?...I will conclude by saying that three parties predominate in these provinces. The revolutionists, an incorrigible race which is always meditating the blackest crimes; the Papalist leaders consisting of good men, of speculators, and of men seeking revenge; the Moderates, who include many good people, apart from the well-to-do classes who...for interested motives...are always opposed to revolutions". D. Spadoni, *Giovanni Mastai, Vescovo d' Imola*, quoted by Monti, p. 45.

but, from the first, his circle of friends seem to have regarded it as a possibility, and they felt that in him, an unflinching churchman and yet a patriotic Italian of progressive sympathies, in him as reconciler, lay the one hope of delivering their country from the interminable unrest of the previous thirty years. Indeed the legend of his carriage being followed by a white dove was perhaps the expression of a prayer rather than an idle fancy.

But the doubt remained; would he or any other man ever be able to steer the small barque of the Temporal Power safely between the immense world influences on all sides of it?

Chapter XVIII

ELECTION OF POPE PIUS IX[1]

The election of a Pope is always, even to non-Catholics, a most interesting ceremony, and one that has survived practically unchanged since the early Middle Ages.[2] That of Mastai has grown almost into a legend. There is, for instance, a picturesque story which is noticed even by anti-Papal historians, that, during the journey to Rome, as his diligence was leaving Fossombrone a snow-white dove came and settled on it and refused to be driven away by the surrounding crowd. There is, too, the authentic story of the last sentences spoken to him by his friend Pasolini when they were saying good-bye:[3]

I cannot help telling you that in my heart of hearts I have a great hope that God has now destined your Eminence to be the new Vicar of Christ, so that from the chair of St Peter you will be able to promulgate and bless the principles which we have discussed together so many times, and to fulfil those prayers which we have so often sent up to Heaven for the welfare of the whole Church and for that of our poor Italy.

To which Mastai replied more or less in the following words:

My dear Count, it is not I who am to be the new Pope. But tell your wife from me that I have taken those books which she gave me at Montericco and put them in my trunk and that I'll get the new Pope to read them.

[1] Principal authorities: Bishop Pelczar, Count Pasolini, Monti, Masi (*Nell' Ottocento*), and the various Archives. The main facts are not disputed.

[2] The elections of the Popes from Benedict XI to Pius VI took place in the Vatican except during the period at Avignon. Pius VII was elected at Venice (1800) during the Napoleonic era. The succeeding Popes were elected in the Quirinal. Leo XIII and his successors have been elected in the Vatican, the Quirinal having been occupied in 1870 by Victor Emmanuel.

[3] Pasolini, I, 71; Masi, *Nell' Ottocento*, p. 160.

At Rome the preliminary meetings of the cardinals were already in progress, and all preparations were being made for the conclave itself. At the Quirinal Palace, one whole wing—that which now extends along the Via XX Settembre (then known as the Via Porta Pia)—had been set apart for the electors. The rooms on either side of the long corridor had been divided up, to correspond with the number of cardinal electors, by means of wooden partitions covered with green or purple cloth according to whether the cardinal inhabiting it had been created by a former Pope or by Gregory XVI. Each cell was furnished with a bed, a table, a press, a few chairs and a crucifix. In order to prevent any kind of communication with the outer world until after the election, the windows were darkened so that the light could penetrate only through the upper panes, and all entrances were walled up, except the principal door and a secondary one which was well guarded both inside and outside. At suitable points were inset "turns", similar to those used in convents, so as to enable the servants to hand in food for both the cardinals and their attendants, without themselves entering the isolated wing.[4]

On the morning of June 14th, 1846, the cardinals, fifty in number,[5] assembled in the Basilica of St Peter to hear the Mass of the Holy Ghost, and the Latin preliminary address: the one to implore the necessary grace, the other to recall their duty. A few hours later they were gathered together in the church of St Silvestro, from whence they walked through the

[4] The accounts of the ceremonial, in this chapter, are all taken from Pelczar, a Roman Catholic bishop.

[5] There were sixty-two cardinals in all, but twelve of them (two Italian and ten foreigners) were not able to reach the conclave in time. Among the latter was the Austrian Cardinal Gaysrück, coming from Milan, with orders, some say, to veto the election of Mastai-Ferretti. According to another account, his orders were to veto any Liberal Pope. However, he only arrived in time to see Pius blessing the people from the Quirinal. At this conclave there were seventeen cardinals of seventy years or over. (Vatican Arch. "Fondo Spada", vol. VI.)

streets in solemn procession to the Quirinal. The way was
lined with a crowd on either side, but nevertheless there
reigned a general silence broken only by the intoning of the
Veni Creator and the rolling thunder of a storm above. The
people were silent because they knew the profound importance
of what was taking place in Rome. Many of them felt that it
was a moment which might become the turning-point in the
history of Italy.

On arriving at the Quirinal the cardinals joined in the
prayer "Deus qui corda" and heard a short discourse; then
there was read to them the bull regarding the election of the
Pope, and also the prescriptions for the conclave, to whose
observance the cardinals and their attendants bound themselves by oath. After that they retired to their apartments,
where they received the ambassadors, prelates and princes of
Rome. At 11 o'clock that night the conclave began: on the
second sounding of the bell, the Maestro di ceremonie
announced the "extra omnes" and all visitors left the place;
the door was locked both from within and from without, and
the street outside was barricaded and watched by a contingent
of Swiss Guards. It was feared that there might be an
attack on the building.

Throughout Italy there were three names that stood out
above all others as probable successors of Gregory XVI: one
was Cardinal Lambruschini, and the other two were Cardinals
Gizzi and Micara. These three men represented very different
schools of thought. Lambruschini, minister of the late Pope,
was a pro-Austrian and a Conservative of the old type, one
of those who believed in repressing revolution by force; he
was a strong candidate, because it was to him that a large
number of the cardinals who were voting owed their own
elevation to the purple. Gizzi and Micara on the other hand
represented more popular ideals. Gizzi was a very kindly
man, small in stature but broad in mind. He was the people's
hope because he was a proved Liberal: to his immortal
honour he had refused to allow a military commission to sit

at Ravenna. He had been so highly spoken of by Massimo d'Azeglio in *Degli ultimi casi di Romagna* that he was known as "d'Azeglio's Pope". Cardinal Micara, too, was a popular candidate mainly because he never feared to speak out his mind regardless of those in high places. He was an old Capuchin friar, "considered one of the most eloquent orators of his time, a man of austere habits, severe, an inexorable despiser of luxury, imperious, violent, of a quick and lively spirit, with eyes full of fire and a long white beard to his waist"; often sarcastic—and his public observations about the ministers recently in power had won him a very general sympathy: it was he who after reading Massimo d'Azeglio's revelations about Romagna had said: "Bravo! E tutto vero!"[6] But he was nearly 71 years of age and somewhat infirm, too old in body to occupy the Papal Chair at such a moment. These were the three candidates most prominent in the public eye. And Cardinal Soglia (says Pellegrino Rossi)[7] was also popular, probably owing to his learning and broad-mindedness.

In Rome, however, there is an old saying about conclaves: "He who goes in a Pope comes out a cardinal", and behind the closed doors it was known that neither Gizzi nor Micara had any chance of success. The election was believed to lie between Cardinal Lambruschini and Cardinal Falconieri, the very learned and deeply respected Archbishop of Ravenna. But Falconieri was unwilling to be elected. He felt unequal to so great a responsibility.

Naturally it is very difficult to be certain of what really took place at the conclave. Almost every writer gives a different account of it; though very few of them were in a position to know. But about one point they all agree; that at first Cardinal Lambruschini was the strongest candidate there. He repre-

---

[6] "Well done! It's all true." D'Azeglio says that during his life in the monastery he saved up a fortune of a hundred thousand crowns, which he disposed of among various charitable establishments; thirty thousand went to the infant schools. *V.* Rendu, *Correspondance politique de M. d'Azeglio,* p. 4.

[7] Paris A.E. Rome, Rossi, June 17th, 1846.

sented the old Conservative school and, if elected, would be a continuator of the policy of Gregory XVI, a champion of the governing clique: he could rely on the support of Austria, and could claim the gratitude of many cardinals who had been appointed during his term of office.[8]

As to Mastai-Ferretti's chances there had only been a little discussion, and that chiefly among those to whom he was personally known. He seems to have had isolated admirers[9] rather than a regular party. His chief friends in the conclave are said to have been Cardinals Amat, Falconieri, Ludovico Altieri and Pignatelli. That men with their family names and traditions should support him seems to suggest that he was considered a sensible and safe Liberal. At the same time old Cardinal Micara, though himself a possible successor, had spoken out like a hero for him. The story is told that after the election had begun, he was lying ill in his cell and Lambruschini came to take his vote. "The battle has begun", said Lambruschini, "and what do you think the result will be?" Micara, with a characteristic flash, replied, "It

---

[8] It is said that in opposition to Lambruschini and his "Genoese party" there was the "Roman party", so-called because most of its members were natives of the Papal State. It was headed by Bernetti, the same whom Lambruschini had displaced from office in 1836, and with him was old Cardinal Micara. What these cardinals wanted was a native of the Papal State and a ruler with a more Liberal policy. As yet they had not selected their candidate, but many of them were thinking of voting for Mastai because he fulfilled both their requirements. It seems that against a strong candidate they were setting up a man of whom comparatively little was known, but about whom all reports were favourable, and who, though of Liberal views, would probably be safe. Bernetti did not receive a single vote during the conclave, so it seems evident that he did not mean to stand himself.

[9] Cardinal Pignatelli, before leaving Naples to come and vote, enquired of Padre Ventura, the well-known Liberal preacher, who was best suited to govern the Church in these times of difficulty. Padre Ventura named Gizzi, Falconieri and Mastai: the first, on account of his well-known rectitude, the second, for his learning, and the third, for his devotion to duty.

God directs the election Mastai will be chosen, but if the Devil takes a hand in it, it will be either you or I ".[10]

On June 15th, at 9 o'clock in the morning, the Maestro di ceremonie gave the direction: "In capellam Domini"; and the cardinals flocked into the Pauline Chapel where all preparations had been made for the election. A silken curtain of purple colour divided the chapel into two parts. The picture above the altar represented the descent of the Holy Spirit on the Apostles. On the steps of the altar stood the throne for the future Pope and around the walls were prepared 52 thrones with green or purple canopies, for the cardinals. In the midst of the quadrilateral thus formed, there were six small tables, each with a chair for those cardinals who were to arrive later; and, standing a little to the far side towards the altar, was a large table with the urn containing all the voting-tickets for the election, the chalice in which to collect the votes of those present, the purse to receive the votes of those ill, and the little balls for drawing lots. Behind the altar there stood a small iron fireplace for burning the voting tickets after each election.

As nothing less than a two-thirds majority is valid, the conclave nearly always begins with several inconclusive elections, after each of which the tickets are burnt in the fireplace and the smoke arising from it is recognised by the people outside as a sign that the voting has not yet given a definite decision.

Forty-seven cardinals were present—three being ill, among whom were both Micara and Gizzi—and, as a two-thirds majority is necessary for success, in this case the number of votes required was thirty-four. Mass was celebrated, with Holy Communion, and an allocution was delivered to the electors. The three Scrutatori were then chosen by lot: the duty of the first was to open the vote; of the second to write down the name inscribed on it; and the third scrutator was to call the name aloud to the whole assemblage. The third lot fell on Mastai. It was to him therefore that was assigned the duty

[10] Pelczar, I, 112. But this story is told by many historians; v. Rendu, *Correspondance politique de M. d'Azeglio*; note to the letter of May 28th, 1847.

of reading out the names on the tickets, so that all might hear them. The first election then took place. It is said that throughout the whole of the proceedings the faces of those present showed how deeply they felt the responsibility that lay upon them; and when the scrutiny began, there was a dead silence throughout the chapel while Mastai called out, one after another, the name written on each vote. It took some time, but at length the list was finished. Fifteen times he had called out the name of Lambruschini, and thirteen times his own.[11] The other twenty-two votes had been divided and scattered, most of them going to Cardinals Soglia and Falconieri. A new election was necessary. Among the older cardinals there was great surprise at the small number obtained by Lambruschini.

On the same afternoon the second election was held. It resulted in Mastai's obtaining seventeen, an increase of four, and Lambruschini thirteen, a decrease of two. This proved that the isolated voters did not want Lambruschini. Again the voting papers had to be burnt.

By then it must have been evident that there remained only one possible chance for Lambruschini—that the conclave should be prolonged until the foreign cardinals could arrive. They were twelve in number, including two Italians from far-off sees. It has since been suggested that most of these might have voted against the native candidate. As far as one can see, most probably this would not have altered the result: but it has always been believed that one of them, the Austrian Cardinal Gaysrück, was coming from Milan armed with the "Esclusiva" or right of veto, and with Metternich's directions to veto any Liberal pope. He was due to arrive on June 17th.

On the following morning, June 16th, the cardinals held

[11] Masi gives this as twelve not thirteen, but Monti has proved that there were thirteen (Monti, p. 56). Pelczar says that Gizzi received two votes at the first scrutiny and that Pius IX afterwards said that he had voted for him, and called him "my Pope". Others say that he received none, because the cardinals refused to be dictated to by Massimo d'Azeglio.

the third election. Mastai received twenty-seven votes and Lambruschini only eleven.

Meanwhile among the people in Rome the result was awaited with intense excitement. A report was current that the popular hero Gizzi was elected, and it was received with such joy that his servants thought themselves safe in allowing all his old cardinal's robes to be burnt on a bonfire as being of no further use to him. This *auto-da-fé* in his courtyard was a great tribute to his popularity, but it is said to have cost him about 6000 scudi, or over a thousand pounds.

On that same afternoon of June 16th the fourth election began. As usual, Mastai was deputed to call out the names, and as he stood there in the centre, outlined against the curtain, it was noticed that his face was extremely pale. In a very short time there remained little doubt as to the result. But when he had proclaimed his own name eighteen times in succession, the strain of conflicting feelings became too much for him; his voice died away, he staggered, and seemed about to faint. He even begged those nearest him to name another scrutator to carry on the work in his stead, but most fortunately the cardinals remembered that this was impossible as it would have invalidated the proceedings. However, they gave immediate proof of their sympathy. Some of them thronged forward to his assistance, and others called to him from their places: "Rest for a moment and recover yourself: we can wait". So after a short pause, he rose and finished the scrutiny, which resulted in thirty-six votes being cast for him, that is to say just two more than was actually necessary for his election.

Hardly had he read out the last name when Cardinal Riario Sforza exclaimed: "Habemus Pontificem", and the signal bell was rung. Instantly the doors opened and the secretary of the Sacred College came in, with various other officials, and then Cardinal Macchi and the three cardinals, heads of orders, turned to the newly elected Pope and put the formal question to him: "Acceptasne electionem canonice de te factam in

Summum Pontificem?" Mastai had been kneeling at the foot
of the altar in prayer. He answered in a still trembling voice:
"Accepto".

It was natural that he should be overcome. This supreme
honour and profoundly sacred trust had come to him almost
entirely unexpected, during the previous forty-eight hours.
The conclave had been one of the shortest on record.[12]

On the following morning—June 17th, 1846—the thunder
of 101 guns announced from the old Castel Sant' Angelo,
that a new Pope had been chosen. It was the forenoon of
a splendid day in the Roman summer, and the people came
in their thousands to the Quirinal, still under the impression
that it was their popular choice Cardinal Gizzi; of Mastai
they knew practically nothing.

When, therefore, the cardinals appeared in the loggia above
the great gateway of the Quirinal Palace, where it looks down
upon the statue and fountain of the horse-tamers, and when
Mastai's name and Papal title were announced to the expectant
crowds below, the proclamation was greeted with a roll of
drums and a sounding of trumpets, followed by another
salute from the guns; and at the same time every bell in
Rome rang out a welcome to the new Pontiff. But the populace
remained silent and distrustful, utterly cold. They had hoped
for Gizzi.

Such a reception from the people whom he had hoped to
serve proved almost too much for Pius,[13] after his previous

---

[12] Pelczar quotes three shorter: Gregory XIII (1572); Gregory XV
(1621); and, in later years, Leo XIII (1878), lasting only thirty-six
hours.

[13] "When the Pontiff re-entered his rooms he was more like a
corpse than a living man: so great had been the emotion of that
moment" (Gualterio, IV, 376). Bishop Pelczar says that copious
tears welled from his eyes, and that twice he covered his face with
his raised hand overcome by emotion, which spread to those around
(Pelczar, I, 119). All the eye-witnesses mention his emotion, and
the silence of the crowd.

forty-eight hours of strain. He was hardly able to give the blessing. His raised hand fell back, and with it he covered his face now wet with tears; but then, mastering his feelings, he lifted it high to heaven—his gesture as supreme priest of God; he extended it towards north and south, east and west, to denote that he was the religious father of the world; and at the same time, in a strong tone, he gave out the formal words: "Benedictio Dei Omnipotentis Patris et Filii et Spiritus Sancti descendat super vos et maneat semper vobiscum". And there must have been a great enthusiasm about his features at that moment when he threw back his head and called for the supreme blessing of God upon his people, for, as he spoke, those around him suddenly realised that he was uttering, not a mere Latin formula, but the true expression of a prayer: and in the hearts of the kneeling thousands there awoke a new hope, the presage of a new phase in the history of their country. It was the hope which was soon to be personified in the cry of "Viva Pio Nono" and to be acclaimed all over the civilised world. The intuition of the people was right; they were witnessing the turning-point in the making of Italy.

NOTE to CHAPTER XV

THE MANIFESTO OF RIMINI—SUMMARY
OF ITS 12 DEMANDS

It demands:

1. A complete Amnesty for political prisoners.
2. Civil and criminal codes similar to those in other European nations allowing publicity of debates and institution of juries, etc.
3. That neither the Holy Office nor the ecclesiastical courts should have authority over laymen.
4. Political crimes henceforth to be dealt with by the ordinary courts.

Clauses 5 and 6 deal with the machinery of government. According to them the *municipal councils* are to be freely elected by the citizens, though subject to the approval of the sovereign. This popular election is mentioned in the Memorandum, Cap. III.

The *provincial councils* will be chosen by the sovereign from lists of three names (*terne*) presented to him by the municipal councils. This suggestion is foreshadowed in the Memorandum.

The *Supreme Council of State* will be chosen by the sovereign from the *terne* sent up to him from provincial councils. It is to reside in Rome: to superintend the public debt: to have a deliberative vote on the estimates and budget, and a consultative vote on other matters.

7. All dignities and posts to be open to laymen.
8. Education to be taken from the hands of the clergy.
9. The press to be free within ordinary limits.
10 Foreign troops to be disbanded.
11. A civic guard to be raised.
12. The government is to place itself in the way of making all social improvements required by the spirit of the age, according to the example of other European governments.

Index

Adelaide, the Archduchess, wife of Victor Emmanuel II, 199
Agitation, d'Azeglio's creed of, xix, 204,232, 234, 238; beginnings of, 214; recommended by Balbo,192; substitute for insurrection, 245
Aglebert, Augusto, 218 note
Aix-la-Chapelle, Congress of, 7 note, 32
Albani, Cardinal Giuseppe, 120, 121
Albertist propaganda, xix, 129, 235 note; Balbo's, 150, 190; Pecchio's scheme for a strong Piedmont, 189 note; d'Azeglio's, in Papal State, 208–9, 215, 224; in *Degli ultimi casi*, 233, 234, 238
Alessandria, mutiny at, 66
Alexander II, the Czar, 31, 33, 72
Alexander III, Pope, 159, 187 note
Alfieri, the poet, 53 and note
Alison, Sir Archibald, 5 note
Altieri, Cardinal Ludovico, 271
Amadeo of Savoy, Count, 200 note
Amadori, Doctor Filippo, 206, 230
Amat, Cardinal, 219, 271; Legate at Ravenna, 223–4
America, 39; branches of the *Giovine Italia* in, 243 and note
Amicizia Cattolica, the, 238
Ancona, 96–7, 208; occupation of, iii and note; rising in, 91; surrender of, 98; French squadron arrives off, 117; French occupation of, 119, 122 and note, 123
Andreini, Rinaldo, 225 note
Angeloni, Luigi, 5
Angoulême, Duke of, 73
Apostolato popolare, the, 243 and note
Armandi, General, 91 and note
Army Plot, the, 83, 84–5
Ascoli, 92
Assisi, rising in, 92
Associazione agraria, 237 note, 254
Associazione nazionale italiana, the, 242

Austria, xiii, xiv, xvi, xvii, xix, 1, 2, 3, 4, 7, 12 note, 20, 22, 24, 25, 27, 28 and note, 29, 30, 31, 32 and note, 33 note, 34, 35, 37, 38, 39, 40 note, 41, 43, 51, 54, 58, 59, 60, 61, 63, 75, 78, 82, 83, 84, 86, 88, 94–8, 103, 105, 107 note, 109 and note, 110, 111, 122, 123, 125, 126, 127, 128 note, 130, 131, 140, 142, 147, 151, 163, 182, 187 and note, 188, 190, 197 and note, 198, 200, 202–3, 210, 217, 223, 232, 233 note, 238, 247, 250, 251, 253 and note, 254, 256, 257, 271; geography of, 31; Austrian Royal houses in Italy, 36; at Laibach, 66–7 note; intervention asked by Gregory XVI, 95–6; order in Papal State impossible without Austrian troops, 100; places troops at disposal of Conference, 110; refuses to evacuate without guarantee, 117; evacuates Bologna, 118–19; re-enters Legations, 121; withdraws troops from Papal State, 134; administration in Milan, 23 note, 183; Balbo's proposal for, 188; occupation of Cracow, 248; veto on Liberal Pope, 273
Austrian Emperor, the, 28 and note, 30, 33, 36, 41, 74 note, 75, 94 note, 107 note, 198
d'Azeglio, Costanza, 65 note, 76, 77 note, 178 note, 205
d'Azeglio, Emmanuele, 77 note
d'Azeglio, Enrico, 178 note
d'Azeglio, Massimo, xviii, xix, 3 note, 19 note, 21 note, 23 note, 58, 63 note, 77 note, 129, 133 note, 143, 144 and note, 147 note, 150–1, 153, 161 note, 170 note, 186, 189, 194 note, 217, 221 note, 225, 245, 253 note, 254, 270 note, 273 note; family and early life, 174–6; officer in Piedmontese army, 176–8; life as an artist, 178–82; his novels, 183; settles in

CPSIA information can be obtained at www.ICGtesting.com
Printed in the USA
LVOW040705030213

318362LV00001B/32/P